LANGU

By exposing our ___ ___ stream or birds singing, we can repair at least some of the damage done by the unwanted and discordant noise of our "civilized" way of life. Perhaps, and even more significantly, we may then elect to move a step forwards (or, more correctly, upwards) by tuning in to the hidden "sounds of the soul." This can be achieved by listening to or learning to intone certain invocations and chants, magical words and mantras handed down from ages past and developed to stimulate very specific effects—calming, healing, elevating, and transforming.

By its very action, participation in sacred sound stimulates our intuitive insight, and greatly enhances our capacity for making correct choices. These tried-and-tested mantras, chants and incantations of high potency come from many cultures and are presented in an easy-to-follow format, with guides for correct pronunciation. While other available "mantra" books are exclusively Hindu/Sanskrit in content, *Words of Power* is the first such work of a universal nature.

Words of Power explores the origin of the first mantra, the many names of Allah, the important sacred phrase common to all ancient cultures, the meanings of the words of power used by Jesus, and how Moses may have used words of power to part the Red Sea. It demonstrates the benefits of various mantrical disciplines, how to harmonize the five bodies, balance the biological centers, and disperse negativity through the power of sound.

There is an urgency in the air, a desperate need for a new positive vision for humankind, based on mutual cooperation, respect, and shared wisdom. The true citizens of the "New Age" are not hidebound by any one creed or indoctrination system, but are free to accept and use the rich heritage of positive practical knowledge handed down by our forebears, regardless of source. Among these priceless legacies are the sounds that speak to our souls and to the universe—they are *Words of Power*.

About the Authors

A professional writer and lecturer, with many books to his credit, Brian Crowley was born in Africa, but now makes his residence in Australia. Since a child he has studied the spiritual philosophies of the East and the West, and over 20 years of research has gone into the creation of this volume of words of power. He is past president of Cape Town Psychic Club, and while in Cape Town he was an influential member of the Theosophical Society. Recently, he has worked in association with Dr. James J. Hurtak, an acknowledged expert in ancient languages and sacred chants and mantras. He also is highly regarded for his knowledge of the game of cricket and has had an avid interest in numerology for over 25 years.

Esther Crowley teaches yoga and has written several books and audio tapes regarding the philosophy and methods of yoga and meditation. She is the author of the first book of yoga in the Afrikaans language. For the past 20 years she has explored other worlds as a "psychic artist," painting spirit guides in pastels.

Brian and Esther conduct regular meditation sessions and "Participation in Sacred Sound" workshops.

To Write to the Authors

We cannot guarantee that every letter written to the authors can be answered, but all will be forwarded. Both the authors and the publisher appreciate hearing from readers, learning of your enjoyment and benefit from this book. Llewellyn also publishes a bi-monthly news magazine with news and reviews of practical esoteric studies and articles helpful to the student, and some readers' questions and comments to the authors may be answered through this magazine's columns if permission to do so is included in the original letter. The authors sometimes participate in seminars and workshops, and dates and places are announced in *The Llewellyn New Times*. To write to the authors, or to ask a question, write to:

Brian and Esther Crowley
c/o THE LLEWELLYN NEW TIMES
P.O. Box 64383-135, St. Paul, MN 55164-0383, U.S.A.
Please enclose a self-addressed, stamped envelope for reply, or $1.00 to cover costs.

Words of Power
Sacred Sounds of East & West

Brian and Esther Crowley

1991
Llewellyn Publications
St. Paul, Minnesota 55164-0383, U.S.A.

FIRST EDITION

Interior Art: Esther Crowley

Special Note:

The words, chants and mantras published herein are offered as examples of words of power used down the ages in various languages, with some combinations of more recent vintage. Although the authors have themselves employed many of these to good effect, publication herein is in no way to be considered a guarantee that they will be effective in the manner described when used by any other person.

Library of Congress-in-Publication Data
　　Crowley, Brian.
　　　　Words of power: sacred sounds of East and West / Brian Crowley and Esther Crowley.
　　　　p.　　cm.
　　　　Includes bibliographical references.
　　　　ISBN 0–87542–135–0
　　　　1. Prayers.　2. Incantations.　3. Chants.　4 Invocation.
　　　　5. Mantras.　I. Crowley, Esther, 1937- .　II. Title.
　　　　BL560.C76　1990　　　　　　　　　　　　90-46086
　　　　291.4'3--dc20　　　　　　　　　　　　　　CIP

Llewellyn Publications
A Division of Llewellyn Worldwide, Ltd.
P.O. Box 64383, St. Paul, MN 55164-0383

Loud rang the voice of God, and lightning spears
Pierced all the heavens; thunder shook the spheres . . .
And when they stood waiting, came the word,
That word that splits the rocks: I AM THE LORD!

Eleazar Kalir (Ashkenazic rite, 9th century)

Dedication

This book is dedicated to James J. and Desiree Hurtak for their priceless influence on our lives and our work and for bringing us to a fuller awareness of the value of sacred sounds as connected with the inter-dimensional work of the B'nai Or.

Books by Brian Crowley

The Springbok and the Kangaroo
Concise Key to Numerology
Currie Cup Story
Calypso Cavaliers
Cricket's Exiles
A History of Australian Batting
A History of Australian Bowling
The Face on Mars (with J. J. Hurtak)
Australia's Greatest Cricket Characters
Australia's Tennis Greats
A Cavalcade of International Cricketers
The Great Aussie Sausage Book (with Erich Schaal)
The Zulu Bone Oracle
Return to Mars (with Anthony Pollock)
Cradle Days of Australian Cricket (with Pat Mullins)
Hotting Up
Numerology: Key to Karma (forthcoming)

Books by Esther Crowley

The Living Waters of Yoga & Meditation
Joga in die Buitelug
Love is Life

Books by Brian and Esther Crowley

Understanding the Oriental Martial Arts
Japanese Gods of Luck (forthcoming)

Acknowledgments

Recognition is given to all those teachers who have inspired and/or instructed us down the years, including: Satya Sai Baba; Swami Muktananda; Swami Sivananda; Swami Venkatesananda; Sri Ramana Maharshi; Rita Williamson of the White Eagle Lodge and Psychic Club, Cape Town; Credo Vuzamazulu Mutwa, Hereditary High Sanusi of the Zulu nation; Nathaniel and other friends of rarer dimensions who have guided us throughout the composition of this book.

We also note the valuable part played in our development by institutions such as the Theosophical Society, Academy for Future Science, Aquarian Foundation, World Goodwill and International Yoga Teachers' Association.

Special acknowledgment is accorded Yehuda Tagar of Adelaide, Australia, for his assistance with the chapter relating to universal sound, and David Godwin for his kindly review of the manuscript and sage suggestions.

Contents

INTRODUCTION

*Mantra: A formula, which, by the power of its
sound, creates certain conditions in the world
of one's soul.*
The Bible of the World

There exists a vast selection of words of power for diverse uses and in many tongues that are far too numerous to include in a single volume. We have concentrated here primarily on sacred sounds drawn from the Hebrew, Egyptian, Hindu/Sanskrit and Tibetan traditions—with some mention of Arabic, Latin and Greek sacred words and phrases of significance.

Highlighted are those words and phrases found personally effective during many hours of meditative practice, in group situations and individually. We also touch on the subject of meditation itself and offer some suggested methods and rituals for those who are unfamiliar with meditation techniques in Chapters 7, 19 and 20.

When it comes to the mantras and invocations themselves, there is some elaboration on historical roots, for it is advisable to have some knowledge and understanding of the origin and meaning of what is to be spoken or sung. The possibility of certain key sounds common to all languages is also touched upon.

We wish to emphasize from the beginning that

this work is not intended as a mere manual of magical words and phrases to be used solely for personal gain. If it stands out as an essentially spiritual experience, no apology is tendered, for all humans are basically philosophical or spiritual creatures, whether they care to admit it or not. When it comes to any assessment of what is known as the Divine, it is reasonably pertinent to record that the Supreme Being, or God, as a concept and as a reality, still seems to remain somewhere beyond mere scientific or theological explanation.

In the end result it would appear to matter little if a person subscribes to the tenets of Judaism, Hinduism, Christianity, Islam, Gnosticism, Shamanism, Witchcraft, Druidism, Magick or any of the numerous other creeds, -isms and spiritual and/or self-awareness and mystical practices available to us. What is probably more important is to learn to discern the good (God) in all and to reserve no energy for the negative (or "bad"), no matter its source. But the choice remains strictly individual. Each of us possesses a capacity for free-will expression in a measure greater than some might care to acknowledge. We are eminently capable of sorting wheat from chaff, gold from dirt, and diamond from glinting glass; and exercise of free will may be, in effect, the Creator's most profound gift to His Creation.

Our own personal conviction is that participation in sacred sound, by its very action, results in stimulation of the individual intuitive insight, and thus greatly enhances the human capacity for making correct choices. In this regard and in many other ways, the invocations and mantras presented below have worked well for us down through the years. It is our sincere wish that those who study this book will benefit as much from their use as we have.

1. WORDS OF POWER

And his sound shall be heard when he goeth in
unto the holy place before the Lord,
and when he cometh out.

Exodus 28:35

In our everyday modern world, sound travels through the air in longitudinal "waves" produced by the vibration of any given object—a beaten drum, a plucked string, an object dropped on the floor, the movement of human vocal chords, in speech or in song. The human ear is capable of picking up a wide range of these sounds, judging them by their "frequency" (pitch), "intensity" (loudness), and "quality" (how they impress the ear of the listener). There also exists a whole spectrum of high frequency sound, which, under normal conditions, remains inaudible to humans but can be heard by certain animals and birds. Even plants are known to respond to sound, showing preference for harmonious music, which aids their growth, and being known to wilt when subjected to loud and discordant music.

Unfortunately, many of the sounds we hear around us are harsh and discordant. On a daily basis, we are not only faced with the threat of physical pollution of our air and water but also constantly bombarded with audio pollution in the form of a multitude of syn-

1

thetic noises, mostly by-products of so-called technical progress. Add the sounds made by people talking, shouting, laughing, children playing—all natural enough, but, at times, and in a crowded modern city, as disturbing perhaps as non-human sounds. And because sound waves can travel through virtually any medium, we really have little control over what we hear. The result: constant exposure to discordant noises makes for potentially serious physiological and psychological damage.

But if this be the case, so too can the reverse be true.

By exposing ourselves to more amenable noises—melodious music, the sounds of nature, a running stream, the sea, birds singing, and the like, we can repair at least some of the damage done by unwanted noise. Perhaps, and even more significantly, we may then elect to move a step forwards (or, more correctly, upwards) by tuning in to the hidden "sound of the soul." This can be achieved by listening to or learning to intone certain invocations and chants, magical words and mantras, handed down from ages past and developed to stimulate very specific effects—calming, healing, elevating, and personally transformational. There are even word and tone patterns designed to initiate communication with dimensions of activity more elevated than our own. The all-embracing aspect of controlled use of sacred sound is summed up most succinctly in Jeanne Miller's *The Vedas: Harmony, Meditation, and Fulfillment:*

> . . . the very sound of words inspired from deep within the heart in moments of worship quickened both men and in the celestial entities invoked a response to loftier thought and influences which in

turn brought the worshipper in harmony with the Cosmic Order, the fountain-spring of truth.[1]

The King of Benares' Elephant

Many of the most familiar of verbal invocations of power emanate from the Indian sub-continent, and an old story about the King of Benares' elephant illustrates the value placed by the inhabitants of India on the chanted or spoken word as a generator of positive or negative vibrations.

It is told that a gang of thieves once sought refuge in the King's elephant-house, where they immediately began to plot their next crime. Their plan was to break into the royal treasury and steal the King's jewels and other precious objects. When asked what should be done if someone got in their way, the leader pointed to his dagger meaningfully and proceeded to give his men explicit verbal instructions.

All the while, the King's favorite elephant was listening raptly to the criminals' talk of robbery and killing. Having learned to trust all humans as his mentors and guardians, he was of the impression that the robbers had come to teach him new tricks.

Next day, to the consternation of all who knew him, he proceeded to attack everyone who came close, including his poor faithful personal keeper, whom the elephant lifted high in his trunk and threw to the floor.

The King was distraught at the behavior of his favorite pet and ordered one of his wisest subjects to investigate the matter. The old sage, scratching around in the straw scattered on the floor of the elephant-house, found evidence of the robbers' overnight sojourn there. In meditation, he learned psychically of the occurrence of the night before and of the fact that the elephant had become negatively programmed by the robbers' talk of violence.

When the King asked what should be done, the wise old *rishi* suggested that he gather a group of the holiest men of the land and that they sit together talking about spiritual matters and singing sacred mantras or chants of power in the elephant stall.

This was duly accomplished, and the elephant was seen to listen carefully to the holy talk and chanting of the rishis. And, after a few days, the King was delighted to observe that his beloved pet had reverted back to the normal kind and gentle animal he knew from before.

The Power of Speech

In ordinary speech we generally employ sound to express meaning in communication. The intonation, however, of certain selected words in the form of mantras, chants and invocations serves to release latent forces from within and from without to be directed for very specific purposes, such as healing, personal uplift-ment and the creation of metaphysical conditions that may lead towards a better understanding of the universe and our place in it.

Since time began, priests, healers, shamans, mystics, medicine men and magicians of all persuasions have been aware of the power of specified verbal formulae, spoken or sung out loud, or intoned silently within. Some have gone so far as to assert that the words, and even the name, used by any individual determines to a great extent that person's fate. The renowned mystic and founder of the Theosophical Society, H. P. Blavatsky, writing on the potency of speech and sound in her monumental metaphysical treatise *The Secret*

Doctrine, points out that names and words can be both beneficent or maleficent, that they are "in a certain sense, either venomous or health-giving, according to the hidden influences attached by Supreme Wisdom to their elements."[2]

The use of sound for specified purposes is universal and historical, and scriptural sources refer repeatedly to the use of words of power. The Old Testament simply abounds in expressions of directed sacred invocation, while the New Testament informs us that Jesus and his disciples used selected words of power for the purposes of healing, casting out of demons, and raising from the dead.

Around the World

A large part of ancient Egyptian literature is founded in the use of magical words and phrases, one well-known instance being the *Papyrus of Ani.* This scroll tells in particular of the employment of words of power by the goddess Isis, who was acknowledged as the mistress of words of enchantment, to negate the effects of poison administered to the great god Ra.

For many of the inhabitants of India and other countries of the East, the intonation of recited or sung mantras is an essential part of daily living. In the *Anugita*, a portion of the *Mahabharata,* one of the two great "epics" of Hindu scripture, Brahmana, the creator deity, informs his wife Sarasvati, goddess of wisdom, learning and eloquence, that *apana,* or "inspirational breath" (speech), transforms intelligence and opens the mind. Another ancient Indian work, the *Atharva Veda* (circa 900 B.C.E.), is filled with spells, incantations and magical formulae to cure diseases and to bring success in warfare. According to the eminent

Indian spiritual teacher Paramahansa Yogananda, there was even once a famous Hindu musician, Tan Sen, who was reputed to have been able to successfully quench fire by the power of his song. In Central America, the Maya were known to favor, among other invocations and spells, the magical phrase *hax pax max* to counter the bite of a rabid dog. Similar sounding formulas and spells were heard in Europe during the Middle Ages and afterwards—for instance, the familiar *abracadabra*, which was used to rid a person of illness or bad luck, and another popular formula for banishing sickness: *hola nola massa*.

The s*angomas* of Africa and shamans and Medicine folk of every other continent all hold certain ancient words and expressions as specially potent. Shamanistic songs and chants form a powerful bonding between the natural and supernatural and serve to heal both the singer and the listener. Famous Arctic explorer Knud Rasmussen has, as one instance only, recorded the feats of a Netsilik Eskimo woman called Uvavnuk who "by the power of her song" was able to disperse negativity so that "all who were present were loosed from their burden of sin and wrong."[3]

North American Indians have long extolled the power of song, particularly in healing ceremonials and for the purpose of rendering themselves apparently invisible to other people. They also have always regarded a name as a distinct part of the personality, and any injury resulting from malicious handling of an individual's name is as serious as a wound inflicted on the physical body.

Island-based people around the world are no exception when it comes to employment of magical verbal expressions. In particular, the famed *kahuna* magician-priests of the Hawaiian Islands have a long tradition of a powerful system of magic that enables them to communicate telepathically among themselves (and with discarnate spirits), astral project, forecast the future, control the weather, heal the sick, and even raise the dead. Vocalization of the so-called *Ha* prayer enables the Hawaiian medicine man to contact intangible worlds for assistance and inspiration and, in extreme circumstances, invoke the dreaded "death prayer" to rid his particular island of an enemy or other undesirable person.

The Japanese *kiai,* the "shout of power" exhaled by a martial arts exponent when making a move or strike, might also be equated with the notion of a word of power. The nearest English translation of the expression could be something like "spirit meeting." Kiai is employed as a focusing technique in karate and other martial arts disciplines, and the sound originates in the diaphragm before being forced up the throat by the muscles of the lower abdomen, the area of the body thought by Eastern *k'ung fu* and karate masters to be the source of all power. This violent exhalation of air in the form of a shout just before or during an attacking movement is designed to bring strength to the body and to inure it against the effects of an opponent's blow. Kiai reflects an attempt to balance spiritual resolve with physical action, and is thus directly related to words of power as discussed in this book. It is said that a master of the martial arts can even stun a small animal or bird with one yell and then revive the creature again with another shout.

Angelic Contact

Claims have even been made of contact with angelic beings through use of words of power in the language known as *Enochian*, the so-called "Language of the Angels," and other "celestial" tongues. Sixteenth-century English astrologer, mathematician and occultist John Dee, with the aid of a psychic named Edward Kelly, used the art of scrying, or crystal-ball gazing, in order to obtain dictation in Enochian direct from discarnate entities who identified themselves as angels. Dee produced an Enochian dictionary, which is still in print, and, some 300 years later, the published rituals of the Hermetic Order of the Golden Dawn (a magical society founded by Kabbalah scholar S. L. MacGregor Mathers and others with the object of maintaining and preserving certain ancient and secret teachings) contained many references to the use of Enochian in magical ceremonies—as invocations for the calling up of angels and the "Chiefs of the Elementals" or nature spirits.

Notwithstanding the claims of Dee and the Order of the Golden Dawn to a specialist language of the Angels, there are a host of known idiomatic expressions in Hebrew, Sanskrit, Tibetan, Arabic and other languages that are purportedly designed for stimulation of contact with "higher" intelligence. Many of these expressions are included in this volume.

2. THE HEBREW CONNECTION

*And Moses was learned in all the wisdom of the
Egyptians, and was mighty in words and in deeds.*

Acts 7:22

Jews and Christians alike will be very familiar
with the 3600-year-old story of Moses or, in Hebrew,
Moishe, which was, in fact, originally an Egyptian word
simply meaning "child"—how he was rescued from a
basket on the River Nile and raised by an Egyptian
princess; how he led the previously enslaved Hebrews
out of bondage from Egypt, took them safely across the
Red Sea over dry land, guided and cajoled them for 40
years while they were crisscrossing the wastelands of
the Sinai Desert, finally bringing them to within sight
of the marvelous land promised them by their singular
God, a country Moses himself was, ironically, never to
set foot into.

Before the Hebrews left Egypt, Moses, in the company of his brother Aaron, who was destined to become
High Priest to the Hebrew Nation, managed to persuade a hard-hearted Pharaoh to let his people go by
performing a series of magical feats that included the
visitation of plagues and other grave disasters on the
Egyptians. Moses was, according to scripture, aided
throuhout this campaign by his singular and mighty

Lord Yahweh, the Hebrews' uniquely monotheistic God. All along the way to the Promised Land, he continued to work his outstanding miracles in superb Old Testament style, in a manner that has, in Judeo/Christian literature, only been equalled by the New Testament Jesus Christ.

Moses and the Magicians

Saint Stephen tells us that "Moses was learned in all the wisdom of the Egyptians, and was mighty in words and in deeds" (Acts 7:22). Most importantly, perhaps, is that the future Hebrew leader was raised as an Egyptian prince, and it is almost certain that his court tuition would have included some lessons in *hekau* or *words of power* (perhaps even from a learned sage of the caliber of old Teta of the goose-head story we tell in Chapter 8).

There is also some evidence that Moses would have later been initiated into the Hebrew religio-mystical tradition now known as *Kabbalah*—an expression which means literally "to receive" and derives from a root word meaning "from mouth to ear," indicating the hidden or secret nature of the discipline.

The miracles of Moses ranged from turning his staff into a snake to parting the waters of the Red Sea so that the Hebrews might pass on dry land.

There are numerous ancient references informing us of the ability of Egyptian magicians to also perform such feats as converting sticks into snakes, and back again, or of parting the waters of a lake or river. Indeed, the Bible tells us that the Pharaoh's sorcerers were easily able to duplicate some, although not all, of the miracles performed by Moses. However, as an indication of the apparently superior power at Moses' command, the snake created from his staff easily devoured those called into life by his Egyptian rivals. Why Moses was apparently more successful as a conjurer than his Egyptian counterparts is perhaps best explained by the celebrated Egyptologist E. A. Wallis Budge in his book *Egyptian Magic:*

> . . . one great distinction must be made between the magic of Moses and that of the Egyptians; the former was wrought by the command of the God of the Hebrews, but the latter by the gods of Egypt at the command of man.[1]

What Budge is trying to point out is that in the Hebrew tradition there is a distinct difference between magic and miracle. Jewish lore states that magic is a mere metaphysical operation that involves a mastery of the so-called World of Formation and can be attained by anyone who is prepared to work hard upon the higher centers of the psyche. Miracles, on the other hand, as performed, for instance, by Moses and Jesus, occur through the operation of spiritual energies emanating from the upper World of Creation via the agency of someone whose psyche has developed more naturally through more emphasis on spiritual refinement and sensitization.

Kabalists consider these spiritual energies as "gifts" from subtler worlds that are not to be used for any occult or magical manipulation on the earth plane. In the Jewish *Talmud* (the word means literally "to study"), a body of commentary on the *Torah*, which is based on the first five books of the Bible, or the *Pentateuch*, it is stated clearly: "He who practices magic will not enter Heaven"—meaning that anyone who concentrates solely on operating in the World of Formation (that is, our physical world and what is known as the astral level) for his/her own gain may become trapped there and find it difficult to progress into the World of the Spirit. Persons who, however, perform miracles are acting only as conduits for higher forces, without any thought of self-gain. This rather rigid interpretation of the operation and control of super-physical forces is, of course, open to debate.

Power of the Word

Legend tells us that Moses carried a staff bearing an inscription of the four-lettered Holy Name of God or Tetragrammaton. Stories abound about this and other words of power he may have used in order to effect his miracles in Egypt and in the desert.

One commentator even claims a Sanskrit-based mantra as the phrase used by Moses to part the Red Sea. The syllables said to have been employed on this historic occasion consisted of a mystical sound formula normally used for protection at a critical time, which has no exact grammatical translation: *Ut-Re-Me-Fa-Sol-La-Ne,* with "ut" as in *put*, and the remainder of the invocation sounding much like part of the familiar musical scale.[2]

A revised version of the well-known story of Moses and the Egyptian overseer caught beating a Hebrew worker reveals a clear example of the "power of the Word." It seems as if the Egyptian attacked by Moses may not have been struck down physically, as we are led to believe when reading the standard English translation of Exodus 2:12: "And he looked this way and that way, and when he saw that there was no man, he slew the Egyptian, and hid him in the sand." According to Rabbi Dr. Philip S. Berg, former head of the Kabbalah Institute, Jerusalem and a notable writer on

Did Moses part the Red Sea using words of power?

Hebrew mysticism, an alternative translation of the Exodus text which directly follows the above quotation confirms that Moses probably killed the Egyptian through the energy transmitted by utterance of a special word or phrase—perhaps even the "Ineffable Name" of the Almighty itself.[3]

If this indeed was the scenario, it is certain that Moses would only have invoked the Holy Name once he had first called upon God to make the actual decision about how to take care of the Egyptian—for in terms of Hebrew law it is forbidden to use the *Name* of God to usurp the *Will* of God.

After the encounter by Moses with the Egyptian overseer, we read in Exodus 2:14 of his confrontation with two Hebrews he found fighting each other, one of whom immediately taunted him by asking (according to the standard translation): "Intendest thou to kill me, as thou killed the Egyptian?"

In the original Hebrew, the phrase "Intendest thou to kill me" reads *halhorgeini ata omer.* In its most literal sense, this would be translated something like: "Are you about to kill me, *you say?*" (our emphasis). According to the Hebrew mystical work known as the *Zohar,* specific use here of the word *omer* ("you say") points to the probability that Moses did in fact kill the Egyptian *using a word of power,* and the whole incident helps to confirm the viewpoint that Moses operated all the while on an elevated metaphysical plane.[4]

Being thoroughly conversant with all of the Names of the Almighty, Moses, it would seem, was eminently capable of slaying someone (or raising a person from the dead) through use of the *Aleph-Beis* (or *Aleph-Bet*), the sacred Hebrew alphabet.

Kabbalah and the Tree of Life

Throughout *Torah* and the inspired kabalistic *Sepher Yetzirah* ("Book of Formation") and *Sepher ha Zohar* ("Book of Splendor"), there is repeated reference to the awesome power of the Word. *Torah* means literally "Teaching" or "Law" (also implying guidance and/ or direction), and although it mainly embodies the so-called Law of Moses contained in the *Pentateuch*, the essence of Judaism implies that *Torah* is revealed continuously both in nature and in history as a dynamic unfoldment. The Written Word is always to be supplemented by the Oral Tradition, which is handed down by succeeding generations, and added to from time to time through individual insight and perception. There is thus always an ongoing development and reinterpretation of the Judaic heritage.

The *Sepher Yetzirah* and *Sepher ha Zohar* are claimed to have been revealed by the actual spirit of Moses to the Rabbi Shimon Bar Yochai, a pupil of the celebrated Rabbi Akiva and a great Jewish mystic of the 2nd century, in a cave at Sfad in northern Palestine. Moses thus continues to appear as the most important figure in the establishment of the Hebrews as a separate race in their own country and as progenitor of the laws and mystical wisdom of his people. The basic mystical system of the Hebrew tradition known as Kabbalah is largely contained in the two mentioned works, which are filled with discussion of the nature of metaphysical or pure energy and its superiority over mere physical power in our world.

Central to kabalistic teachings are the concepts of: A Transcendent God, the *Ayin Sof* ("Without End"); Ten *Sephiroth* or Divine Attributes of the *Ets Cha-yim*, the Tree of Life, with an eleventh anti-Sefirah or non-

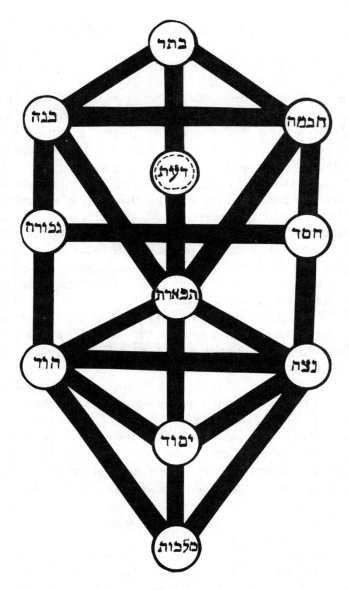

The Tree of Life of the Kabbalah; original Hebrew script.

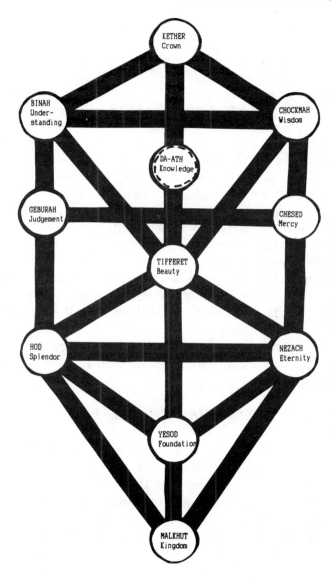

The Tree of Life of the Kabbalah; English translation.

Sefirah known as *Da-ath*—Knowledge that emerges out of nowhere and comes direct from God; Four Worlds of: Emanation (*Azilut*), Creation (*Beriah*), Formation (*Yezirah*), and Action (*Asiyyah*—our physical world); and most important of all in the present context: A Living Language of Light, the *Aleph-Beis*, represented by the 22 letters of the Hebrew alphabet.

Although we may experience a semblance of changeability in the lower worlds of Formation and Action, all is, in fact, always in Divine Order, and the Sephiroth of the Tree of Life provide us with a blueprint for every physical and metaphysical event. Moreover, in the two lower worlds in particular, Divine Will is firmly based on Mercy (*Chesed,* one of Ten Sephiroth), balanced with Justice (*Geburah*)—which might be equated with the Eastern Karmic Law principle, which leads inexorably towards eventual balance in all things. In the kabalistic context, above all else there rests the principle of Divine Grace through which the existing laws of reward and punishment are immediately adjusted for any person who sincerely recognizes any misdemeanors, and repents.

Christian Kabbalah

Amongst Jews of the scattered diaspora, the kabalistic tradition of Moses and Shimon Bar Yochai enjoyed a revival in 11th- and 12th-century Spain, following hundreds of years of limited and mostly hidden use. The well-known Moses de Leon and other Jewish kabalists of Spain believed that by singing mystical chants in Hebrew they were transported bodily to Jerusalem. Another resurgence of Kabbalah practice came about in the 16th century, this time in Palestine itself, where Isaac Luria, the "Holy Lion" of Sfad, was a notable teacher of the system.

The Middle Ages saw an interest in Kabbalah develop among Christian occultists who considered the system to be tantamount to the Yoga of the West, some prominent students being Cornelius Agrippa, Philippus Paracelsus and the German Jesuit priest cum scientist of the 1600s, Athanasius Kircher. Another possible Kabbalah-oriented candidate of the so-called "hermetic century" was the famed Michel de Notredame or Nostradamus. The mysticism of the Hebrews has, in effect, supplied the foundations of modern Western occultism. Some other personalities of note down the centuries who have been influenced by kabalistic lore include the so-called "man who never dies," the Comte de Saint Germain, Dr. John Dee (communicator with the "angels") and his colleague Edward Kelley, the mysterious Count Cagliostro, the famous lover Casanova, and the "unknown philosopher" Louis Claude de Saint-Martin.

It is highly likely that much earlier in the 1st century the enigmatic Greek Apollonius of Tyana, an almost Christ-like personality but theoretically a pagan, studied and practiced Kabbalah, as would have Simon Magus (or Simon the Magician), who is referred to in Acts of the Apostles.

Down the ages, the influence of kabalistic principles has been profound, and traces can be found in almost every occult practice extant. When occultism became fashionable in Britain during the 19th century, names like Mathers, Yeats, Waite, Crowley and Dion Fortune became closely associated with its use. MacGregor Mathers, author of *The Kabbalah Unveiled*, a new translation of the *Zohar*, was, with several other Christian kabalists, a founder of the famous Hermetic Order of the Golden Dawn, which had lodges in England, Scotland and France. W. B. Yeats was, of course, also a famous poet, while A. E. Waite produced the most used of all modern Tarot decks, the Rider-Waite edition, which is filled with kabalistic symbology. The rather unpopular but powerful occult adept Aleister Crowley, who was born in the year (1875) that H. P. Blavatsky founded the Theosophical Society, produced his own Tarot set based primarily on Egyptian lore. He did, however, use Hebrew kabalistic procedure in many of his rituals. Dion Fortune (real name: Violet Firth) published some of the still most widely read books on occult or psychic self-defense as well as about Kabbalah.

A Crowley disciple, Frances Israel Regardie did much to enshrine the Golden Dawn kabalistic connections for use by the general public when he published a four-volume work detailing the order's secret rituals. Occultists of the Golden Dawn used the kabalistic Tree of Life as a matrix or grid for comparing archetypal images of other mythologies and religions for use in magical ritual and ceremony. For example, *Chokmah,* the Father or Wisdom principle of the Tree, was aligned with Odin (Scandinavian), Zeus (Greek), Jupiter (Roman) and Ra (Egyptian). The Golden Dawn system could be applied to any type of magical ritual. For the record, Eliphas Levi, the French occultist and author, was the first to align the ten Sephiroth with the 22 cards of the Major Arcana of the Tarot.

The Middle Pillar

Central to much modern-day kabalistic practice is stimulation of the so-called "Middle Pillar," or Pillar of Equilibrium, in ritual and in meditation. This refers to the five Sephiroth or Divine Attributes depicted on the central column of the Tree of Life mentioned above. The "tree," as already noted, embodies a total of ten Sephiroth in its lowest presentation (in the Jewish system there are countless further "trees" extending forever "upwards" into the higher heavens).

The Middle Pillar or Center Column is known by occultists as the magical equivalent of the "Middle Way" and represents the pathway through which the Holy Spirit or *Shekinah* energy descends to illuminate our human consciousness in a balanced manner. This action should never be confused with the *Kundalini* power that arises from the base of the spine to stimulate the seven chakras or energy vortices of the physical body, which is described in Chapter 11.

The five powers or attributes incorporated into the Middle Pillar are: *Kether* (Crown), *Da-ath* (Knowledge), *Tifferet* (Beauty), *Yesod* (Foundation) and *Malkuth* (Kingdom).

There are a number of Middle Pillar Meditations in use. Sounding of certain Hebrew words and/or phrases can be essential in creating the required conditions for proper activation of the Middle Pillar energies. A suggested ritual is given in Chapter 7, following a full discussion of various Hebrew expressions of power and of the so-called "Language of Light" itself in Chapters 3 through 6.

The Middle Pillar phenomenon pointedly illustrates the underlying principle behind all kabalistic work. Basically, the task of the kabalist is to aid in the unification of the higher worlds with the lower world by striving to draw the Divine Light down through the World of Formation into the World of Action (our physical world) via his or her own body.

Perhaps most importantly, this work of unifying our lower world with higher dimensions means that mystics of all and any persuasions are able to meet on common ground in a spiritual world to acknowledge that the same reality exists behind apparently differing theories and practices. All are able to converse together in unity in the Higher Heavens, no matter their individual religion or system of mystical operation.

We are convinced that this act of unification can be appreciably enhanced through use of pre-selected sacred sounds in the form of mantras, chants and invocations in several ancient languages, including the language of the original kabalists, Hebrew.

3. A LANGUAGE OF LIGHT

*The alef-bet is a cable representing the
missing link between the sending of a message from the
physical to the metaphysical level.*
—Dr. Philip S. Berg
(The Kabbalah Connection)

The concepts presented above relating to the power of the word will not be too unfamiliar for anyone who has made a serious study of the Hebrew alphabet, its letters, and the words and phrases that can be constructed from them—*and of the effects which may be generated by their use.* Just as the ancient peoples of Asia used their *mantras* and the Egyptians their own *hekau*, or words of power, for a variety of predetermined purposes, so too did the Hebrews of old (as have their descendants to this day) use words of power—for protection, for healing, and for the initiation of personal transformation, and ultimate transcendence.

Jewish lore tells us that Bezalel, the son of Uri (meaning "light"), who is mentioned in Exodus 31 as the builder of the Tabernacle in the Wilderness, knew how to combine the letters with which Heaven and Earth were created. If these letters (or sounds) were to be removed for an instant, our universe would return to the state of an absolute vacuum. When the Hebrew sages taught that God created the universe with ten utterances, their objective was to lead us to the knowl-

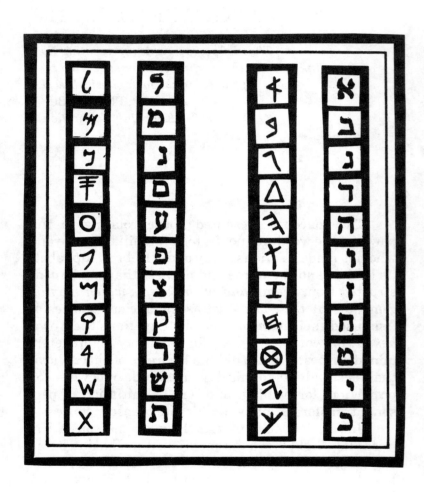

Genesis of the Hebrew Alphabet: The 22 letters of the Hebrew alphabet in the early Temple Script and in their modern form.

edge that the very existence of each creature and object—angelic, human, animate and inanimate—is dependent upon the spiritual content of divine speech.

Sacred Speech

To the Jewish kabalist, speech is the medium of God's revelation, which makes language itself sacred and an object of mystical contemplation. The 22 letters of the Hebrew alphabet are considered profound realities, component parts of a "Living Language of Universal Light" as well as primal spiritual forces that are, in effect, the building blocks of Creation. In no way should they be taken merely as a haphazard collection of consonants. Each Hebrew letter serves as a specified channel connecting Heaven with Earth in some form or another. Through contemplation of correct combinations of letters, the devout may eventually ascend into abstract levels and gain ecstatic mystical experience and prophetic vision.

Because of the Jewish belief that the Hebrew alphabet, the *Aleph-Beis* or *Aleph-Bet*, predated Creation, and is, so to speak, the protoplasm of the universe, the letters themselves, and the order and manner in which they are utilized, are of crucial significance. Even their separate parts contain meaning, some being combinations of two or more of the other letters. The study of Aleph-Bet letter combinations is known as *Tseruf*, and can be compared in some respects with the esoteric study of music. One kabalistic analysis of our physical resonance system sees the sound of the sacred words traveling from ear to heart, on to the spleen, center of emotion, and then upwards and out through the crown of the head. The various parts of the body serve as strings on an instrument; the effect created by holy sounds varies according to their preparation and fine tuning.

As is the case with other ancient languages (notably Sanskrit, Tibetan, Egyptian and Chinese), Hebrew sacred chants formulated down the ages carry the power to arouse spiritual forces that range far beyond the imagination of the ordinary person in the street. Indeed, Hebrew is considered by kabalists and others to be a truly transcendental "flame-language." As in the Hindu experience, purification of the divine power within is attained through correct and persistent usage of sacred sound, resulting in the accomplishment of amazing feats of a physical and paraphysical nature.

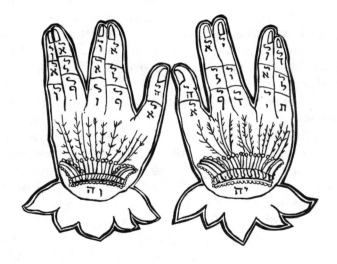

Mystical use of the Hebrew letters: A figure from Shefa Tal by the 17th-century German kabalist Shabettai Horowitz depicts the channels of divine emanation in the form of hands. Each wrist bears two letters of the Hebrew name of God, and from these issue 28 "sources of emanation" in the form of combinations of letters.

The Power of Language

An outstanding example of the overall power of language is provided by the revival of Hebrew as a daily form of speech in 1948, when Israel was declared an independent state. For thousands of years, succeeding generations had kept Hebrew alive primarily as a religious language for use in the synagogue, in ritual prayers in the homes of Jews, and in the written form. Although some attempts were made to return to Hebrew speaking during the early part of the 20th century, in normal day-to-day communication in pre-Israel Palestine the Jews resident there used mostly Yiddish (a language developed from East European and Russian roots and closely approximating some German dialects), with Arabic as a second *lingua franca*, plus whatever tongue happened to be spoken in the country in which they previously resided. During earlier times, when the Jews returned from Babylonian captivity (around 538 B.C.E.), the general language in use throughout the Middle East was Aramaic, closely related to Hebrew and still in use at the time of Jesus and afterwards.

Official adoption in 1948 of the vibrant ancient Hebrew language as the spoken tongue of the newly independent Israel served as an immediate unifying force for Jews of many national ties, who spoke diverse tongues and who had taken part in the great return or *aliyah* ("going up") to their ancestral homeland from the death camps and ghettos of Nazi Europe and from many other locations scattered elsewhere around the world.

Hebrew, now used as a daily language of communication, served to promote a highly charged and dynamic national energy, which was witnessed in the way the new Israelis fashioned a veritable Garden of Eden out of the arid desert sands of Palestine within a very short period of time.

Hebrew—a Computer Code?

As is the case with Sanskrit mantras, careful articulation of Hebrew prayers and chants is considered of prime importance (although there are, naturally, variances in enunciation from region to region and country to country). There even have been some claims that the sounds contained in the Hebrew language might represent some kind of basic computer code used in establishing our present round of human existence, beginning some 6,000 years ago.

Just such a theory was seriously postulated in December 1983 by Dr. Philip S. Berg, then esteemed Director of the Institute for Kabbalah, Jerusalem, in a paper entitled "Extra-Terrestrial Life in Outer Space: Forces Behind the Future" during the *Forecast 1984: Multidisciplinary Congress on Prophecy* at the Jerusalem Hilton, Israel. Dr. Berg cited Hebrew as a probable computer code for programming our "walking biocomputers," or bodies, and argued that the kabalistic *Zohar* provides a perfect system for contacting extraterrestrial intelligence. Our own extrapolation is that those who learned the system could learn to control the universe, the aim being to program (or reprogram) our physical bodies into "Superluminal Light Bodies" capable of traversing higher universes. Referring to Hindu terms, this would mean that it would no longer be necessary, nor advisable, to reincarnate repeatedly in order to strive for spiritual perfection.

Support for this concept is provided by Dr. James J. Hurtak of California (another speaker at the *Forecast 1984* meeting), who has written extensively about a "special archangelic alphabet of Metatron known historically in Kabbalah as *ketav einayim*, 'eye writings.'" Use of this "greater language," of which Hebrew is claimed to be a form, may, it seems, take us considerably beyond the Hindu experience of *Nirvana*, or Eternal Bliss, by removing us completely from our "Earthly Cross of Space and Time" so that we may co-exist (and co-create) with higher forms of life in the biblically termed "Many Mansions of the Father's Kingdom," or Realms of Light of the *B'nai Or*, the Universal Brotherhood of Light. The name *Metatron* represents a visible manifestation of the Supreme Deity. The *ketav einayim* are composed of small circles and lines shaped like flames, a "greater language of creation through which the elements of life are projected."[1]

Hurtak also cites a biophysically oriented connection that links the four letters of the Tetragrammaton, or Holy Name of God, namely *yod, hey, vau, hey*, with the DNA-RNA matrix, which principle governs the life of all organisms and their hereditary genetic characteristics. The claim is that, correctly intoned, the Tetragrammaton and other sacred names serve to biophysically program or reprogram the human body. Hurtak, however, includes in his commentary several other languages in addition to Hebrew that can aid in this transformational process—namely Tibetan, Sanskrit, Egyptian and Chinese.[2]

Startling scientifically correlated support for the concept of Genesis (and possibly other books of the Old Testament) as some kind of code book written by some ultra-terrestrial intelligence has been offered by the California-based Meru Foundation and its team of scholars and scientists led by Stan Tenen. Using satellite computer linkups with researchers in a number of countries, results achieved so far by the Meru group point towards the Hebrew letters in the first of the Five Books of Moses as being positioned in a prearranged pattern, which has nothing to do with the story itself. This *Aleph-Bet* configuration apparently provides sophisticated data relating to topics such as quantum physics, cosmology, astronomy, time, gravity, and the DNA system, among others.[3]

Unusual research by Dr. Moishe Katz and colleagues at the Institute of Technology in Haifa, Israel, adds further weight to the argument that the *Torah* contains meaning that runs beyond its narrative detail. Having typed the entire Five Books of Moses into a computer, Dr. Katz abolished all spacing and created a stream of Hebrew letters. His next discovery has been calculated as a 38-million-to-one probability. Taking the number 49 (7 x 7), which represents the kabalistic number of the maximum spiritual level, and commencing with the first word in Genesis *B'reshiyth*, "In the beginning," Dr. Katz commanded his computer to skip every 49 letters, and mark the 50th.

The first four letters so marked clearly spelled out the word *Torah*!

In another experiment, the Israeli researcher used the Genesis 28 story of Jacob and the ladder, plus the number 26—the kabalistic value for the Tetragrammaton itself. His letter-skipping system immediately produced two easily recognizable words: *Mikdush* ("Temple") and, again, *Torah*. As the Temple and the Law or Scriptures represent the basic twin pillars of Judaism, this was more than astounding. In ongoing research, numerous other intriguing anomalies relating to hidden messages in the Bible have been

*The High Priest chanting Qadosh, Qadosh, Qadosh, Adonai
Tzeba'oth—"Holy, Holy, Holy is the Lord God of Hosts."*

reported by Dr. Katz and his coworkers.[4]
Perhaps Dr. Philip Berg is not too far off the mark
when he claims that the Bible, linked with the *Zohar*,
contains "the entire system for contacting extra-terrestrial intelligences."

Hebrew Pronunciation

As is the case with Sanskrit and Egyptian, vocalization of the Hebrew language can be a difficult task for
Westerners, particularly when it comes to the more
guttural sounds. A simplified guide to pronunciation of
a few key letters that differ greatly in sound from their
English counterparts is given below for readers totally
unfamiliar with the language. Anyone seeking true
perfection in enunciation is advised to seek out a good
Hebrew teacher, or utilize one of the many books and/
or audio-tape presentations available on the subject.
Key sounds are:

ch = as in Scottish *loch* (the Hebrew letter
chet)
dz = as in adze (*zayin*)
kh = as in Khmer (*kaph*)
tz = as *ts* in cats (*tzaddi*)
q = guttural q as in Qoran (*quf*)

Meanings of the 22 Hebrew Letters

Every letter in the Hebrew alphabet carries many
special meanings, and a full chapter might be devoted
to each. However, for present purposes, brief interpretations of the 22 basic components of the *Aleph-Bet* are

listed below, with special emphasis placed on the more important letters. The meanings given are a synthesis taken from several sources, including the wonderful exposition on the Aleph-Bet by Rabbi Michael L. Munk of New York in his *The Wisdom in the Hebrew Alphabet* (Mesorah Publications Ltd., Brooklyn, NY, 1983), a book which is heartily recommended to all who wish to study in depth the myriad spiritual nuances that highlight the Hebrew Language of Light and provide a code book of spiritual and temporal conduct for all.

1: א *Aleph*
Numerical Value: 1

Traditionally "first"; "sacrificial ox"; and "one thousand." As the first of all the Holy Letters, and symbol of God's Oneness and Omnipotence, *aleph* is a three-in-one presentation. Its upper right segment consists of a *yod*, the first letter in the Name of the Divine. A second *yod* in the *aleph's* lower left segment signifies the Creator resident within His creation. The central diagonal connecting pillar is the *vau*, symbol of transformation. *Aleph* thus represents the process of spiritual transformation from human to super-human and is linked with the belief in absolute monotheism—that there is but one true living God.

2: ב *Bet*
Numerical Value: 2

Translating literally as "house," *bet* is the first letter of the first word in the Hebrew bible (*B'reshiyth*—"In the beginning"). Also the first letter in the first word of any Jewish Blessing: *Baruch* ("blessed"), as in *Baruch ha Shem* ("Blessed is the Name [of God]"). *Bet* symbolizes the Duality and Plu-

rality of Creation, the two worlds of the Jewish faith—
"This World" and the "World to Come"—and emphasizes the fact that our pre-eminent task in This World is
to prepare for the World to Come.

3: ג *Gimmel*
Numerical Value: 3

Traditional meanings: "prize"; "reward"; "fund."
Esoterically, this is a symbol for Kindness and of Completion, standing for the Creator's overwhelming and
eternal beneficence or *Chesed* ("Mercy").

4: ד *Dalet*
Numerical Value: 4

Literally, "door"; also meaning "weakness." It represents dimensions in space and time: the four physical
directions—north, south, east and west—and the
metaphysical "Four Worlds"—*Emanation, Creation,
Formation,* and *Action.*

5: ה *Hey*
Numerical Value: 5

"The Spirit of the Lord." It symbolizes Divinity and
Gentility. This letter appears twice in the full Name of
God and, together with *yod,* forms the Divine Name
YAH. According to tradition, the World to Come was
created through utterance of the letter *yod.* This World
was created through the sound of *hey,* which is pronounced as a mere exhalation of breath, requiring little
movement from tongue or lip.

6: ‏ו‎ *Vau*
Numerical Value: 6

Traditionally this symbolizes "Humanity" and the "Restoration of Judgment." As the third letter in the *Ha Shem*, the Holy Name, *vau* represents Completion, Redemption and Transformation. It is the letter of continuity, uniting Heaven with Earth. When used with certain vowels (as in the probable pronunciation of the Name of God), *vau* can be an almost silent letter, more approximating a vowel than a consonant. A soft, vowel-like *vau* denies validity of the harsh-sounding *Jehovah* as an English translation for the Hebrew Name of God (about which more later). As the letter *yod* is also a so-called half-vowel, *Iyahweh*, with the *w* and both *h*'s uttered softly, may be closer to being correct as a possible pronunciation of the Ineffable Name.

7: ‏ז‎ *Zayin*
Numerical Value: 7

Means "a spear" or "male appendage." Closely linked with the mystical number seven (and all of its many connotations), *zayin* signifies Spiritual Struggle, as well as Spiritual Sustenance.

8: ‏ח‎ *Chet*
Numerical Value: 8

The *chet* or *chai* is the traditional symbol of "Life" and, ironically, of "sin." It is also the sign of Transcendance and of Divine Grace, pointing to the possibility that a human being can transcend the limitations of physical existence.

9: **ט** *Tet*
Numerical Value: 9

Meaning "to sweep out (by judgment)," *tet* epitomizes Goodness and Humility—the objective "goodness" which it is the Creator's prerogative to define and
delineate, not humankind's.

10: **י** *Yud*
Numerical Value: 10

Literally, "hand" and symbol of the Jew. It also
means "monument" or "share." Although the smallest
letter in the Hebrew alphabet, *yod* contains as much
meaning as the rest of the Hebrew alphabet combined.
Yod signifies Creation itself and all of the Metaphysical processes and, on its own, stands as an important
symbol for the Creator.

11: **כ** *Kaph*
Numerical Value: 20

This translates directly as "palm (of the hand or
tree)" and is the symbol of Crowning Accomplishment—with a dual meaning that encompasses both the
beginning and the ending. *Kaph* also relates to the
principle of the "four crowns": *priesthood*; *kingship*; the
Torah, or Word of God; and a *good name*.

12: **ל** *Lamed*
Numerical Value: 30

Meaning literally "to learn," this is the sign of Wisdom and of Purpose. Central letter of the Aleph-Bet
symbolizing the "King of Kings," the "Supreme Ruler."

13: מ *Mem*
Numerical Value: 40

Traditionally, *mem* has several direct meanings: "waters," "people," "nations," "languages," "tongues." It is the mystical symbol of the Revealed and of the Concealed. Also the first letter in the names *Moishe* (Moses) and *Mashiach* ("Anointed One"), equated by some with a coming Messiah. Moses was given the revealed evidence of the Creator's sovereignty over His creation; the Messiah represents the concealed part of the Celestial rule to which Humanity submits in faith alone.

14: נ *Nun*
Numerical Value: 50

Can be taken to mean "gaffing hook" (for fishing) and "to waste away." It is a letter sometimes used as a substitute letter in order to disguise a name. In its mystical sense, *nun* represents Everlasting Faithfulness and the Emergence of the Soul. Just as the soul is a spark of the Divine, so is God's grace available to all.

15: ס *Samekh*
Numerical Value: 60

Samekh means "to trust," "depend upon," and "support." It symbolizes Divine Support and Protection and is associated with the process of Memory. This important letter of the Aleph-Bet also depicts Abundance and Completeness.

16: **ע** *Ayin*
Numerical Value: 70

This means "eye," "wellspring," "source," or "center" and is linked with the Egyptian Eye of Horus (see Chapter 10). *Ayin* is, therefore, the symbol of Perception and Insight, of the Physical Eye and of the Spiritual Eye. It illustrates symbolically that the human eye can be taken as a microcosm of the universe.

17: **פ** *Pey*
Numerical Value: 80

Meaning "mouth," this letter represents both Speech and Silence and is closely linked with the art of Healing. The ultimate purpose of Creation is for humankind to learn to sing the praises of the Almighty, and to study the *Torah*.

18: **צ** *Tzaddi*
Numerical Value: 90

As the first letter in the word *tzaddiq*, or "righteous man," *tzaddi* stands for Righteousness and Humility. But although every *tzaddiq* expresses righteousness in a uniquely individual way, true righteousness can exist only in God.

19: **ק** *Quf*
Numerical Value: 100

There are numerous traditional meanings for this letter, including: "to buy (or to sell)"; "eye of needle"; and "ape, or monkey." Esoterically, it is the sign for Holiness, both human and Divine, and a symbol for abstinence and control. *Quf* also represents the various Growth Cycles of our world.

20: ר *Reysh*
Numerical Value: 200

Literally, "head," "chieftain," or "supreme one," paradoxically *reysh* can also be taken to mean "to become impoverished." It stands for the Challenge of Choice—Greatness or Degradation—between which elements there is a very fine dividing line. *Reysh* also represents the fact that the wicked retain the potential to repent at any chosen moment.

21: שׁ *Shin*
Numerical Value: 300

Means "tooth" and is the symbol of Divine Peace, Power and Mastery, but also of Corruption and Falsehood. One of the holiest letters in the Hebrew language, it appears on its own on the *mezuzah* attached to the doorpost of all Jewish households as the sign of *El Shaddai*, the Holy Spirit.

22: ת *Tau*
Numerical Value: 400

Literally, this means "mark" or "sign," and it is also a symbol for "vehicle of sacrifice." *Tau*, as the final letter in the Hebrew alphabet, represents completion of the Spiritual Cycle and is a sign of Truth and Perfection. It denotes the final spiritual destination for humankind and is closely associated with the preceding letter *shin*.

4. MASTER OF THE GOOD NAME

And I appeared unto Abraham, unto Isaac, and unto Jacob, by the name of God Almighty, but by my name Yahweh was I not known to them.

Exodus 6:3

When Moses first asked the Lord by what name the Israelites should call Him, the reply was *Ehyeh Asher Ehyeh*—"I Am That I Am." Moses was subsequently instructed to tell the people that "I Am" had sent him to them (Exodus 3:13-14). Further along in Exodus 6:3, we learn that the forefathers of Moses, namely Abraham, Isaac and Jacob, knew the Lord as *El Shaddai* ("God Almighty," and also used to denote the "Holy Spirit") and not by His actual name, which is represented in scripture by the four Hebrew letters *yod, hey, vau, hey,* written יהוה in Hebrew, and generally translated into English as YHWH.

In his initial confrontation with the Pharaoh, described in Exodus, Moses informs the haughty Egyptian ruler that he (Moses) had been sent by the unnamable God of the Hebrews, *Ha Shem*—"The Name." According to tradition, Pharaoh scoffed at this information and pointed out that there was no such god in his Egyptian list of deities. He then asked Moses as to where this nebulous god of the Hebrews might exist. The reply was that, although the Lord was everywhere

41

in the world, He remained securely hidden and capable of contact only in the hearts of those who sought after Him. The *Shekinah*, or Divine Presence (also equated with the female principle of the male Godhead), chooses to be revealed only to those who seek the Lord with all of their heart and all of their soul.

The Ineffable Name

The true declaratory four-lettered Name of God is known as the Tetragrammaton, or *Shem Ha-Meforash* (literally "Special Name of the Lord"). It appears exactly 6,832 times in the Old Testament and is held to possess unbounded power sufficient, it is said, to shake the very foundations of Heaven and Earth and to in-

The four-lettered Tetragrammaton as found inscribed on ancient pottery shard (circa 700 B.C.E.) uncovered in an ancient burial cave 20 miles (32 kilometers) southwest of Jerusalem.

The Ineffable Name of God in modern Hebrew characters.

spire even the angels with astonishment and terror! However, it has not been uttered aloud by a devout Jew ever since the time of the destruction of Solomon's First Temple at Jerusalem by Nebuchadrezzar, king of Babylon, in the summer of 587 B.C.E.—the sole exception being when the High Priest vocalized The Holy Name once a year, on the Day of Atonement, but only when alone in the secret place in the Temple known as the Holy of Holies. This practice fell away completely following the leveling of the refurbished Second Temple by the Roman general Titus in 70 C.E. The now unused Ineffable Name became known as the "Lost Word."

Up to present times, when anyone reads aloud from the *Torah* or other scriptural source, a substitute name is used, usually *Adonai* ("my Lord") or simply *Ha Shem* ("The Name"). In daily usage, Jews frequently use the phrase *Baruch Ha Shem*, "Blessed is The Name."

There are several other terms signifying God in the Old Testament, including the curiously plural *Elohim* ("gods"; "divine beings"), which might be compared with the Arabic *Allah*, which is also strictly a plural expression. In its singular form, *Elohim* becomes *El* or *Eli* as in *Eli, Eli*, "My God, My God," used by Jesus on the cross. *Eli* also translates as the noun "Divinity." Another variation, *El Eliyon*, is usually translated as "The Most High God." The title *Adonai Tzeba'oth*, Lord Sabaoth or Lord of Hosts, brings to six the major names used for God in the Bible. To sum up, these are: the four-lettered unspoken Tetragrammaton YHWH itself, *Adonai, Elohim, Eli* (or *El Eliyon*), *Adonai Tzeba'oth* and *Shaddai* (or *El Shaddai*), the last mentioned being the name for God used by the early Hebrew Patriarchs.

Using the Holy Name

When at the turn of the 17th century Eastern European Jews were being persecuted and massacred by the thousands, there was born in a little village close to the borders of three countries, Russia, Turkey and Poland, one Israel ben Eliezer, who was later to become known as the *Baal Shem Tov*, "Master of the Good Name." As founder of the charismatic Jewish Hassidic sect and bringer to the persecuted Jewish people of a new ecstatic religious expression in which members danced and chanted in glorification of the Lord, the Baal Shem was acknowledged as a miracle worker, as much as Jesus was some 1800 years before him.

Like Jesus, the creator of Hassidism was reputed to walk on water, exorcise evil spirits, and heal the sick by his touch—although, unlike the traditional Jesus of the Gospels, the Baal Shem was twice married.

There were, however, other similarities. As was the case with the parents of Jesus, the Baal Shem's mother and father were reputedly visited by an angel prior to his birth (both of his parents were already 100 years old when their amazing son was born). In accordance with the Jewish custom of thousands of years, the Baal Shem married young, at eighteen, but his first wife soon died and he remarried. In his fortieth year he revealed himself as a messenger of God.

An old Jewish axiom taken from the *Mishna* (the codified version of the traditional oral law) states that "when one's knowledge is greater than one's deeds, the knowledge is futile." The Baal Shem Tov always taught that actions were more important than the mere accumulation of knowledge. Most importantly, legend tells us that, by *using the Holy Name*, he could physically bring back to life a person who was at death's door. He would also use *The Name* to re-infuse with the spirit of the Creator those who were mentally and spiritually ailing.

In the following quote, "New Age" Hassidic writer Reb Zalman Schachter encapsulates the method and basic philosophy of the Baal Shem Tov, especially in relation to the subject under discussion—the power ascribed to the so-called "Ineffable Name" of God:

> He was capable of using the Divine Name for purposes of *changing things as they were, to what they ought to be*, because there is always such a discrepancy between how things are and how they ought to be.[1] (our emphasis)

Pronouncing the Name

Even if Jewish tradition compels devout Jews not to intone the Holy Name out loud, considerable force can still be generated through its silent use as a mind-focus in meditation, in all or any of its different forms. Non-Jews and Jews no longer bound by traditions imposed in the 1st century may, of course, be quite happy in trying to verbalize the Name of God without offending any personal inhibition—the only problem being that no one is absolutely sure how "The Name" should be pronounced!

The practice by Jews for so long of never uttering the Ineffable Name probably led directly to its later strictly Christian *mistranslation* as *Jehovah*. In the Phoenician and early Hebrew alphabets, all vowels except *aleph*, the first letter, were not written down. As a result, there is really no knowing the true original pronunciation of The Name, other than through knowledge of its sounding gained inspirationally. Around the

7th century C.E., a group of scribes known as the Massoretes (their name was derived from the Hebrew word for "tradition") introduced a set of vowel signs into the Hebrew language, which were written in and around the consonants so as not to interfere with the traditional sacredness of the individual letters. Much later, in our present era, the incorrect Jehovah interpretation came about as a result of the Jewish practice of inserting vowel points relating to the word *Adonai* (Lord) whenever the four letters of the Tetragrammaton were encountered. Christian translators took these as vowel points relating to The Name itself. The later change to *Yahweh* by some translators may have moved closer to a more correct interpretation.

What was apparently overlooked by most Christian translators was the fact that the consonants *yod*, *hey* and *vau* sometimes cease to carry consonantal form and are used instead to indicate the principal long vowels. This is particularly true in the case of a final *hey*, which, when placed as the last letter in any word, is always silent and extends the final vowel sound (i.e., as in Isaiah, Elijah).

In his *Wars of the Jews* (5:5:7), the Roman/Jewish historian Josephus states clearly that the sacred name consisted of four vowels. The much respected 11th-century kabalist, Solomon Ben Yehuda Ibn Gebirol (known also as Avicebron, the undisputed master Jewish sage of his time), points to a Holy Name of seven vowels in his writings on the *Zohar*. Taking all this into consideration, it is unlikely that the Divine Name in its original consisted of anything else but *all vowels* (thus discounting completely any harsh-sounding consonantal version, as in Jehovah).

There are a number of interesting theories and associations which may point towards a reasonably accurate key to correct vocalization of the Ineffable Name. As we will learn in Chapter 9, the Egyptian word for the source of all being (written in hieroglyphs as four vowel signs) might be vocalized something like *IAAW.* Distinguished poet and mythologist Robert Graves argues for a distinct link between Egyptian priestly hymns to the gods (which he confirms as consisting of the uttering of *seven vowels in succession*), the secret name of the transcendental god of the mythical Greek Hyperboreans, some Celtic and other connections, and the Ineffable Name—which he suggests could be sounded as *IAOOUA*, with accents on the second *O* and final *A*.[2]

There is certainly some similarity in sound between the Egyptian *IAAW* and Graves' *IAOOUA*, and if our supposition that the Holy Name consists of all vowels is accurate, the latter (Graves' *IAOOUA*) may well come near to the original pronunciation.

In his *Egyptian Magic*, E. A. Wallis Budge, who was once Keeper of the Egyptian and Assyrian Antiquities in the British Museum, tells of a magical formula using the Sacred Name found on a parchment fragment of a Graeco-Egyptian magical work. The full invocation includes, among others, the following appellations that can be identified as related to the Most High: *IAOOUEI; Adonai; Iao; Ieo; Baroukh* (Hebrew for "blessed"); *Sabaoth;* and *Eloai.* According to the script, the magical formula in question "loosens chains, blinds, brings dreams, creates favor," and may be used "for whatever purpose you will."[3]

Whatever the precise sounding may be of the Ineffable Name of God, the fact remains that, traditionally, it is held to carry more power of a universal, all-embracing nature than any other word or name, in any and all of the numerous languages of Earth—and, for that matter, perhaps in any and all of the tongues of the entire universe.

As the uncertainty remains regarding correct pronunciation of the full Holy Name, for those who have no difficulty with the notion of its vocalization, a chant emphasizing the four individual Hebrew letters might be used in order to draw from On High intense, revivifying energy, for redispersal into the world around. It might be intoned thus:

Yod—Hey—Vau—Hey
[Yood—Hayi—Wau—Hayi]

Note that each letter may, in effect, be a vowel and that *yod*, on its own, represents one of the many names of God. It is thus pronounced softly and with due respect. According to Rabbi Michael L. Munk, the sound of the letter *hey* is a "mere exhalation of breath" requiring "little effort, no movement of lip, tongue, or mouth." The letter symbolizes, in its form and in its sounding, the effortless Creation of the world. *Vau* is a linking letter connecting Heaven with Earth, and it should be vocalized with a soft *W* sound.

Some Kabalistic Connections

We have been told that the use of words of power is an essential part of the study of Kabbalah, the mystical side of Judaism. One kabalistic teaching is that each word in scripture is capable of being broken down into a meaningful sentence, which process can add untold power to the "Word." For instance, *B'reshiyth* (meaning "In the beginning"), the first word in Genesis, can be transformed into the sentence *B'reshiyth Rahi Elohim Sheyeqebelo Israel Torah*, translated as "In the beginning the Elohim saw that Israel would accept the law."

This tells the kabalist that the presence of the Divine is manifested in every single word of the written *Torah*. The *Torah* is, in effect, the Hebrew Old Testament, but the word itself means more literally "The Teaching," and is sometimes taken to represent the full body of Jewish scripture. Originally, there was the Written Law (*Torah*) and the Oral Law, which was codified into the *Mishna* around 200 C.E. An interpretation of and commentary on the *Mishna*, known as the *Talmud*, was compiled circa 400 C.E.

A kabalistic system, known as *Temura*, allows for the alteration of the sequence of the letters in a word to change its meaning, *and its effect*, which can be perhaps from hurtful to beneficial. A suggested example was put forward publicly by kabalist David Sh'alev in Jerusalem in 1983 when he suggested that the letters contained in the Hebrew name of the forthcoming year, known as *Tashmad*, meaning "destruction," be rearranged to read *Shamdat*—and thus turn 1984 from a "Year of Destruction" into a "Year of Religion." There is, of course, no way of ascertaining whether Mr. Sh'alev's efforts ensured a relatively safe passage for the world during 1984. What is interesting to note, however, is that the title *1984* was chosen by George Orwell for his famous prophetic novel on the advice of a Jewish publisher who was fully conversant with the negative meaning of the Hebrew calendar year.

In order to set up new channels for the inflow of Divine Light and Love from On High, kabalists work frequently at rearrangement of the letters of the Tetragrammaton itself. There are 12 possible permutations, all of which hold the interpretation "to be." These are known as the "Twelve Banners of the Mighty Name," and have a correspondence in the Twelve Tribes of Israel and in the 12 signs of the zodiac.

Readers may wish to note several other connections involving the important number 12, namely: 12 disciples of Jesus; 12 Apostles of Osiris; 12 princes of Ishmael; 12 Olympic deities; 12 Governors of the Manicheans; 12 knights of King Arthur; and the 12 Labors of Hercules (which symbolize 12 steps of Initiation that approximate the zodiacal signs).

The 12 possible combinations of the four Holy letters (YHWH) are given below, reading as YHWH, left to right, in the non-Hebrew Western fashion. Anyone who feels no inhibition about using the sacred letters in verbal form, and who feels they can handle the energy induced, may be prompted to chant the variations of the four letters as an alternative to simply invoking the standard YHWH, as given above:

YHWH YHHW YWHH HWHY HWYH HHYW
WHHY WYHH WHYH HYHW HYWH HHWY

A Warning

Mention has been made of the strict Jewish prohibition involving the use of the Holy Name. Exodus 20 tells us that when the Jews were making their arduous way through the desert following escape from Egypt, God gave Moses Ten Commandments on Mount Sinai. The third of these injunctions reads:

> Thou shalt not take the name of the Lord thy God in vain; for the Lord will not hold him guiltless that taketh his name in vain.

This statement represents a clear warning that (if it is to be used at all) the Ineffable Name should never be vocalized lightly or irreverently, either in an oath, or particularly if intoned as part of any kind of magical practice relating to a desire for personal acquisition of any kind. The choice as to its use remains strictly with the individual, but caution regarding the possible consequences attached to misuse of the Holy Name cannot be emphasized too strongly.

We know of at least one prominent modern spiritual teacher of original orthodox Jewish background who actually recommends fully vocalized use of the Hebrew letters of the Holy Name as an absolute necessity in the current era and as an indispensable aid to the continued spiritual evolution of humankind itself. From our own experience, we have found that, in order to temper the great power that is "drawn down" by use of the four letters of the Tetragrammaton, it is advisable to prefix any utterance of the letters with the words *Baruch Ha Shem* [Barukh Hah Shem], "Blessed is the Name."

5. PRAYERS FOR ALL OCCASIONS

*Blessed art thou, O Lord our God,
King of the Universe . . .*
Preface to Jewish prayers

There exists a host of Hebrew words and phrases of considerable authority and influence, and most of the chants and prayers recorded in this book are based on traditional Hebrew prayers and affirmations that have in one form or another been spoken or sung by the faithful for thousands of years. A few are included that have been received inspirationally in more recent times. These remain, however, well-rooted in age-old basic principles and meanings, and embrace well-defined uses.

As is the case with most other religious systems, the Hebrew tradition offers a prayer or affirmation for every conceivable occasion—from the *Sh'mah*, center point of every morning prayer ritual, and the Jewish "good luck" expression *mazel tov* (which more literally translates as "good constellation of stars," in an astrological sense), right through to the sacred prayer for the dead, known as the *Kaddish*. The selection that follows below and in the next chapter should be considered primarily as an introduction to some of the more well-known and most frequently uttered sacred

53

phrases in a language that has been in continuous use since the days of Abraham, Isaac and Jacob, Moses, Elijah and Jesus, right up to the present day, when Hebrew is once again the official day-to-day language of the Jewish people.

Sh'mah Yisrael

Morning and evening, for as long as he lives, when he is *davening*, or swaying and praying, the devout Jew will recite the prayer known universally as the *Sh'mah*, each and every day. It is the very first verse taught a child at the knee of his parent, and the last phrase uttered with the final breath of life before departing this world for the next. It was recited daily in the Temple in ancient times and is enclosed in the *mezuzah* that marks the entrance to every Jewish home to this very day, as is commanded in Deuteronomy 6:9. The mezuzah is a small wooden or plastic case attached to the right-hand side upper half of the front doorpost in a slanting position, just above eye-level, containing a tiny, handwritten parchment scroll bearing the Sh'mah prayer. On entering or leaving the home, a devout Jew will touch the mezuzah and then lightly kiss his fingers to show respect for God's Word, which it contains.

The Sh'mah is an especially important prayer as it embodies the Jewish creed, the affirmation which stands above all others and declares for everyone to know that the God of Israel is the One, true, living God—notwithstanding the possibility that He may choose to reveal Himself in so many different, and at times, contradictory, ways. On a broad scale the Sh'mah, spiritual Israel's highest prayer, can be considered as a call to faith which provokes response from all the faithful, of this world and of other worlds, and of this and other dimensions of reality. In its deepest esoteric sense it can be considered as the very "breath of God." Its utterance is a reminder that we fulfill God's function in every breath we take, and its continued use down the ages is a confirmation of our link with the beginnings of Creation.

A profound illustration of the absolute awe surrounding the use and importance of the Sh'mah is contained in the story of Rabbi Hutzpit, one of the ten Jewish sages massacred by the Romans after the destruction of the Temple in 70 C.E. Reb Hutzpit was said to be 130 years old, and a man of handsome and commanding appearance, like an Angel of the Lord of Hosts. When people pleaded that the old sage be spared execution, the Roman Emperor asked the Jewish religious teacher his age.

"One hundred and thirty less one day," replied Reb Hutzpit, "and I ask you to wait till my birthday."

"What difference does it make to you if you die one day earlier or later?" retorted the Emperor.

Came the reply: "I will be able to say the Sh'mah twice more, morning and evening, before I die and thus be able to proclaim the sovereignty of His unique and awesome Name over all other rulers."

The Emperor was infuriated. "How long will you impudent and stubborn people continue to believe in your God! He no longer has any power to save you. If he did, he would have already wreaked his vengeance, as you say he did on the Pharaoh."

On hearing this blasphemy, Reb Hutzpit burst into weeping and rent his clothes, saying:

"Woe to you, O Emperor! What will you do on the day of reckoning when the Lord will exact retribution from Rome and all of its gods!"

Shaking in his fury, the Emperor cried, "How long must I debate with this man?" and gave the order for the brave Reb Hutzpit to be stoned and then hanged.

The opening line of the Sh'mah is taken from Deuteronomy 6:4: "Hear, O Israel, *Ha-Shem*, Who is our God, is the One and Only." The full Jewish creed is a linking together of Deuteronomy 6:4-9, 10:13-21 and Numbers 15:37-41. The English King James Bible version of this composite text that provides the foundation stone of the Jewish religious tradition would read as follows (Deuteronomy 6:4-9):

Hear, O Israel: The Lord our God *is* one lord:
And thou shalt love the Lord thy God
with all thine heart,
and with all thy soul,
and with all thy might.
And these words, which I command thee this day,
shall be in thine heart:
And thou shalt teach them diligently
unto thy children,
and shalt talk of them
when thou sittest in thine house,
and when thou walkest by the way,
and when thou liest down,
and when thou risest up.
And thou shalt bind them for a sign upon thine hand,
and they shall be as frontlets between thine eyes.
And thou shalt write them
upon the posts of thy house,
and on thy gates.

The word *Israel* means "God wrestler." This interpretation introduces the concept of wrestling with the lower mind until victory and an elevation into the realm of the higher mind is attained. For any person, of whatever faith, who chooses to "strive with the Divine" (i.e., the sincere spiritual seeker), use of the Sh'mah takes on an especially important significance. When singing it out loud, or within the silence of the heart, there can occur a distinct heightening of spiritual awareness, carrying the consciousness beyond the merely ordinary into realms of inspiration, prompting a sense of renewed strength and refreshing individual purpose that is firmly based in the all-embracing oneness of creation.

The Sh'mah can be written phonetically and chanted as follows:

Sh'mah Yisrael!
[Sh'**mah Yis**-ro-ail]
Adonai Elohainu Adonai Echad
[Ad-o-**noy** El-o-hayi-noo Ad-o-**noy** E-**chad**]
Barukh Shem K'Vod Malkuthor La'Olam Va-ed
[Ba-rookh Shem K'Vod Mal-ku-**torh**
La'Oi-**lam** Va-**ed**]
Adonai Hu Ha'Elohim
[Ad-o-**noy** Hu Ha'El-o-**heem**]

Hear O Israel!
The Lord our God, the Lord is One!
Blessed be His name,
Whose Glorious kingdom is for Ever and Ever.
The Lord, He is God!

The written Hebrew version of this daily invocation is:

שמע ישראל יי אלהינו יי אחד

ברוך שם כבוד מלכותו לעולם ועד

It is customary, at times, to chant only the first two lines of the Sh'mah as an invocation on its own. However, in its deeply esoteric sense, the full chant has been considered by some as a formula or key to open a "Gateway" into a higher kingdom of Light (meaning "Superluminal Light") that takes the human consciousness into dimensions existing way beyond the material universe. The Sh'mah has also been described as the "Wall of Light" that will be placed around the righteous as protection at the time of destruction that will come at the End of Times.

A Universal Blessing

An ancient Hebrew affirmation of great worth that may be more familiar to non-Jews is taken from Numbers 6:24-26, and was, according to scripture, given by God to Moses to pass on to Aaron for use as a perennial blessing over the children of Israel:

Y'varekeka Adonai Vi'Yish'Mereka
[Y'va-**reh**-khe-kha Ad-o-**noy** V'Yish'Me-**reh**-kha]
Y'ar Adonai Panav Aileka V'Yichuneka
[Y'**air** Ad-o-**noy** Pa-**nav** Ai-ley-kha
V'Yi-chu-ney-kha]
Yisha Adonai Panav Aileka V'Yashem Leka Shalom
[Yi-**sha** Ad-o-**noy** Pa-**nav**
Ai-ley-kha V'Ya-**shem** Ley-**kha** Sha-lom]

The Lord bless thee, and keep thee;
The Lord make his face shine upon thee,
and be gracious unto thee;
The Lord lift up his countenance upon thee,
And give thee peace.

This especially powerful invocation is used as the final prayer at any Jewish *Bar Mitzvah* ceremony. This is the ritual all Jewish boys must go through at age 13 (and in modern times, some girls around age 12—in which case it is called a *Bas Mitzvah*), when they are ready to understand the *mitzvot*, or commandments and duties of being an adult Jew. On the first Sabbath after his thirteenth birthday, in a special synagogue ceremony, the boy, on what is considered to be one of the most important occasions in life, is called upon to read aloud from the sacred *Torah* scrolls.

When chanted before and/or after any meditation or mantra chanting session, it serves to clear away unwanted vibrations and to prepare the participants for what lies ahead, fostering at once protection and peace.

Shalom! ("Peace!")

A Greeting, and a Plea for Peace

Possibly the most universally known word in the Hebrew language is the lilting and lovely *Shalom* (in Arabic: *Salaam*), which signifies both "peace" and "greetings." Used as a daily invocation, or as an introduction to meditation, the word *Shalom* produces an effect similar to that generated by the Sanskrit phrase *Om Santi* (see Chapter 14). Shalom, of course, incorpo-

rates the Sanskrit "First of all mantras," *Om*. It signifies both a concept and a power, and repeated use of
this one word, sung out loud or phrased silently within
the heart, will eventually draw towards the user that
great "peace which passeth all understanding":
Shulamit Shalom. Its calming effect operates on all
levels, and it is, like Om, one of the key sounds of the
Universe—and also one of the simplest to intone:

Shalom

[Sha-lom]

Peace

A variation of the Shalom greeting (it is also used
for "goodbye") is *Shalom Aleichem*, "Peace be with
you." A number of well-known songs, of varying tempos
and styles, have been created around these two words
that call for peace on Earth and peace within the souls
of everyone living upon it. The Shalom Aleichem is virtually identical to the Arabic equivalent *Es-salaam
aleikum*.

Shalom Aleichem

[Sha-lom A-laiy-chem]

Peace be with you

When Eating and Drinking

Before and after every meal, most Jews say a
B'rakha, or a blessing. The word *B'rakha* comes from
the first three words used in just about every Hebrew
prayer: *Barukh Ata Adonai*—"Blessed is the Lord."
Two main mealtime prayers are pronounced in most
Jewish households on the Friday night before Sabbath
(which falls, of course, on Saturday) to accompany

breaking of the bread and blessing of the sacrificial wine.

As the famous Last Supper attended by Jesus and his disciples occurred on the Passover Sabbath, it is probable that these were something like the exact words used by the initiator of the Christian faith:

When breaking the bread:

Barukh Ata Adonai Elohainu Melekh Ha'Olam
[Ba-rookh A-**tah** Ad-o-**noy** El-o-**hayi**-noo Me-lekh Ha'O-**lam**]
Ha Motzi Lechem Min H'Aretz
[Ha Mo-**tzi** Le-chem Min Ha'Ah-**retz**]

Blessed art thou, O Lord our God,
King of the Universe;
Who bringest forth bread from the earth.

When blessing the wine:

Barukh Ata Adonai Elohainu Melekh Ha'Olam
[Ba-rookh A-**tah** Ad-o-**noy** El-o-**hayi**-noo Me-lekh Ha'O-**lam**]
Borey Pri Ha' Gafen
[Bo-ray Pree Ha'Ga-fen]

Blessed art thou, O Lord our God,
King of the Universe;
Who createst the fruit of the vine.

There are several variations to the B'rakha, in accordance with the ritual requirements of specific Jewish festivals and holy days. Of special note is the important *Pesach*, or Passover ritual, which celebrates remembrance of the Jews' successful flight from captivity in Egypt. This consists of a long, involved set of Pass-

Jews at prayer at the famous Wailing Wall at Temple Mount, Jerusalem. The recapture of this site by Israeli forces on June 7, 1967, represented the culmination of a vow and a dream that was perpetuated each year at Passover for almost 2,000 years with the utterance of the phrase "Next year in Jerusalem!"

over mealtime prayers known as the *Haggadah*. According to the mystical *Zohar*, the peculiar structure and order of the blessings said during Pesach act as a metaphysical bonding or spiritual cable for the transfer of energy from higher dimensions to lower planes of activity. This element of elevated activity serves to carry use of the B'rakha way beyond the bounds of a mere form of mealtime grace and into the realms of mystical communion with the Creator of all things. The symbolism contained within the "Last Supper" story of Jesus (who was at base a devout Jew who upheld the spirit as well as the letter of Mosaic Law) is enhanced by the supernatural depth of meaning associated with the B'rakha, and in particular, with the Passover Blessing.

For the record, and as an oddity, it has been suggested that the term *abracadabra* (used as a mystical formula down the years by magicians and showpeople) may be derived from a combination of Hebrew words that includes the B'rakha—and originally meant "pronounce the blessing." Alternative sources for abracadabra are the words *b'rukh barak*, "cast forth lighting" (to scatter evil), taken from Psalm 144:6, or a distorted combination of Hebrew/Aramaic expressions relating to the Trinity of Father (*Ab*), Son (*Bar*) and Holy Spirit (*Ruach Ha-kodesh*).

All Roads Lead to Jerusalem

Perhaps the most historically potent set of words ever uttered by Jews during the Passover, or at any other festival—and other than the Ineffable Name of the Almighty Himself—is the phrase *Le shanah ha ba'ah b'Yerushalaim!*: "Next year in Jerusalem!" This short declaration is and has been sincerely affirmed each year at the time of Passover in just about every Jewish household, all around the world, ever since the fall of Jerusalem to the Romans in 70 C.E.

After that cataclysmic event in Jewish history, the people of Israel were dispersed among the nations on a scale never before conceived, and the diaspora, or dispersion of the Jews, was to last right into the 20th century, when the Jews finally began to return to their homeland in meaningful numbers. The proclamation, in 1948, of Israel as an independent Jewish State served as part fulfillment of a vow that has been repeated by millions of Jews for centuries. The final taking of Jerusalem by Israeli soldiers during the Six-Day War of 1967, other than being a major emotional event for all Jews, saw final completion of an age-old task set in motion almost 2,000 years before. The question that can be asked is: Without the repeated wish to return, would the Jews have held their resolve to do so for so many decades?

6. HEBREW CHANTS OF POWER

Enoch, who from mortal flesh
Was turn'd by God to flame,
Sits like a teacher in the height,
Imparting to the Sons of Light
The song which they declaim:
Holy, holy, holy is the Lord of Hosts.
—Amittai ben Shephatiah (11th century)

One of the most familiar, to Christians in particular, of Hebrew sacred chants will be the phrase which translates: "Holy, Holy, Holy, is the Lord of Hosts" in English and *Sanctus, Sanctus, Sanctus, Dominus Deus Sabaoth* in its Latin version. The solemn recitation of the Hebrew version of this great verse of power, *Qadosh, Qadosh, Qadosh, Adonai Tzeba'oth*, forms a central and sacred moment in every Jewish synagogue service. The words of this important chant are taken from Isaiah 6:3 and constitute part of a spectacular experience enjoyed by the most quoted of the Old Testament prophets after having been taken up into the Higher Heavens. While listening to the angels intoning "Holy, Holy, Holy," Isaiah witnessed the Almighty Himself seated on His throne in all His glory.

The Old Testament text which introduces this dramatic event relates how during his experience Isaiah was purged of all sin by a *Seraph* of the Lord. In Jewish lore, the *Seraphim*—the angels of love, light and fire—are noted as the highest order in the angelic kingdom. Their leader is none other than the Archan-

65

gel Michael or *Mik-kah-el* himself, whose name means "who is as God."

There is also a close link between the song heard by Isaiah and the fiery Archangel Metatron, the Angel of the Presence, whom some say was once the biblical character Enoch or Chanokh and to whom, in his angelic role, the verse at the head of this chapter is directed.

The Celestial Song

The Seraphim whom Michael commands are said to surround the Throne of Glory at all times. They intone unceasingly *Qadosh, Qadosh, Qadosh, Adonai Tzeba'oth, M'lo Kol Ha'aretz K'vodo* (Holy, Holy, Holy is the Lord of Hosts; His glory fills all the Earth) as a celestial song which can be likened to the music of the spheres. Revelation 4:8 also speaks of this mighty praise-song to the Father in a slightly altered version that reads: "Holy, Holy, Holy is the Lord of Hosts, who was and who is and who will be forever."

As is the case with the *Sanctus* in Roman Catholic and other Christian liturgy, the full Hebrew chant is used frequently by the Jews and, in particular, as part of a morning prayer ritual. Its immediate effect is to project an aura of protection around the user for the day ahead, and for all days to come. The *Qadosh* mantra can, in fact, be numbered among the most powerful of all chants of power available to us. It is said that any living creature, human or non-human, exhibiting basically negative or destructive tendencies will find it difficult, if not impossible, to remain in the presence of any other person who sings *Qadosh, Qadosh, Qadosh,* making it, verily, a phrase to be used to even "judge the angels," to see whether they truly be of God (see I Corinthians 6:3).

Anyone who cares to intone this chant should not be too surprised if the sound appears to beat in time with the human heart, as if in tune with some universal biological clock. According to one source, this profound incantation "... ties together all the bio-rhythms of the body with the spiritual rhythms of the Overself body, so that all circulatory systems operate with one cosmic heartbeat."[1]

The chant is given below in Hebrew characters, followed by a guide to pronunciation. It is preferably used at the start and ending of any mantra/meditation session. While intoning the words, it helps to visualize a golden helmet of protection being placed around the chanter's head, through which only that which emanates from the highest possible source will penetrate into the consciousness; and through which anything at all of a negative nature is unable to penetrate.

קדוש קדוש קדוש יי צבאות מלא

כל הארץ כבודו

Qadosh, Qadosh, Qadosh,
[Qa-**dosh**, Qa-**dosh**, Qa-**dosh**]
Adonai Tzeba'oth;
[Ad-o-**noy** Tze-ba-**ot'h**]
M'lo Kol Ha'aretz K'vodo
[M'lo Khol Ha'**ah**-retz K'vo-**do**]

(Repeat entire chant 12 or 24 times for best effect)

Holy, Holy, Holy,
Is the Lord of Hosts;
His glory fills all the Earth.

It can be noted that, in biblical Hebrew, the letters *bet* and *vet* are represented by the same symbol בּ . In modern Hebrew, the word *Tzeba'oth* is generally sung more like *Tzvai-ot'h*, but our personal preference has always been to use *Tze-bay-ot'h*, which is possibly closer to the original.

The Most High

The more important phrases in the Hebrew language remain those that deal with one or another aspect of the Creator—usually in the form of one of His Holy Titles. There are several of these, any of which can be used to invoke divine energy flow and to attract to the chanter from above the all-embracing Light, Love and Power of the Almighty—for the Lord is near to all who call upon Him sincerely.

A selection of some of the Names of the Most High follows. For maximum effectiveness, it is recommended that each should be separately vocalized in combinations of 12 or 24:

El Eliyon
[El Eli-**yon**]

The Most High

El Shaddai
[El Sha-dhai]

The Almighty

Eli Eli
[Aye-li, Aye-li]

My God, my God

Adonai
[Ad-o-**noy**]

Lord

Barukh Ha Shem
[Ba-Rookh Ha Shem]

Blessed is The Name

Ruach Elohim
[Roo-**ach** El-o-**heem**]

Spirit of the Godhead

An especially significant mantra of similar nature to the above is used by the Hassidic mystics (whose founder *Baal Shem Tov*, "Master of the Good Name," has been mentioned in Chapter 4) for protection in times of danger and crisis, and for spiritual inspiration through invocation of the Holy Presence:

Ribono Shel Olam
[Ri-bo-**no** Shel Oi-lam]

Lord of the Universe

Influence of the Holy Spirit

In traditional Hebrew terms the power of the Almighty is carried into our world via the agency of the Holy Spirit, the *Ruach Ha Qodesh*. An example of a physical manifestation of this Power of the Spirit is contained in the Exodus story concerning the pillar of cloud by day and pillar of fire by night which led the Hebrews during their desert sojourn following the Exodus from Egypt. There is also a close link here with the more esoteric teachings of Kabbalah in that the Exodus story can be equated with the twin pillars which stand at either side of the frontier of the unconscious (*Netzach*, Eternity or Victory, and *Hod*, Reverberation or Glory).

The *Zohar* informs us that when Israel faced the forces of Amalek in battle at Rephidim, Moses, his brother Aaron, and Hur stood on the top of a hill facing the enemy and simulated the three pillars of the Tree of Life—while Joshua led the Hebrew army on the plain below. Moses held his arms outstretched, representing the central column of the Tree, the Pillar of Equilibrium, and the link between the energies invoked by his two companions. He was supported by Aaron as the right pillar and Hur as the left pillar of the Tree. The arousal of their combined energies served to create a conducting channel for the inflow from above of the *Shekinah* power of the Holy Spirit to aid the Hebrews in their battle (Exodus 17:10 and following also refers to this).

It is highly probable, of course, that the three Hebrews on the hill overlooking the battle against Amalek also invoked words of power embodying the names of God and of the Holy Spirit.

Kabalists hold that the unutterable Name of God expresses a duality in the Godhead, consisting of a male and a female aspect. The second female aspect of God is known as *Shekinah* and can be equated with the concept of the Holy Spirit. In fact, the daily prayers of the orthodox Jewish liturgy commence with the words: "To the One Name, the Holy, blessed be He!—and his Shekinah."

On a personal level, any individual usually recognizes the "Pillar of Light" of the divine Shekinah presence at the moment true illumination has been attained—and also, paradoxically, when a position of abject psychological stagnation and darkness has been reached.

The inflow of the force of the Holy Spirit will then serve to aid in stimulating a quantum leap of consciousness to take the aspirant forward and upward towards his or her next personal level of conscious operation and achievement, whatever that may be at any given time.

The next chant has been developed for anyone who wishes to connect with the Divine Presence in order to stimulate the downpouring of the healing, inspiring and transformational "gifts" of the Holy Spirit. However, the express warning is given that, prior to any excessive vocalization of this sacred phrase, and in order to benefit fully and safely from the sudden inflow of supra-natural energy that may result, it is advisable to make a strong declaration of a sincere desire to *receive in order to give*. This action is in line with ancient kabalistic law which affirms that anyone who develops this "desire to receive in order to give" will experience a "cup that is always full," without any danger of overexertion. An uninhibited flow of energy and power from above will pass safely through the bodily vehicle of the individual concerned (raising the level of personal perception in the process) and then move out into the world in the form of Love, Light and Healing.

Any contrary action involving a desire to *receive for self only* could result in adverse consequences, including the danger of temporary "self-destruction." Because of the high voltage involved (in spiritual energy terms), any attempt to hinder free flow of the Shekinah power for selfish reasons could lead to a "blowing" of bodily metaphysical fuses. The resultant deleterious physical effect could be temporary or permanent, depending on the intensity of the experience.

For the record, the Shekinah experience is not to

be equated directly with the *djed* pillar phenomenon of Egyptian origin, nor with the *Kundalini* experience of the Indian mystical system. Shekinah unfoldment concerns energy entering the bio-physical system from a higher level of beingness; the other two mentioned experiences relate to energy already present, but lying dormant within the existing physical and/or psychical framework of the individual.

It is recommended that a pillar of light or fire, representing the downward flow of the "Gifts of the Spirit," be visualized while intoning this chant:

Shekinah Ruach Ha Qodesh
[Sh'**khee**-nah Roo-**ach** Ha Qo-**desh**]

Divine Presence of the Holy Spirit
(Repeat 12 or 24 times)

An alternative chant for attainment of personal peace and balance, while also invoking the influence of the Holy Spirit, incorporates the duality principle plus the word *shalom* (peace):

Shekinah Shalom, Yod Hey
[Sh'khee-nah Sha-lom, Yood Hay]
Shekinah Shalom, Yod Hey
[Sh'khee-nah Sha-lom, Yood Hay]
Shekinah Shalom, Yod Hey
[Sh'khee-nah Sha-lom, Yood Hay]
Yod Hey, Yod Hey
[Yood Hay, Yood Hay]
(Repeat 3 times)

The Peace of the Divine Presence
(Devised by Esther Crowley)

Limitless Light

An especially beneficial meditation chant consists simply of the three Hebrew words, *Ayin Sof Ur*, a phrase which describes the "Limitless Light" of the Eternal, the all-seeing, all-hearing synthesis of the multitude aspects of the Creator God. Translated literally, *Ayin Sof* means the "Absolute," or "the All." *Ur* translates as "light," and is also, incidentally, the name of the birthplace of Abraham, first patriarch of the Hebrews.

This phrase is best chanted softly, 12 or 24 times, while the chanter visualizes a pyramid of pure Superluminal Light descending from above to cover the head. This action will assist in propelling the consciousness into a higher realm of reality, a domain of peace and light, where all is known and there are no limitations.

Ayin Sof Ur
[Ai-yin Sof **Oor**]

Limitless Light of the Absolute

Sacred Healing Chants

An important use for any words of power is the healing of physical, psychological and/or spiritual ailments. Many of our actions in life are devoted to "healing" in some form or other. Whenever we strive for harmony in our activities and relationships, we work with the healing processes of life. Later we will learn of specific mantras in Sanskrit and other languages designed to aid in the attainment of good health and balance. There are several healing supplications in the Hebrew *Siddur* or *Daily Prayer Book*, most of which are rather long and complicated, especially for anyone unfamiliar with the language. The understated abridged version of one of these chants has proved, however, to be highly effective as an easily learned substitute:

R'phanu Adonai V'Narophay
[R'phai-**nu** Ad-o-**noy** V'Nay-ro-phai]
Khi El Melekh Rophay Ne'Eman V'Rachman Atah
[Khi El Me-lekh Ro-phai Ne-E-man
V'Rach-man A-**tah**]

Heal us, O Lord, and we shall be healed;
For thou, Almighty King,
Art a faithful and merciful Physician

An extremely powerful Hebrew healing mantra invokes the name of *Geburah*, one of the more prominent Angels of Healing, whose name colors one of the *Sephiroth* of the Tree of Life—that of Judgment. This severe aspect is reflected in the action taken by the Geburah influence to break the "seven seals" of the body, cleansing and balancing, in effect, the seven bodily chakras so that divine energy may flow unrestricted throughout the physical and paraphysical system. The name *Geburah* translates directly as "divine power" or "strength."

For maximum effect, the chant presented below should be intoned aloud six times. Then add the name or names of those who need healing—and then repeat the chant six more times. This great healing mantra is particularly effective when used during group healing sessions.

Shel Shem Geburah
[Shel Shem Ge-bu-**rah**]

In the Name of Geburah

The sword of Michael inscribed with "Flame Letters"
of the Hebrew alphabet.

Angelic Protection

As part of their prayer ritual before retiring at night, some Jews might be heard intoning a plea that they be afforded protection by the four mighty archangels—Michael, Gabriel, Uriel and Raphael—and that they should never overlook the protective and nurturing presence of the Almighty above. Traditionally,

Michael is acknowledged as the greatest of all angelic beings, with perhaps only Metatron, the "Angel of the Presence," as a rival in seniority—although, in fact, the two may be different aspects of the same "Power."

Michael (whose name, we have learned, means "who is as God") is accepted by Jews, Muslims and Christians alike as the prince of angels and as a mighty protective force who can be called upon at any place or time. As the acknowledged sustainer and protector of our particular part of the universe, Michael might be equated with the Hindu deity Vishnu. The great "sword of light" wielded by Michael has the "flame letters" of the Hebrew language inscribed upon it, and is used to cut asunder the veil of darkness and ignorance that separates us from our true identities as "beings of light."

When calling upon Michael for assistance, it is recommended to use one of the ancient forms of his name, the oldest known archaic version of which is given below. The name of Michael can be invoked by anyone who feels threatened by negative forces, at any place, and at any time:

[Mik-kah-eylu]
(Repeat 12 or 24 times for best effect)

Gabriel ("God is my strength") is another highly regarded angel, in both Judeo-Christian and Muslim tradition. He is at once the angel of vengeance and mercy, death and resurrection, annunciation and revelation. He and Michael are the only two angels mentioned by name in the Old Testament. Gabriel appeared to Miriam, or Mary, mother of Jesus, and to Mohammed, to whom he dictated the *Qoran, sura* by *sura*.

Uriel ("fire of God") is, according to Jewish lore, the archangel of salvation and a messenger of God who is reputed to have given the mystical teachings of the Kabbalah to humankind.

Raphael ("God has healed") is acknowledged as the greatest healing angel of our planet, and can be invoked separately to aid the sick. Legend tells us that he was the angel sent by God to cure Jacob of injury after the father of the Twelve Tribes of Israel had wrestled with another angel, identified by various sources as Metatron or Michael.

The ancient Hebrew nocturnal chant invoking guardianship from all four mighty archangels runs as follows:

B'Shem Adonai Elohai Yisrael
[B'**shem** Ad-o-**noy** El-o-**hayi Yis**-ro-ail]
Mimini Michael
[Mi-mi-**ni** Mik-kah-**el**]
U'mishmoli Gabriel
[Oo'mish-mo-**lee** Gabh-ri-**el**]
U'mulifinai Uriel
[Oo'mool-i-fa-**nai** Oo-ri-**el**]
U'mayachorai Raphael
[Oo'may-a-cho-**rayi** Ra-pha-**el**]
V'al Roshi Shekinath El
[V'ahl Ro-**shee Shay**-kee-naht **El**]

In the Name of the Lord, God of Israel:
May Michael be at my right hand;
Gabriel, at my left;
Before me, Uriel
Behind me, Raphael;
And above my head, the Divine Presence.

7. SOME HEBREW MEDITATIONS

O how love I thy law!
It is my meditation all the day.
Psalm 119:97

A study of words of power can be a rewarding exercise, but even more so if the newly learned words and phrases are put into practical use. Many books can be written concerning the origin, use and effects of specified mantric words and phrases, but it remains impossible to convey to any individual the full impact of the sounds created unless that person takes the time and trouble to learn the intonation and meaning of the words used, and then personally vocalizes them. Moreover, this final act of sounding a mantric word or phrase should be performed wholeheartedly, with firm intent, and without any limitations placed on expected results. In other words, from the beginning a certain amount of faith is necessary, and, as is generally the case in almost any field of human endeavor, a positive attitude will generally produce positive results.

Also of prime importance is that there be a grasp of the meaning and potential effect of the chosen words or phrases. As in common speech, invocatory statements can be constructive, destructive or ineffective, depending upon the actual words and tone employed—

and the intent of the user. Although certain sacred sounds carry an inherent power of their own, no matter how or by whom they are verbalized, a firm belief in their efficacy serves to amplify further the energy charge they carry.

Offered in this section is a small selection from the many Hebrew mantra meditations that have proved of particular personal value down the years, covering several stated purposes, which are delineated as we move along. Feel free to modify any of these to personal taste, perhaps incorporating some other of the many mantras, chants, and invocations presented in earlier chapters not included below. It is a matter of tuning in to the higher self for guidance and then utilizing those sounds that appear to be most relevant to any particular person or persons and occasion.

This rule applies to mantra singing in any language. The only recommended criteria for a truly successful performance are: (1) A good knowledge of the meaning of the mantra chosen; (2) Some grasp of the intonation of the sounds to be expressed; (3) A relaxed and uninhibited approach to the meditation as a whole.

The meditations here presented may be used by any person singly or in group meditation. In group situations, one or more members can take on the responsibility of guiding the others through the visualization and chanting. Alternatively, each of the group members might prefer to take turns in moving the meditation along as specified. At the start, it may be necessary to read out in full the explanatory notes given before each meditation. Choose a comfortable position while meditating—stand erect, sit in a chair or cross-legged on the floor (perhaps in the yogic lotus position), but do not lie down. Those not actually reading from the text can sit or stand with eyes closed, as this aids the concentration. We have generally remained stationary during our meditation sessions, either standing or sitting, but there are practitioners who recommend alteration of posture—adopting perhaps several different yoga-type positions as the meditation progresses. This we must leave to personal taste and choice.

The meditations usually vary in length from around 15 to 30 minutes, depending on how much time is devoted to "entering the silence."

In group meditation, the saying of a prayer or affirmation by three of the participants prior to the start aids in establishing an "energy base."

After meditation, it is useful to share individual experiences gained during the meditation process.

Where there is any uncertainty regarding pronunciation of any given mantra, refer to Chapter 3.

In Chapter 11 we note use of the *bija*, or Sanskrit seed sounds, for simultaneous balancing of the seven biological chakras, or energy vortices, in order to bring about an energizing of the body and a heightening of mental and intuitive faculties. Certain Hebrew phrases can be utilized as part of a meditation session for similar effect. This procedure also can lead to a simultaneous opening or piercing of the seven seals or centers so that the participant's consciousness may be raised into the more elevated eighth and ninth chakras, and beyond.[1]

Hebrew Meditation 1
Balancing the Centers

Breathe in deeply, and exhale. At the base of the spine, visualize a red pyramid, situated at the first chakra. Using an act of mental visualization while

Balancing the Centers—Breaking the Seven Seals

breathing normally, inhale in a stream of white light, the *Ain Soph* or Limitless Light, through the third eye at the forehead. Direct this pure white light down the spinal column until it reaches and covers the red pyramid at the base of the spine, like a white capstone. Holding this white capstone firmly in place to balance and activate the root chakra, intone three times the sacred phrase *Adonai Tzeba'oth*, "Lord of Hosts"—pronounced Ad-o-**noy** Tze-ba-**ot'h**:

> *Adonai Tzeba'oth ... Adonai Tzeba'oth ...*
> *Adonai Tzeba'oth*

Now visualize a six-pointed orange star, the Star of David, in the area of the second chakra—close to the spleen or organs of procreation. As before, take in a stream of white light through the third eye at the forehead and direct this white light down the spinal column until it reaches and activates and balances the six-pointed orange star, representing the sacred seed. Keeping the center of procreation firmly imbued with the white light, chant three times the sacred phrase *Ehyeh Asher Ehyeh*, "I Am That I Am"—pronounced Ay-**yeh** Ah-**shehr** Ay-**yeh**:

> *Ehyeh Asher Ehyeh ... Ehyeh Asher Ehyeh ...*
> *Ehyeh Asher Ehyeh*

At the solar plexus—the third chakra—hold a mental picture of a yellow crystal. Inhaling again a stream of white light through the third eye, take this down the spine to mingle with the yellow at the solar plexus, and then bring the white light up again to the third eye to form the double-helix of the DNA system, the programming cornerstone of life. As the solar plexus center becomes balanced and activated, project yellow arrows of light out in all directions, and say three times *Mashiach*, "Messiah"—pronounced Mah-**shee**-yach:

> *Mashiach ... Mashiach ... Mashiach*

Now, visualize a crystal of glowing emerald green, the color of rebirth, at the fourth or heart chakra. Breathing in white light again through the third eye, direct this light down to the heart center to mingle with the emerald green. Visualize an opening up of the heart center in six directions, three pointing upward and three downward, to balance both the physical and transcendental self. Then, while emitting emerald green rays outward from the heart, intone three times the sacred word *Melech*, meaning "King"—pronounced Melekh:

> *Melech ... Melech ... Melech*

At the throat chakra, the fifth center, visualize a turquoise-colored crystal radiating light. Inhaling white light again through the third eye, take this light down to mingle with the turquoise at the throat so as to balance and revitalize the throat center. Then send turquoise arrows outward and chant three times the word *Adonai*, meaning "Lord"—pronounced Ad-o-**noy**:

> *Adonai ... Adonai ... Adonai*

Now focus on the third-eye position, the seat of the sixth chakra. Visualize the Hebrew Name of God inscribed on the forehead in the form of flame letters in royal blue—*Yod, Hey, Vau, Hey* (alternatively, visualize the English letters YHWH in blue flames). Intone the letters of the Holy Name silently within the mind (or if preferred, say them out loud) three times, as the third-eye center becomes alive with the light of the Creator:

*Yod Hey Vau Hey... Yod Hey
Vau Hey... Yod Hey Vau Hey*

Hold a mental image of a purple crystal pyramid capstone directly over the seventh chakra at the crown of the head, and then extend this downward to complete the pyramid and thus enfold the entire body in a purple light. All centers are now balanced and the seven seals have been pierced, activating all chakras in unison. Chant three times the phrase *Melech Sh'mayyim*, meaning "King of the Heavens"—pronounced Me-lekh Sheh-mai-yeem:

*Melech Sh'mayyim... Melech
Sh'mayyim... Melech Sh'mayyim*

We now move beyond the seven physical centers to align them with the metaphysical or paraphysical chakras. Mentally create the image of an inverted crystal pyramid of white light at the crown chakra above the head. Place a scintillating diamond inside this upturned pyramid. This represents the eighth chakra through which we connect with other space-time dimensions and the Lords of Light. Holding the image of the pyramid and diamond above the head, intone three times the words *Ain Soph Ur*, "Limitless Light of the Absolute"—pronounced Al-yin Sof **Oor**:

Ain Soph Ur... Ain Soph Ur... Ain Soph Ur

The eighth center is now fully activated and in balance with the seven lower centers. At the ninth chakra, beyond the eighth, visualize an intensely bright light and chant three times *Ain Soph*—"The Absolute":

Ain Soph... Ain Soph... Ain Soph

The ninth chakra is now operative and consciousness projects only upward through the inverted pyramid at the top of the head. By activating the eighth and ninth chakras in conjunction with the seventh chakra, we initiate a physical quantum leap that takes us beyond the imperfect karmic cycles of the solar spectrum. Now chant three times the word *Ain*—meaning "Nothingness," and go into meditation:

Ain ... Ain ... Ain

GO INTO THE SILENCE FOR 5 TO 10 MINUTES

Note: If the meditation is to be closed at this point, the following procedure is suggested (or go on to the next meditation).

With eyes closed, mentally let go of the inverted pyramid at the ninth center, and then the diamond at the eighth center. Hold, however, the form of a pyramid capstone of purple light at the seventh center at the crown of the head. Extend once more this purple light over the body, enfolding it in the protective energy that projects downward from the capstone above the head. This purple pyramid of protection can be renewed by an act of will at any time.

Amen ... Amen ... Amen ... and Amen!

Hebrew Meditation 2
Harmonizing the Five Bodies

We now harmonize the five bodily vehicles, which surround the physical body of each person like so many sheaths. The outermost of these bodily vehicles—the Electromagnetic Body—codes the physical body directly into other consciousness regions, other dimen-

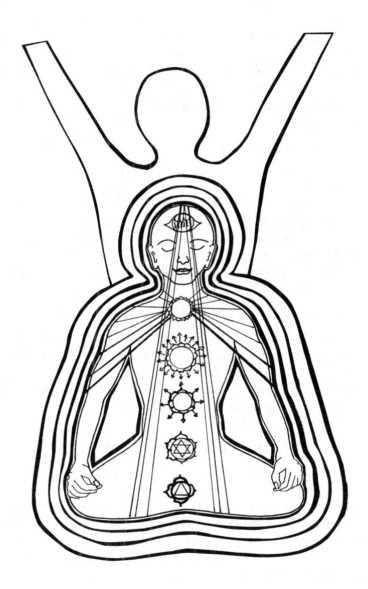

Harmonizing the Bodily Vehicles

sions. To fine tune this Electromagnetic Body, say three times the phrase which invokes the plurality of the Supreme Being as a Creator: *Eloha-Umma*—pronounced El-o-hah **Oo**-mah. (*Note: Eloha* is singular for *Elohim*—"Creator Gods"; *Umma* is an Aramaic word referring to God's covenant with his "Community of Light.")

Eloha-Umma . . . Eloha-Umma . . . Eloha-Umma

The Electromagnetic Body aligns itself with the Will of the Supreme Creator and with the next of our outer bodies: the Epikinetic Body. This is the energy vehicle required for teleportation and projection within the physical universe. Allow the vibrations of the sacred phrase *Eloha-Umma* to bring balance to the Epikinetic Body—and to align with the Electromagnetic Body:

Eloha-Umma . . . Eloha-Umma . . . Eloha-Umma

The tuning of the Eka Body follows. This is the bodily vehicle of higher consciousness, utilized for time travel while still retaining contact with the physical body. Balancing of the Eka Body with the other bodily vehicles is again achieved by repeating, three times, the words *Eloha-Umma*:

Eloha-Umma . . . Eloha-Umma . . . Eloha-Umma

Next comes alignment of the Inner Gematrian Body, the "light geometry" body, or *gewiyyah*, which frees creative life from slavery to the flesh and offers a positive point of connection with the Overself. Bring this Inner Gematrian Body into alignment with the Electromagnetic Body, the Epikinetic Body, and the Eka Body by saying three times *Eloha-Umma*:

Eloha-Umma . . . Eloha-Umma . . . Eloha-Umma

Finally, visualize the four newly aligned inner bodies becoming raised together to merge into a fifth body—-the "mantle of many colors," or *Zohar* Body. This is the transcendental bodily vehicle designed to carry a person beyond the boundaries of immediate relativity into the Higher Dimensions of the Heavenly Jerusalem. It is the true Body of Light, which becomes activated during phrasing of the words *Eloha-Umma*, again three times:

Eloha-Umma ... Eloha-Umma ... Eloha-Umma

Now enter into the silence of the spirit for 5 to 10 minutes:

Eloha-Umma ... Eloha-Umma ... Eloha-Umma

MEDITATE IN SILENCE FOR 5 TO 10 MINUTES

When coming out of the silence, chant once more:

Eloha-Umma ... Eloha-Umma ... Eloha-Umma

If the meditation is to be closed at this point, use the following procedure (or go on to the next meditation).

Hold the form of a pyramid capstone of purple light at the seventh center at the crown of the head. Extend this purple light downward, over the body, enfolding it in protective energy. This purple pyramid of protection can be renewed by an act of will at any time.

Amen ... Amen ... Amen ... and Amen!

Certain chants and mantras have been devised for the specific purpose of drawing down energy from "On High" (using metaphysical terms) into our own plane of activity—to activate personal transformation for healing processes, or in order to direct this spiritually enhanced power into the world at large for the benefit of all. To accomplish any of these aims, it is normally necessary for the individual or group concerned to elevate initially their own personal awareness level so that effective contact may occur, and in order that the downward flow of energy may be safely channeled.

Ancient language forms, such as Hebrew, Sanskrit, Tibetan, Egyptian and Chinese, serve to prime the thought vibrations that normally flow in and out of the third-eye center and open vibratory channels which allow an individual to communicate directly with Higher Intelligences through telethought communication.

This concept of using language to connect with extraterrestrial intelligences is fully in line with ancient teachings which record encounters by various personalities with beneficent extraterrestrial "Beings of Light." Excellent examples, in the Hebrew experience, are contained in the stories of *merkabah* or vehicles of divine light sighted by the prophet Ezekiel and others.

The Hebrew-language mantra meditation given below has been used by us for several years, with adjustments from time to time to suit any specific occasion. It has proved, at once, not only to facilitate intuitive and inspirational communication but also to initiate a feeling of spiritual, mental and physical reinvigoration.

Hebrew Meditation 3
Inviting Down the Power

The first act in "Inviting Down the Power" is to place around the head of any person or persons taking part in this meditation a helmet of perfect protective light. This headgear of Superluminal Light is created through sounding of the familiar "Holy, Holy, Holy is the Lord God of Hosts," in Hebrew, the so-called "Celestial Song" (see Chapter 6).

Chant 6 or 12 times the words *Qadosh, Qadosh, Qadosh, Adonai Tzeba'oth*—pronounced Qa-**dosh**, Qa-**dosh**, Qa-**dosh**, Ad-o-**noy** Tze-ba-**ot'h**—and mentally place around the head a helmet of perfect protective light through which only that which emanates from the highest possible source is able to enter into the consciousness, and through which nothing at all of a negative nature will be able to penetrate.

Qadosh, Qadosh, Qadosh, Adonai Tzeba'oth
(Repeat 6 or 12 times)

Now invite the Supreme to enter into the physical consciousness, and into the whole being, by intoning 24 times the ancient Hebrew temple blessing *El Eliyon,* meaning "The Most High"—pronounced El Eli-**yon**:

El Eliyon
(Repeat 24 times)

Visualize the downward extending flow of Light and Power in the form of a pyramidal pillar of pure light from On High which envelops and permeates all the bodily vehicles. Thus, bathed in the Fire of the *Skekinah* Light, say 12 times: *Layoo-esh Skekinah*— "Pillar of Light of the Holy Spirit Presence"—pronounced Lay-oo-aish Sh'khee-nah:

Layoo-esh Shekinah
(Repeat 6 or 12 times)

MEDITATE IN SILENCE FOR 5 TO 10 MINUTES

Coming out of meditation, repeat the *Qadosh*

mantra 6 or 12 times:

> *Qadosh, Qadosh, Qadosh, Adonai Tzeba'oth*
> (Repeat 6 or 12 times)

If the meditation is to be closed at this point, use the following procedure (or go on to the next meditation).

Hold the form of a pyramid capstone of purple light at the seventh center at the crown of the head. Extend this purple light downward, over the body, enfolding it in protective energy. This purple pyramid of protection can be renewed by an act of will at any time.

> *Amen... Amen... Amen... and Amen!*

The importance attached to the Middle Pillar of the kabalistic Tree of Life has been outlined in Chapter 2. The five-pointed central column can be aligned with the human body, commencing above the head (*Kether* or Crown), moving down to the back of the neck (*Da-ath* or Knowledge), the heart (*Tiphereth* or Beauty), the base of the spine (*Yesod* or Foundation) and between the feet (*Malkuth* or Kingdom). The object of any Middle Pillar exercise is to draw downward the power of the *Shekinah*, the Holy Spirit, in order to illumine the human consciousness.

The meditation just presented might be considered a short-form version of the Middle Pillar exercise, and we have found it eminently adequate in our own meditation sessions as a vehicle for attracting energy from higher levels. We have also used the following ritual, which may differ from some of the other Middle Pillar meditations in current use, but which, again, we have personally found to be highly effective.

What is for us of prime consideration is to keep in mind at all times that it is advisable to carry one's attention and concentration beyond the so-called "ninth hour" or "gate" of the Name of Yahweh—which relates to mere generalizations on the "theory of creation"—in order to receive revelation direct from the living "messengers of light" of Yahweh/Yeho-wah in a truly personal way.

Hebrew Meditation 4
The Middle Pillar

Stand erect, with feet slightly apart, and hold a mental image of a pyramid of perfect protective golden light, its apex just beyond the top of the head and extending downwards to encompass the entire body. Chant 6 or 12 times the words *Qadosh, Qadosh, Qadosh, Adonai Tzeba'oth*—[Qa-**dosh**, Qa-**dosh**, Qa-**dosh**, Ad-o-**noy** Tze-ba-**ot'h**]—"Holy, Holy, Holy is the Lord of Hosts":

Qadosh, Qadosh, Qadosh, Adonai Tzeba'oth
(Repeat 6 or 12 times)

Now activate the *Kether* entry point for Divine Energy—the pure white light of the Shekinah—just beyond the crown of the head by intoning 6 or 12 times the God-name *Ehyeh*, "I Am," pronounced Ay-yeh, followed by the name of the Archangel of the Presence, *Metatron*, who is connected with the Crown Sephira at the apex of the Pillar of Equilibrium:

Ehyeh Metatron
(Repeat 6 or 12 times)

Feel the downward flow of Shekinah energy as a pure white light that enters at the top of the head. Direct the flow towards the back of the neck, the seat of

Da-ath or Knowledge. Become aware that the inflow of spiritual knowledge supersedes all physical knowledge. Chant 6 or 12 times the holy names *Yahweh Elohim*, pronounced Yah-weh El-oh-heem, meaning "Divine Lords of Light and Learning":

Yahweh Elohim
(Repeat 6 or 12 times)

Accept the energy of the Shekinah light into the heart, the center of Beauty or *Tiphereth*, and intone the Hebrew name of Jesus—*Yeshua*—and of the Archangel *Michael* [Mik-kah-eylu] 6 or 12 times:

Yeshua Michael
(Repeat 6 or 12 times)

Move the balancing Shekinah energy down to the base of the spine and intone the phrase *Shaddai El Chai* [Shah-dai-i El Chai-i]—the Almighty Living God—followed by the name of *Gabriel* [Gah-bri-el], Archangel of the Sephira *Yesod*, the Foundation—again 6 or 12 times:

Shaddai El Chai Gabriel
(Repeat 6 or 12 times)

Finally, bring the white light energy of the Holy Spirit down to a point between the feet, vocalizing 6 or 12 times the phrase *Adonai H'Aretz* [Ad-o-**noy** H'Ah-retz]—Lord of the Earth—followed by the name of the Archangel *Sandalphon* [Sahn-dal-fon]—who guards the Sephira *Malkuth* and holds at bay the forces of negativity, and who is the twin brother of the Archangel Metatron:

Adonai H'Aretz Sandalphon
(Repeat 6 or 12 times)

As above, so below. The five Sephirotic centers are now truly aligned with the Shekinah force balanced between Metatron at the Crown or *Kether* and *Sandalphon* at the Feet or *Malkuth*.

Hold this balance for a few moments and then begin slowly to raise the arms upwards and outwards—like the wings of a bird or an angel. While doing this, visualize emanations of light forming a coat of many colors around your body, starting at the feet—the color luminous red—moving towards the base of the spine—glowing yellow—upward to the heart—emerald green—to the back of the neck—royal blue—and, finally, above the head—the violet flame of cosmic order—and all of the myriad hues that fall between each of the five main colors. Lower the arms.

Clothed in the rainbow garments of the *Zohar* Body of the Shekinah Light, your human consciousness can now be raised to come into direct contact with the *B'Nai Or*, the Brotherhood of Light, and the *B'Nai Elohim*, the Teachers of Light, so that Divine Inspiration and Divine Energy will flow freely into your spirit, your soul, your mind, your body.

STAND THUS CLOTHED IN COLOR, IN SILENCE, FOR 5 TO 10 MINUTES

If the meditation is to be closed at this point, use the following procedure (or go directly on to the next meditation).

Let go of the garment of many colors. Visualize a pyramid capstone of purple light at the crown of the head. Extend this purple light downward, enfolding the body in protective energy, and say 6 or 12 times:

Qadosh, Qadosh, Qadosh, Adonai Tzeba'oth
(Repeat 6 or 12 times)

The meditation that now follows was received inspirationally by Esther Crowley around eight years ago, and has been used by us very effectively in group meditations ever since. It is designed to anchor the Light flowing from On High and then distribute this energy out into the world.

The Shield referred to holds the shape of the *Mogen David*, the six-pointed Star of David, and is known in its fuller sense as "Shield of the Guardians of the Apocalypse." Its function is to provide protection and healing on a global as well as on a personal level.

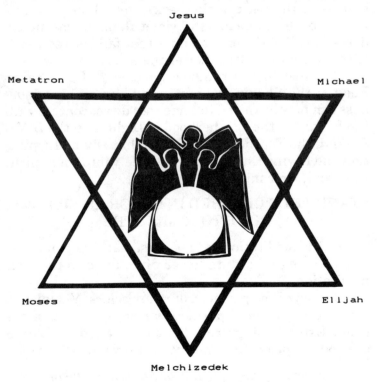

The Shield of the Guardians

Hebrew Meditation 5
Shield of the Guardians

Standing or seated, repeat the following affirmation:

I Am That I Am!
Ehyeh Asher Ehyeh!
We release the heart, mind and spirit,
free of all limitation, into the infinite.
We call by name the Archangels:
Michael + Gabriel + Uriel + Raphael.
Our God is the God of Angels;
Our God is the God of Light.
Together with men, women and children,
and interplanetary souls of like mind
throughout the Universe,
we, of collective mind, combine to project
a Rainbow of Light:
to surround the country in which we reside;
to link up with all countries;
to encircle the world;
to encompass the Universe.
Peace is here; peace is now!
We live in our *Zohar* Bodies of Light
in the New Jerusalem,
united with God:
Yahweh ... Yeshua ... Shekinah ...
and with the *B'nai Or*,
the Brotherhood of Light.

Now create a mental image of a huge, flaming six-pointed star consisting of two interlocking triangles or pyramids. This is the Shield of the Guardians of the Apocalypse, which, when activated from higher dimensions of light, holds the entire planet under protection. Understand the symbolism involved: The downward-thrusting triangle or pyramid represents the inflow of Light and Love from the Creator's Kingdom Above; the upward-thrusting triangle or pyramid symbolizes our human attempt to take ourselves off the cross of space and time so that we may co-exist with the Brotherhood of Light in the Higher Heavens. The Shield is activated by the sounding of the names of its Guardians. The downward-thrusting triangle is carried towards us by the power contained in the sacred names of: The Great Initiator, *Melchizedek* [Mel-ki-tzedek]; the Angel of the Presence, *Metatron* [Me-ta-tron]; and the Angel who is both the Builder and the Protector of our part of the Universe, *Michael* [Mik-kah-eylu]. Repeat each of these names three times:

Melchizedek ... Melchizedek ... Melchizedek
Metatron ... Metatron ... Metatron
Mik-kah-eylu ... Mik-kah-eylu ... Mik-kah-eylu

The power of the upward-thrusting triangle that takes us off the cross of space and time is activated by the sacred names of the Christ or Messianic Trinity: Moses, Jesus and Elijah—*Moishe, Yeshua* and *Eliahu* [Moi-**she**, Ye-**shu**-ah, Eli-ah-**hoo**]:

Moishe ... Moishe ... Moishe
Yeshua ... Yeshua ... Yeshua
Eliahu ... Eliahu ... Eliahu

As we chant once again these six great names of power, we visualize the Shield of the Guardians vibrating with energy, as it extends to enormous size and forms a protective shield over the entire planet Earth:

Melchizedek.... Melchizedek.... Melchizedek
Metatron... Metatron... Metatron
Mik-kah-eylu... Mik-kah-eylu.... Mik-kah-eylu
Moishe... Moishe... Moishe
Yeshua... Yeshua... Yeshua
Eliahu... Eliahu... Eliahu

Begin to visualize Soldiers of Light descending from on high—ten... one hundred... one thousand... ten thousand... a hundred thousand... one million... ten million Soldiers of Shining Light—and they join forces with us to enfold the planet with Light and Love. The flow of energy now settles and the great Shield of Protection and Healing is in place, resonating all the time with the energy grid system of planet Earth. Going right into the silence, we intone the word *Shalom*—Peace—softly six times:

Shalom... Shalom... Shalom
Shalom... Shalom... Shalom

ENTER INTO SILENT MEDITATION FOR 5 TO 10 MINUTES

Now come out of the silence using the great word of peace again six times:

Shalom... Shalom... Shalom
Shalom... Shalom... Shalom

Hold the form of a pyramid capstone of purple light at the seventh center at the crown of the head. Extend this purple light downward, over the body, enfolding it in protective energy. This purple pyramid of protection can be renewed by an act of will at any time.

Amen... Amen... Amen... and Amen!

8. WORDS OF POWER IN ANCIENT EGYPT

Behold these words of power are mine . . .
—Tem-Khepera
The Papyrus of Ani, *The Book of the Dead*

The ancient Hebrews had an important and strong connection with the Land of the Nile from the time of Joseph of the coat of many colors and before, through Moses and the Exodus. Jesus was, of course, another notable Jew to fall under the Egyptian influence early in his life.

With its awe-inspiring pyramids, mystifying sphinx and numerous other massive stone monuments at places like Thebes, Karnak, Luxor and Abu Simbel, Egypt has long been regarded as a land of marvel and mystery. In ancient times, the land of *Khemt* (literally "black"—the color of the River Nile mud) was an acknowledged home of gods, men and magicians who used words of power, or *hekau*, to create specified natural and supernatural effects.

The famous Egyptian *Book of the Dead* contains numerous references, including entire chapters, devoted to spells and charms of influence and command. Indeed, the Egyptians believed that words were concrete things, and if an individual's personal words of power were stolen, that person would become vulner-

101

able to all manner of abuse and attack.[1]

Teta and His Words of Power

One of the thousands of old papyrus scrolls translated by Egyptologists tells a marvelous story about a certain disciple of the god Thoth. A sage and magician of great repute, Teta, who was already 110 years old, allegedly ate 500 bread-cakes and a side of beef and drank 100 draughts of beer each day.

Because of the old man's ability to perform amazing acts using selected magical words, he was brought before Khufu, second King of the 4th Dynasty, more familiar as Cheops, builder of the Great Pyramid at Giza, near Cairo. Khufu was seeking a lost papyrus roll on which was inscribed words of power used by the great pyramid builder Imhotep, constructor of the Step Pyramid at Saqqara. These spells of Imhotep were believed to safeguard a pyramid against all forms of natural or supernatural calamity. This negative activity was usually attributed to Set, the Evil One.

Apart from his prodigious eating habits, and among numerous other astounding abilities, Teta, the venerable adept in Thothian mysteries, was capable of wielding complete influence over wild beasts. He was also said to be able to join to its body a head that had been completely severed, *by using certain words of power*.

Khufu's son Herutataf (himself famous as a learned man) brought Teta to his father after a lengthy journey by boat and litter. As a start to what was to be a dramatic sequence of events, the Egyptian ruler then ordered that a condemned prisoner be beheaded so that the old man could demonstrate his powers. Teta, however, begged of the King that a goose be used instead, so saving the prisoner.

The bird's head was duly severed and laid on one side of the King's chamber, with the body of the goose placed on the other side of the room. The ancient sage then began to utter a string of potent phrases and, to the amazement of all present, the goose sprang up and waddled directly towards its head—which itself began to move towards the body—eventually to rejoin its owner.

The papyrus transcript then tells us that the bird stood up and cackled.

The magician Teta repeated his wonderful feat for King Khufu, using another bird described on the papyrus as a *het-a-a* bird. He then performed the miracle for a third time, now using his magical words to replace the severed head of an ox.

Finally, Teta instructed Khufu regarding the lost papyrus of Imhotep, which the old man suggested was hidden in a casket of flint in the great Temple of Amen-Ra at Heliopolis. He also told the Pharaoh that the one who finally discovered the casket would first dedicate three marvelous pyramids that would stand to the end of time, and then himself sit on the throne of Egypt. Teta also identified the family from which the finder would come, which person Khufu immediately had brought to live under his protection.

User-kaf, eldest son of the family in question, did indeed discover the missing casket of flint and the papyrus roll of Imhotep. As a young priest, he read Imhotep's famous words of power at the dedication of the Great Pyramid of Khufu, and again at the dedication of the pyramids built for the two sons of Khufu who followed him as pharaohs—Khaf-ra and Menkau-ra. Following the death of Menkau-ra, the patient User-kaf, in fulfillment of the prophecy of Teta the magician, be-

*The Ibis-headed Thoth—scribe of the gods, inventor of hieroglyph-
ics, and the deity who pronounced the words that brought about
creation. The inscription top right reads medu-neter, "words of god,"
the Egyptian symbol for hieroglyphics.*

came first Pharaoh of the 5th Dynasty.

The three great pyramids of Khufu, Khaf-ra and Menkau-ra were to become regarded as the first of the Seven Great Wonders of the ancient world, and stand to this day, 5,000 years later, as further vindication of the prophecies of Teta, user of words of power and disciple of Thoth, who spoke the words that started creation.

In the Beginning

Egyptian lore tells us that the god Thoth played a crucial role in the earliest Nile traditions, in the development of a language of power, and in the act of creation itself. Ancient Egyptian literature is filled with references to a Supreme Deity under various titles (among them: Temu, Ptah, Khepera, Ra) who first created for himself a place in which to dwell by uttering his own name *as a word of power*, and then created the heavens, the celestial bodies, the gods, Earth, people, animals, birds and other creatures as concepts in his mind. It was the god Thoth, as representative of the intelligence of the Prime Creator, who translated into words these divine thoughts or ideas.

When Thoth spoke these "words of power," creation commenced.

The *Book of the Dead* tells us that the principal phrase spoken by Thoth on this awesome occasion was: *Kheper medet nebt Tem*—"There came (or come) into being the words of Temu."

As the "Master of Secrets," Thoth was scribe to the gods and a kind of World Teacher who taught the doctrine of the "Inner Light" of the Creator to the priests of the Egyptian temples. He was, together with the jackal-headed Anubis, god of mummification, one of the two major gods of the Egyptian funerary cult. Thoth was also acknowledged as a great magician, an *Ur heka*, or "Great One of Words of Power."

There are numerous references in the *Book of the Dead* to Thoth's command of potent speech, particularly in relation to the eventual resuscitation of the deceased after physical death. He is usually portrayed in reliefs as a man with the head of an ibis bird, after which he takes his Egyptian name, *Tjehuti*. In one semi-human aspect he was seen as vizier to the god Osiris, and later to Horus, son of Osiris. In another, he was reputed to have reigned over Egypt as king for 3,226 years.

Hieroglyphics and Hermetic Literature

In addition to his afterlife activities and other roles, Thoth was also known as the "Lord of Wisdom," especially when it came to the application of divine laws and to the use of sacred words and writings. Another of his roles was as the god of chronology and counting and, even more significantly, he was the reputed inventor of *medu-neter*, or hieroglyphic writing—the "words of god."

Because of a system of double meanings for each symbol, the sacred hieroglyphs represent the secret language of the Egyptian Mysteries. This possible dual interpretation for each hieroglyph has caused some confusion among translators of old papyri and wall paintings, and occasionally has brought forth garbled accounts of Egyptian mythology.

Other than being one of the acknowledged authors of the famous *Book of the Dead*, Thoth was, according to the Neo-Platonist Iamblichus, credited by the Egyptian prehistorian Manetho, a high priest living in

Lower Egypt around 300 B.C.E., as the compiler of 36,525 books containing the entire wisdom of the world. This massive body of writing was said to encompass the full range of material needed for education of priests and seers, including historical, geographical, mathematical, medical, and prophetic data. If a floating decimal is used, the figure 36,525 is, incidentally, remarkably close to the sacred cubit measurement of a base side of the designed perimeter of the Great Pyramid at Giza (365.24 = the number of days in our solar year). This measurement is duplicated in several other places in the Great Pyramid, notably in the King's Chamber, which leads to the possibility that Manetho may be hinting that Thoth himself designed the Pyramid. This proposition also posits a possible connection with Hebrew lore, which claims that the pyramid was built by the Patriarch Enoch (Hebrew: *Chanokh*) who is reputed to have lived 365 years, 88 days, 9 hours, expressed numerically as 365.24.

Thoth also enjoyed a messenger aspect, which led the Greeks to equate him with their own god Hermes under the appellation Hermes Trismegistus. This connection has led to the description of the metaphysical literature of Thoth/Hermes Trismegistus as the "Hermetic works." The modern term "hermetically sealed" derives from Thoth's apparent proclivity towards being able to create tightly sealed boxes. In esoteric terms, the word *hermetic* also means, of course, secret or "sealed."

To add to his now lost literary mysteries, Thoth is also listed in many works as a possible compiler or initiator of the original Tarot card deck, the symbolism and allegory of which is reputed to embody a synthesis of all the sciences, with infinite permutations capable of solving all problems.

The early 20th-century occultist and magician Aleister Crowley, a member of the Order of the Golden Dawn, with the help of an artist, Lady Frieda Harris, produced a guide to the Tarot and a deck of cards filled with erotic images known as *The Book of Thoth*. It remains unknown, however, whether Crowley received any inspiration from original Thothian writings. As part of his numerous magical rituals, Crowley also used various Egyptian mantras, including that taken from the so-called "Stele of Revealing."

Some Parallels

The Thothian story about the start of creation through utterance of certain potent words is to some extent paralleled in The Gospel According to St. John statement "In the beginning was the Word." St. John goes on to inform us that this Word "was made flesh," and that our Earth and all of its fauna and flora were created via a divine utterance. Several creation myths from around the globe echo this "first sound" phenomena.

For instance, the Indian *Upanishads* (philosophical treatises from around 600 B.C.E. based on the even more ancient *Rig Veda*) relate that *mantra* evolved out of the primeval ether or *Parma Akasha*—and that the universe came into being in the uttering of a primal sound related to *vach*, the human voice and feminine aspect of the originating Eternal Principle.

In the *Popul Vuh*, the sacred book of the Quiche Maya of Central America, we read: "(in the beginning)... there was only immobility and silence in the darkness, in the night.... *Then came the word.*" A Guatemalan legend tells of the two gods Hurakan and Gucumatz, hovering over the water-covered planet

Earth: "They said: *'Earth!'* and immediately the Earth was created."

Hebrew tradition relates that the universe was created with ten Godly utterances, the actual building blocks of creation being the spiritual motives behind the speech, and a similar version of the creation myth is given in the Nag Hammadi scroll *On the Origin of the World*: "His thought was made complete by the word and it appeared as a spirit moving to and fro over the waters. . . . Afterwards, the ruler thought within his nature, and he created an androgynous being *by means of the word.*"

A number of references to the use of an "all-powerful Word" to initiate the Earth's formation and/or creation of living creatures are contained in the Apocrypha and Pseudepigrapha of the Old Testament, notably in *The Wisdom of Solomon* (18:15; 9:1) and *The Syriac Apocalypse of Baruch* (21:4), while the Church of Latter-Day Saints' *Book of Mormon* informs us of the following: "For behold, by the power of his word man came upon the face of the earth, *which earth was created by the power of his word.*" (Jacob 4:9)

In a lighter vein, there is a Gnostic Egyptian myth that refers to a rather humorous Creator who laughed seven times to bring into being the universe and its inhabitants. The same story mentions a string of "magic words"—*Bessen Berithen Berio*—used by this happy God. Their meaning is, unfortunately, lost.

Papyrus transcript: "The sage spake certain words of power."

Ritual Magic and Words of Power

Ritual magic, or *za*, permeated all aspects of ancient Egyptian civilization, not only the expected areas of medicine, healing and prophecy. To the Egyptians, magic was regarded as an exact science. All gods, people, creatures and objects were considered to be imbued with a definable spiritual force that at once could be contacted, and controlled—when the correct words of command were utilized. There was a distinct belief in divine guidance and divine involvement in all human affairs.

The first of three major basic principles governing Egyptian magical science was that sound itself possessed an *intrinsic dynamic force*. It was widely held that by simply uttering the name of a being or an inanimate object that being or object could be called into existence, thus paralleling the very act of original creation. A reigning pharaoh would preface any new decree with the words "I am the Great Word"—indicating that he was capable of conferring life. A magician would begin all spells with the words *peret herou*, literally "that which comes forth at the voice."

It was also believed that utterance of a specified incantation could lead to power over wind, rain, storm and tempest, and even over the motions of river and sea. Correctly intoned, *hekau* (words of power) might also produce food for the hungry, banish illness from a patient, and provide protection from all manner of dangers and disasters, sometimes even death. Spells and incantations took on a particular significance when used by the deceased to negotiate safely the many pitfalls encountered beyond the threshold of death.

Even the gods themselves were obliged to abide by words of power uttered by a mortal. Every Egyptian received two names, the great name and the little name, of which only the second was ever made public. Knowledge of the secret name of any god, devil or person was considered to be the key to true mastery over that being or individual, and a name was considered as important as the *Ka* of a person, the soul itself. The worst fate that could befall any being was to see his or her name misused or destroyed, for it could be as much the objective of a curse as of a blessing.

The very letters of a name carried their own force. When an Egyptian magician spoke, he used sound like an artist, creating a word picture of marvelous strength and influence. It followed naturally that magical writing in hieroglyphs was believed to carry a power of its own, and because of the symbols used (animals, plants, parts of the human body), this form of writing was considered of a timeless nature.

Images and Amulets

For the most part, magic in ancient Egypt was used as a form of self-defense. The god of supernatural power, Heka, was said to have been created from "light." Sacred scripts were known as *Baou Ra*, "powers of Ra, the god of Light." The proportion of spiritual "light" present in a magical operation determined whether it could be regarded as "white" or "black."

Second in importance to sound in ancient Egyptian magical science was the use of an amulet—an image or model of a god, person or object. Pictures and figures of various shapes and forms, plus the performance of certain ceremonies (the third basic principle operative in Egyptian magic), were employed to invoke supernatural powers. Formulae consisting of words of power were inscribed upon amulets and statues, with

Amulets

the sacred scarab or *hepra* (usually made of lapis lazuli) a favorite among the many animal life forms thus
utilized. Healing statues, in particular, were not considered effective unless they carried a name of power.
An example of Egyptian ritual magic relating to
the use of words plus a physical form is demonstrated
by the so-called "execration figurine," which was inscribed with the name or names of persons considered
enemies, then smashed and thrown away in the hope
that a similar fate would befall those named.

The Egyptian Language

Although some early Greek writers had displayed
varying degrees of knowledge about the meanings of
hieroglyphics, it was not until 1798, when Napoleon
Bonaparte took a force of 38,000 men to Egypt in an attempt to annex the land of the Pharaohs (almost as
many men as Alexander commanded when he set out to
conquer the entire East), that some real progress was
made in translating the ancient Egyptian texts. After
some initial success in capturing Cairo, Napoleon was
destined to failure against Britain's Admiral Lord Nelson in the great sea battle of Abukir. To add to the
French leader's woes, a devastating Egyptian eye pes-
tilence blinded many of his soldiers, and he sailed home
a disappointed and disillusioned man. France was
eventually forced to hand over Egypt to the British in
1801.

However, when Napoleon arrived in the Land of
the Nile, he had with him several French scholars and
archaeologists, who enjoyed a unique first taste of the
marvels of Egypt's abundance of antiquities. Their
most outstanding discovery was the famous Rosetta
Stone, or Rosetta Pillar as it was first called. It was

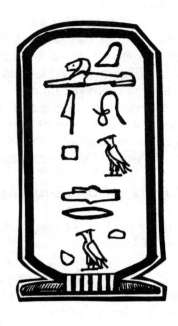

Cartouche of Cleopatra's name from the Rosetta Stone

found near the Rosetta mouth of the Nile in 1799 by a
Captain Bouchard. This approximately four-foot-high
slab of black basalt bore a carved decree in honor of the
Pharaoh Ptolomy V Epiphanes, King of Egypt from 205
B.C.E. to 182 B.C.E., in three separate scripts: 14 lines of
hieroglyphics; 32 lines of so-called *demotic*, non-picto-
rial Egyptian script used on business documents; and
54 lines of Greek. The text referred to certain great
works of the Pharaoh, including the conferring of benefits upon priests, the setting aside of large sums for
temple and irrigation construction projects, and the
giving of tax rebates to the people.

By 1824, a brilliant young French linguist, Jean-Francois Champollion—who had taught himself to read, and had accomplished his initial feat of language decipherment at the age of five—was the first to decipher the hieroglyphics on the stone obelisk. One of two words first translated by him from its pictographic presentation was the name of the famous Cleopatra (pronounced more correctly, *Krwiopadrat*—the nearest sound to *l* in the Egyptian tongue being *rw*), Queen of Egypt, and favorite subject of many a tale of royal love and intrigue. The other key word initially deciphered by the brilliant French linguist was the name *Ptolomy*, the husband-brother of Cleopatra.

An interesting side note relating to language connections is that the hieroglyphic inscription for the second letter in Cleopatra's name is the pictograph representing a lion—its sound *rw* symbolizing the roar of the animal concerned. It seems more than a coincidence that "lion" is spelled in English beginning with a letter that represents the Egyptian *rw*. More will follow later about other interesting language links that suggest a "universal" sound connection.

Some Notes on Egyptian Pronunciation

Unfortunately, Champollion's decipherment and the work of later Egyptologists did not lead to any exact knowledge of the correct pronunciation of ancient Egyptian. As is the case with Hebrew and most other ancient tongues, the original Egyptian vowel sounds are not certain. However, some attempt at correct vocalization of the language has been gradually reconstructed by using Greek and Coptic expressions which approximate the Egyptian, as well as evidence from texts in various languages written with cuneiform characters.

A synthesis of research and meditative inspiration has been used in determining a guide to pronunciation of the reconstructed Egyptian words and phrases of power here presented.[2]

It is not always easy for a Westerner to reproduce some of the apparently throat-based Egyptian sounds. A case in point is the sound represented by the letters *ch*, which is similar to that in the Scottish word *loch*. As another example, there are three forms of *a* in Egyptian, all distinctive, and one of which actually sounds like the "o" in *bottle* when spoken by an English Cockney. Note the following:

ȧ = truncated *a* as per the "o" in *bottle*, if pronounced by a Cockney

a = *ah* as in *bath*

ạ = *i* as in *mine*

ḥ = *ch* as in *loch*

dj = *dge* as in *badge*

kh = *q* as in *Qor'an*

ṭ = *tch* as in *batch*

u = *oo* as in *mood*, but more elongated

ụ = *u* as in *bud*

9. LIFE—A PRELUDE TO DEATH

O ye gods, who hear speech!
Papyrus of Ani

For the Egyptians, their country was the center of the world with their people as its only rightful inhabitants. Furthermore, life on Earth was considered as merely a prelude to the hereafter, and provision was made for death on a scale unmatched anywhere else in the world. The Egyptian *Book of the Dead*, or *Pert-em-Hru* (more correctly "Book of the Coming Forth by Day" or "Book manifested in the Light"), is probably the oldest book in the world and contains a vast storehouse of ritual relating to the afterlife. A person was meant to memorize the ceremonial spells for use to escape from the tomb after death, reach the Osirian heaven, and pass the required tests set there in order to become an accepted member of the divine bureaucracy.

This collection of hymns and prayers, spells and incantations, has been compiled from ancient papyri, from inscriptions on sarcophagi, and from the walls of pyramids and other tombs. It is replete in the use of magical words and phrases, and special emphasis is placed on the use of names of power in the sections that deal with the soul's travels through the "Halls" inhab-

117

ited by various gods and goddesses.

The Oldest Prayer in the World

An outstanding example of the importance placed by the Egyptians on death rites, and possibly the oldest known prayer in the world, is recorded in the *Book of the Dead* as part of the significant Ma-at ritual—during which the newly deceased faces a row of 42 gods in *Usekht Ma-ati*, the Hall of Ma-at or Hall of Double Right and Truth. Ma-at was the ostrich-plumed goddess of Truth and Divine Order, or the personification of physical law and moral rectitude. She was also daughter of the sun-god Ra and female counterpart to the deity Thoth, and, as such, she was a participant with Thoth in the creation saga. In the Halls of Ma-at,

Ma'at, goddess of Truth and Divine Order.

the soul of the deceased person, through use of various rituals and incantations, is separated from his or her sins, and thus finally becomes able to "see" the "Lord of Mankind."

Ani, our principle character in the *Book of the Dead* drama, was the royal scribe of Thebes around 1320 B.C.E. and a high ecclesiastical dignitary associated with the priests of the god Amen, who was known as the "hidden one." His confession after death to the assembled gods is contained in the 78-foot *Papyrus of Ani* scroll, which is perhaps the finest copy extant of the Egyptian *Book of the Dead*. Another classic Egyptian scroll, the *Papyrus of Nu*, asserts that the subject prayer was in use in the time of Menkau-ra of the 4th Dynasty, circa 3700 B.C.E. As it was still fashionable during the Ptolemaic period, when Cleopatra reigned around 30 B.C.E., this famous funerary ritual had by then been in use for nearly 3500 years—which must make it almost certainly the oldest known prayer in the world.

In the prayer of Ma-at, the supplicant recites what amounts to a negative confession ("I have not robbed," "I have not caused pain," "I have not committed fornication," "I have not stirred up strife," "I have never cursed God," and so on) and asks that no false witness be borne against him, that his character be not blemished, that no lies be talked about him, and that his heart be not separated from him. This ritual listing of allegedly uncommitted misdemeanors and sins is in interesting contrast to the generally purgative confessions of other cultures, such as the Jewish Day of Atonement or *Yom Kippur* confession known as *Viddui*, the Japanese Shinto *Ohoharahi* or "Great Purgation," and the Indian Brahmanic ceremony of *Avabhrta* during the annual expiatory rite of *Varunapraghasa*.

It is of interest to note that, basically, the Egyptians believed in a singular, monotheistic god, who possessed many aspects and attributes. They perceived this Supreme Deity as an active force in their own world, commanding, guiding and inspiring them. Free choice also played its part—the evil in this world considered the consequence of humanity's forsaking of the Creator's will.

Gods and Good Fortune

When studying Egyptian words of power, it is of particular importance to note the difference between the similarly spelled words *neter* and *nefer*. *Neter* can be taken as a common Egyptian title for any particular god. It is, however, a word with many meanings, including: "god-like," "divine," "sacred," "power," "strength," "guardian" and "watcher." With its single letter change, the expression *nefer* relates to "happiness," "good fortune," "perfection," "beauty," or the granting of a boon by a god.

Neter remains an extraterrestrial concept; nefer is the terrestrial manifestation of *sehemu*, the powers of the divine.

The separate Egyptian "gods" possessed personality, but lacked individuality. It might be claimed that these individual *neteru* merely represented personifications of the various aspects of a single Creator that included the many and varied features of nature and the cosmos. This is in line with another interpretation of the word *neter*, which places it as "masters of nature."

The plural *neteru* can claim some comparison with the Hebrew biblical reference to God as *Elohim*, which is also plural and means literally "Gods."

Some Egyptian Chants for Daily Use

For the most part, the invocations given in the Egyptian *Book of the Dead* are rather long and complicated. In keeping with the introductory nature of this present work, a small selection of simplified Egyptian language chants are offered in this chapter and the next for use by the reader. These have been devised by the authors, but are based on original ancient Egyptian textual information. Some background data is given in each instance for fuller understanding of the chants given so that they may be most effectively utilized.

In accordance with the neter/One God principle, the phrase noted below has been composed as an Egyptian language mantra that signifies the interrelationship between terrestrial and extraterrestrial forces. It has been designed for constant repetition in order to attract protection, inspiration, happiness and good fortune—and a "bonding" with higher forces. If used in alliance with any particular Egyptian deity's name, it will draw towards the chanter the attributes of that chosen deity.

The underlying principle operative behind the uttering of any invocatory statement remains the same, no matter the language chosen. Of overriding importance is the sincerity and intention of the invoker. Remember always that there is a universal law which states that all energy transmitted outwards, positive or negative, eventually returns to its original source.

Nefer-Neṭer-wed-neh
[N'fr N'tjir wed neh]

The perfect god grants life

Ptah—the Great Cosmic God

Ptah was a name used for the Egyptians' great cosmic god, who was one of several deities credited with the original creation of the universe. He was known as "Lord of Life," and his name also has a secondary meaning which translates as "to break open." This alludes to an ability to initiate a "breakthrough" into higher realms of consciousness while dispersing surrounding negativity, much in the way of the Hindu god Shiva.

In a mirror image of the Hindu triune, Brahma-Vishnu-Shiva, the deity Ptah is a member of an Egyptian trinity that embraces three especially important attributes: creation (Ptah), death (Sekher) and resurrection (Asar or Osiris). This Egyptian trinity representation symbolizes the resurrection prospect that eventually becomes the heritage of the righteous person.

One of Ptah's major symbols is the well-known *ankh*, the sign of eternal life. Its hieroglyphic representation is taken from a sandal tie, and from a metaphysical point of view the ankh is possibly the most powerful of all Egyptian ritual objects.

Sounding of the word *ankh* plus the three names of Ptah can stimulate a profound protective force on all levels of human activity, and help set into motion a process of transformation of the individual from human into super-human.

Ankh-Ptaḥ-Sekher-Ȧsar
[Ainq P'tach S'qer Os'r]

Ankh-Ptah-Sekher-Osiris

Hieroglyphic form of the chant Ankh-Ptah-Sekher-Asar.

Ra—the Sun-God

The deity Ra, the Egyptian falcon-headed sun-god as creator and sustainer of the world, is possibly an older subject for reverence than Ptah. Ra is a personification of the sun at noon and was known as the creator of gods and of humans. His emblem is, of course, the unmistakable sun's disc.

The fact that the Egyptians chose a supreme sun-god is rather unusual, as most African peoples tended to revere a moon deity as the prime object of worship. The Pharaoh Userkaf, the first King of the 5th Dynasty, whose rise to power was predicted by the famous magician Teta and whose tale is told in Chapter 8, was the first notable priest of Ra and the first Egyptian ruler to take on the title "Son of Ra."

A mantric phrase embodying the name Ra (pronounced Reh) is designed to draw towards the user the life-giving warmth of the sun and the protection of a deity/power who was supposed to have spent the hours of darkness fighting *Apepi*, the serpent and personification of evil, always rising triumphantly every morning to shine anew in the sky.

Ra-Neṭer-Âtef-Nefer
[Reh N'tjir O'tef N'fer]

The Divine god Ra is gracious

Initiation, Activation, and Resurrection

Spiritual operations connected with the Egyptian gods or attributes of the One God are frequently associated with the concept of the *Ba*, the "spirit," which can be symbolized as the dove, especially in its relation to the "gifts of the gods," or in Judeo-Christian terminology, the "Holy Spirit." The word *Ba* is not to be confused with the expressions *Ab* (heart) or *Ka*—which is related to the vital energy of the physical universe and similar in some ways to the Hindu *prana*, but much more personal. *Ka* is perhaps best described as representing the corporeal transmigrating human soul. It is

Hieroglyphic representations of (top to bottom):
Ka—the transmigrating human soul; Ba—the spiritual soul;
Akh—the divine essence; IAAW—the source of all being.

also linked with the astral body, which remains separate but, during this lifetime, indivisible from the perishable physical body (*khat*) and is activated mostly when a person is asleep.

It can be noted here that, although considered to be of a supernatural nature, *Ka* was for the Egyptians essentially a force resident in our physical world as a transmitter from one lifetime to the next of hereditary characteristics and the like.

The concept referred to as *Ba*, that portion of the Universal Spirit which can become an integral part of the human being, may be aligned with the idea of an interdimensional "body of light," or divine double, which is needed by a human to enter into higher realms of evolutionary participation. The *Ba* vibration is highly potent and will be discussed more fully below as part of a meditation mantra which also incorporates the *Bak* or hawk (symbol of Horus) and the legendary phoenix or *Bennu* bird, which is said to rise from its own ashes after self-immolation by fire.

In addition to the more earthly *Ka* and the dualistic *Ba*, the word *Akh* was used to describe the extraterrestrial divine essence of Egyptian gods and kings. *Akh* was the radiant light symbolized by the ibis bird and, with *Ba* and *Ka*, formed an indivisible trinity of powers emanating from the source of all being, known as *IAAW*. The term *IAAW* posits a curious analogy with the Hebrew ineffable Name of God, generally pronounced *Yahweh* or *Jehovah*, but consisting of four consonantal Hebrew letters, *yod, hey, vau, hey* (see Chapter 4). It was believed by the Egyptians that every person has his or her image in *IAAW*, being, as it were, a mirror reflection of the Absolute—a concept which is certainly not out of touch with Judeo-Christian teachings. A secondary meaning for the word *iaaw* is "glorification" or "praise."

Another word used for God by the Egyptians was *Wr*, pronounced "oor" or "ur," which is almost identical to the Hebrew word for "light," meaning Superluminal or holy "Light."

An especially significant Egyptian-language mantric phrase relates to the attributes and principles of the *Ba* (dove), *Bak* (hawk), and *Bennu* (phoenix). Employment of these three potent words in a repetitive chant can transport the user into a mystical state in which is simulated an experience involving the threefold nature of existence: birth, death, and rebirth into a higher form.

The *Book of the Dead* includes three separate mystical ceremonies involving the symbolism of the Ba, Bak and Bennu, entitled, respectively: "Opening of the Tomb to the *Ba*-soul and Shadow," "Making the Transformation into the God Hawk,"and "Making the Transformation into the *Bennu* Bird."

The *Ba* is usually portrayed in Egyptian art as a human-headed falcon. However, in its alternative dove aspect, *Ba* represents the vehicle of spiritual sanctification—the down-flow of divine power into the kingdom of humans which activates the spiritual or higher self of any individual.

Bak as the hawk and sign of Horus is symbolic of a vehicle of spiritual action within our physical universe—or the effort made by any individual to attract the presence of the *Ba*. It also holds many personally protective qualities on the physical, astral and spiritual levels.

The *Bennu* or phoenix bird, which according to hermetic lore is reborn from its own ashes, represents a vehicle of time-translation, symbolizing spiritual and physical "rebirth" into a new "body of light," capable of traveling in higher regions of creation. It is at once a symbol of Ra and of Osiris, the heavenly and the human.

It is recommended that the chant which follows be sung repetitively at a pace in time with the individual chanter's own heartbeat. Its effect is to stimulate a personal experience of spiritual transformation. This effect is initiated by stimulus from "above" (*Ba*), is carried forward into resultant activation of the physical condition (*Bak*), and culminates in a highly charged feeling of spiritual resurrection or transformation (*Bennu*). This mantra based on Egyptian terminology is specially recommended for group chanting.

Ba-Bak-Bennu
[Bah Bahk Ben-noo]

The Dove; the Hawk; the Phoenix

The sleeve note of a recommended audio-tape version of this chant offers the following interpretation:

"The 'rebirth' of the spirit through the Holy Spirit / *Shekinah* Dove; the protection of the soul through the Eagle; and the awakening of body, soul and spirit through the Phoenix power of resurrection."[1]

10. THE PILLAR OF OSIRIS

Praise be unto thee, O Osiris,
Lord of Eternity;
Un-nefer, Ḥeru-khuti!
"Hymn to Osiris,"
The Book of the Dead

To assist in the perfection of the spirit-souls of those who had moved into the Realm of the Dead, it was customary for the still-living Egyptians to recite the names of the gods at funerals and other feasts. Sixty-six such names are listed in the Theban Recension of the *Book of the Dead*, beginning with Osiris-Kenti-Amenti, one of the many appellations of Osiris, the Egyptian "savior" and most significant of all Egyptian deities. Osiris is usually depicted as a bearded personage, either green or black in color, wearing the Crown of Upper Egypt and swathed like a mummy. In his hands are the flail and a crook, insignia of the power over the underworld vested in this dying and resurrecting god.

There is little doubt that as accepted king and judge of the netherworld he is the most important figure in Egyptian mythology. One of his numerous descriptions even alludes to an extraterrestrial origin, placing Osiris as a Lord Creator from *Sah* (the constellation Orion). It is, therefore, not surprising that vocalization of the name of Osiris in various contexts provokes considerable power on several levels.

Lord of Eternal Life

Having himself been resurrected from the dead, thanks to the dedicated efforts of his consort and sister, the goddess Isis, Osiris is clearly equated with the concept of eternal life. There is indeed a Christ-like "raising from the dead" element in the scenario presented in the Egyptian Ritual of the Dead, which places prime emphasis on the reuniting of the deceased with Osiris the Redeemer. It has also been claimed that the legend of Osiris, and that of his spouse Isis and son Horus, is the story of all creatures on Earth: birth, life, death and rebirth.

The djed pillar surmounted by the ankh with two hands representing the Ka, or soul, holding the sun disc of Ra.

Osiris, as deity of eternal life, is inexplicably linked with the symbol referred to as the *djed*—the "pillar of Osiris." This supportive djed-pillar represents, among other things, the actual spinal column of the legendary Osiris and is, according to ancient texts, the origin of the "Fire of Life." This Fire of Life can, of course, be related in Hindu terms with the *Kundalini* power that rests at the base of any individual's spine, awaiting awakening at the appropriate time and under suitable conditions (see Chapter 11). The djed itself can be likened to a spiritual or etheric version of the human backbone.

Another interpretation of its symbolism holds that it exemplifies the entire process of psychogenic evolution, beginning at the base of the column with the start of life in the form of micro-organisms, and working its way up the ladder through the forms of fish, reptile, mammal, and finally, human being. These various stages of evolution are represented by the sequence of enclosed horizontal bars on the lower part of the djed. The series of broad horizontal platforms that commence in the upper portion of the column are indicative of repetitive human incarnations and continued upward progress. The narrower segments separating these platforms symbolize between-lives periods, when the soul is resident in the world of the spirit.

Some representations of the djed column of Osiris include two arms, one holding a hook, the other a flail, at the conjunction of the lower and upper portions. This signifies the point in time when the human became a moral being, something beyond the animal world of purely biologically motivated feelings and desires.

The *ankh* or *crux ansata*, Egyptian symbol of eternal life, is often seen placed on the top of the djed, with a second set of two arms issuing therefrom, holding a disc representing the sun. As a set hieroglyphic form, the two arms indicate the *Ka*, or transmigrating human soul. The solar disc can be equated with the sungod Ra, and is the model for the highest possible perfection of human intelligence.

Hieroglyphic form of the chant Asar-djedu (Pillar of Osiris).

The following mantric phrase, dedicated to Osiris and incorporating the djed principle, consists simply of a repetition of the words *Asar-djedu*. It is to be used in order to promote strength of will and purpose, leading towards a yearning for true wisdom and understanding so as to nurture spiritual transformation and growth. During chanting, and under appropriate conditions relating to the personal development stage of the chanter, a tingling warmth may sometimes be felt traveling up the spinal column; this is caused by the raising of the "Fire of Life" of Osiris.

Àsar-djedu
[Os'r dje-doo]
Pillar of Osiris

Isis and Her Words of Power

Isis, whose name literally means "seat," was the devoted wife of Osiris and the most popular goddess in the Egyptian pantheon. She is also a role model for many later Mediterranean and Middle Eastern goddesses, and even possibly for the Buddhist Avalokitesvara or Kuan Yin. Known in the *Book of the Dead* as Ast, the goddess Isis is hailed in various ancient Egyptian texts as "the woman of magical spells" and "the mistress of words of power, or enchantments." She is also described as having turned aside countless calamities with the "magical power of her mouth." One passage in the *Book of the Dead* describes how "the words which she stringeth together destroy diseases, and they make to live those whose throats are stopped up (i.e., the dead)."[1]

As goddess of both Earth and moon, sister-wife of Osiris, and mother of Horus, Isis possessed virtually limitless powers. She was said to hold sway over Earth, sea and heavens, and even the underworld. As goddess of birth, she decided the fate of mortals from an early stage in their lives.

Hieroglyphic form of the phrase Erta-na-hekau-apen-Ast
(May I be given the Words of Power of Isis).

Utterance of a phrase invoking her name, *Erta-na-hekau-apen-Ast* ("May I be given the Words of Power of Isis"), can be used to initiate immediate aid and protection and to provoke intuitive hints for action for anyone facing any form of threat, be it from physical danger or disease or of a psychic or spiritual nature.

Ertạ-na-ḥekau-ȧpen-Ȧst
[Err-tai no che-kah-oo o'pen Ost]

May I be given the Words of Power of Isis

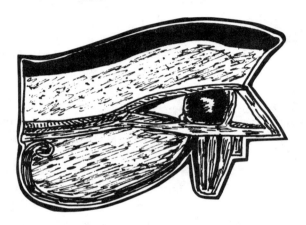

The Udjat—"Eye of Horus" (from an amulet circa 600 B.C.E.).

The Eye of Horus

The sky god Horus, or Heru, son by magical means of Isis and an already slain Osiris, is portrayed in Egyptian art in the form of a falcon or hawk (*bak* or *hor*). Horus was in his own right the center of an important cult and the role model for Egyptian earthly rulers, who considered themselves to be deities. His emblem, the hawk, was, according to Budge, possibly the first living creature to be venerated by the early Egyptians.

As is the case with his father Osiris, some sources have placed Horus as an extraterrestrial supra-natural figure—a model for the super-human who has acquired higher consciousness. The distinctive "Eye of Horus," or *udjat*, is mentioned frequently in Egyptian literature, and is not to be confused with the human "third eye" discussed in Chapter 11. The udjat was considered by the Egyptians as a device used by advanced beings on other planes to view events in our world—the "Eye of the Lord," so to speak. Magical amulets against injury bearing the Eye of Horus were usually made of lapis lazuli, a favorite medium for ornaments bearing inscriptions of words of power. Some were plated in gold.

Each of the four accredited sons of Horus—Hapi, Tuamutef, Khebhsenuf and Amset—represents an essential part or function of the udjat, the all-seeing eye. The four children of Horus are also associated with the four corners, or Cardinal Points, of the world, much in the way of the Japanese *Shitteno*, or guardians of the four points of the compass.

There are two distinct types of udjat eye: the right and the left; one white, the other black, representing the Sun and the Moon, or Ra and Osiris, respectively. Any artist's representation of the eye itself incorporates a combination of the human eye and the markings of a falcon's or hawk's eye. As an amulet, the udjat was considered at its most powerful during the summer when the sun is at its strongest. The Greeks later took over the symbol and even developed an udjat ceremony to catch a thief involving the use of the Eye of Horus symbol and the chanting of certain magical words.

*The hawk-headed Horus approaches his parents, Osiris and Isis.
In the background, on a lotus flower, are the four sons of Horus.*

A short invocation—*Heru-Udjat*—calling upon the all-seeing Eye of Horus, can be utilized as a personal protection mantra of particular use against psychic attack of any kind, and also for the promotion of strength and vigor.

Ḥeru-Udjat
[Che-roo Oo-dgot]
Eye of Horus

Transformation of the Soul and Psyche

Aside from those of his qualities already discussed, Horus can be considered as a prototype for emulation by any aspirant who seeks eventual transformation of soul and psyche from human into superhuman. The initiation chant presented below calls on the user to sacrifice all personality considerations to Temu, the self-created "maker of the gods" and representative of the source of all life, in order to achieve the divine status of his son Horus, the "perfected one," who transcends all normal human consciousness.

The prime function of this dynamic mantra is to uplift the consciousness into realms of mental and supra-mental activity that ranges far beyond the physical. There follows a quickening of the pace of the inner ordeal, which usually precedes discovery of the Infinite behind the finite.

Sa-Su-Temu-Ḥeru-Hȧkenu
[Sah Soo Tem-moo Che-roo Ho'ken-noo]

Make an offering to the son of Temu—
Horus, the praised one

The sleeve note of a recommended musical variation of this chant describes it as the Egyptian/Coptic:

"Appasionata... The passions of personal ordeal and the discovery of the Heavenly Father behind the enigma of creation, opening unending vistas of space."[2]

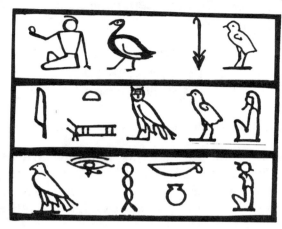

Hieroglyphic form of the chant Sa-Su-Temu-Heru-Hakenu (Make an offering to the son of Temu—Horus, the praised one).

There are several other significant interpretations to be attached to the various individual expressions in the phrase *Sa-Su-Temu-Heru-Hakenu*. As well as meaning "make an offering" and "son of," the word *Sa* represents the name of the *neter* (god) of Feeling. Its several other meanings include: "back" (associated with the energy running along the spinal column, as in the djed column); "life-preserver" (referring to protective gear worn by herdsmen driving animals through swampland—and relating to the overall notion of protection); and "a guardian" (which serves to emphasize the protective nature of the word). The *Sa* hieroglyphic was frequently used on an amulet for warding off unfriendly forces.

Heru-Hakenu is, incidentally, also one of the many names of Thoth—he who spoke the first words of creation—and a distinctive symbol for "Initiation." The word *hakenu* means literally "praise him." The word *heru*, other than representing the name of Horus, also means "beings celestial."

The Seven Unalterable Powers

In line with the Hindu seven bodily chakras, or energy entry and exit points, the ancient Egyptians spoke of seven "ineffable powers," which approximate the chakra system. As is the case with the Sanskrit *bija* sounds, the names of these powers can be used to activate the chakras, either in unison or separately as required. However, before these words of power are used, and in order to understand the function of the body's energy vortices fully, it is recommended that a thorough study be made of the chakra system as described in Chapter 11.

The names and attributes of the Seven Egyptian Powers are:

1. *Ikh* [Eeq]: placed at the seventh chakra, at the crown of the head. It is the reflected image of the Divine; the gateway to higher dimensions.

2. *Mer* [M'rr]: corresponds to the sixth chakra, at the third eye in the middle of the forehead. It represents the awareness of the essential duality of existence.

3. *Sehem* [Se-chem]: relates to the fifth chakra, at the throat. It is the generating or liberating center.

4. *Heper* [Che-p'r]: embodies the fourth chakra, placed at heart level. This is the center which opens up the pathway to spiritual transformation.

5. *Àb* [Ob]: literally "heart," but equated with the third chakra, at the solar plexus. It is the center of occult emotional activity, linked with the desire body.

6. *Tekh* [Teq]: connected with the second chakra, situated at the organs of procreation. It represents the individual's capacity for absorption of the vital universal power.

7. *Sefekht* [Se-f'qt]: also known as *Sheshat* [Shehsh't]; corresponds to the first chakra, the root chakra at the base of the spine. It epitomizes the "power of crystallization," or manifestation on the physical level.

11. MANTRA YOGA

Shabdanishtam Jagat
(The universe is manifested through sound)
Sanskrit Sun Mantra

The mystical aim is to utilize the
power of sound vibrations to influence
modalities of consciousness.
—James Hewitt
The Complete Yoga Book

The results of sound generated at a particular pitch have been clearly demonstrated by singers and violinists who have used a persistent note to break a glass; or through the shattering of windows by a jet airplane's sonic boom. Experiments using sand sprinkled over a tightly stretched drum have revealed the formation of geometrical shapes and attractive plant-like forms when harmonious sounds or positive, happy words are sung or spoken close by. When disharmonious sounds are used, the patterns formed are generally chaotic. Science has indeed confirmed that every form in our universe, animate and inanimate, exhibits its own vibratory rate. It follows that knowledge of any such given rate of vibration may be used in creating an effect upon the subject form.

Sacred Sound

The sages (or, respectively, *rishis* and *lamas*) of India and Tibet have long recognized the human voice as potentially the most perfect of all vehicles of sound.

One of the verses of the *Rig Veda* (a collection of sacred hymns completed around 900 B.C.E.) informs us that many who can see do not "see" the Word; and many who can hear do not "hear" it.... "Yet for another it reveals itself like a radiant bride yielding to her husband." (Hymn 10.71:4)

In terms of the Vedic experience, sacred sound, which is capable of initiating a biological effect on the human physiology, originates in the form of a flash of "light" in the innermost center of an individual, and this "shining" duality leads towards illumination. To praise is thus considered to illumine.

This concept is echoed in Western scripture and provides an illustration of the principally subjective nature of holy sound.

In Hindu terms, sound is broken up into three basic categories: *sa-ama-anya*—everyday sounds of the physical world; *varna*—the spoken word linked with the flow of the human heartbeat; and *mooka*—the "Sound of Silence," represented by the divine primeval *Om* (or, more correctly, *Aum*).

Traditional Indian music embraces 120 *talas*, or time measures, but remains nonetheless firmly based on the human voice range of three octaves, with emphasis on melody rather than harmony. Above all, Indian music in all its forms, both instrumental and sung, is a particularly spiritual experience, placing personal harmony with the Absolute above mere symphonic excellence.

Yoga

For many, the practice of yoga is indivisible from the practice of mantra chanting. The meaning of the word *mantra* will be more fully dealt with in the following pages. *Yoga* is the name given to various systems designed to raise the consciousness of an individual and develop a union with the *Atman*, the higher self or pure consciousness, which can be equated with *Brahman*, the impersonal and imageless life force behind all being. Atman lies beyond human ego and, in effect, yoga can be called "union with Atman and/or Brahman."

In no particular order, as all are equal, the best-known Indian yoga disciplines are:

Yoga type:	Union with Atman/Brahman through:
Jnana yoga	knowledge and discernment
Bhakti yoga	love and devotion
Karma yoga	action and service
Kundalini yoga	arousal of psychic forces
Tantra yoga	physiological discipline
Hatha yoga	bodily mastery and breath control
Raja yoga	mental mastery and meditation
Yantra yoga	use of vision and form
Japa yoga or Mantra yoga	use of voice and sound

Although there appear to be divisions in yogic practice, this is not in actual fact the case. All forms of yoga are interrelated, and elements of each appear within the separately titled disciplines. For instance, before *Kundalini yoga* can be effectively practiced, it is usually necessary for the participant to have some knowledge and mastery of *Hatha yoga* and/or *Jnana* and *Raja yoga* so as to achieve the required understanding of body and mind control. Those leaning towards *Tantra yoga* as a means of raising their level of perception would by necessity need to have some knowledge of all of the following: *Jnana yoga* (for discernment); *Hatha yoga* (bodily control); *Raja yoga* (mental control); *Karma yoga* (understanding of the laws of cause and effect); *Kundalini yoga* (correct manipulation of psychic power); *Bhakti yoga* (to achieve the necessary love and devotion for sexual partners—for the practice of *Tantra yoga* places prime emphasis on the union of male and female); *Yantra yoga* (correct visualization); and finally, but most importantly, *Japa yoga* (for understanding of the use and effect of sound in yogic practice).

Indeed, *Japa* or *Mantra yoga* is used in most systems, and is, of course, the form of yoga with which we are here most concerned.

Japa Yoga

A simple definition of the terms *Japa yoga* or *Mantra yoga* might be: "the use of certain syllables, words, or phrases, for the purpose of influencing individual consciousness." We have already noted that in ordinary speech we employ sound to convey meaning. *Mantra yoga* is concerned with sound as "being."

Swami Sivananda, in his book *Japa Yoga*, the definitive work on the subject, sums up in a few words the effect created by divine sound or mantric invocation: "The recital of a mantra brings everlasting peace, infinite bliss, prosperity and immortality."[1]

Born into a rich family in 1887, Sivananda was a medical doctor of note before he settled down to study yoga under the great sage Jivanmukta at the age of 37. Out of his ashram at Rishikesh grew the worldwide Divine Life Society. Sivananda has published over 300 volumes on the various types of yoga and has disciples of all faiths around the world. According to him, in the present age, which is known as *Kaliyuga* (the Iron

Age), Japa yoga alone is the easy way to a realization of Divinity: "Life is short. Time is fleeting. Those who simply eat, drink and sleep and do not practice any Japa are horizontal beings only."[2]

The great guru of Rishikesh, who passed over into *Mahasamadhi* in 1963, was a stern taskmaster who entreated his pupils to do Japa for many hours and told them to repeat their holy mantras as much as 50,000 times a day!

Japa is, in effect, the repetition of any mantra or Name of God that forces the mind to move towards the spiritual. A common literal translation of the Sanskrit word *mantra* is "the liberating thought." Another definition is: "instrument or vehicle of thought." Although similar to it, a mantra cannot be totally equated with the Western concept of prayer. A prayer is usually a supplication, a request made by the supplicant. The mantra is regarded at once an invocation, a benediction, an affirmation and a promise.

A mantra can be chanted out loud or sung silently within the mind. Sivananda notes three types of Japa: *Manasika Japa*, or Mental Japa; *Upamsu Japa*, or Japa employing a humming sound; and *Vaikhari Japa*, or loud, audible Japa. Used as a single word or as a collection of words in verse form, whether physically vocalized or mentally evoked, a mantra sets in motion a predetermined chain of effects directly related to the words spoken aloud or in the mind.

The main object of mantric intonation is to carry the consciousness into an elevated state beyond the mere material. Some Indian yogis even produce the desired effect by simply writing out certain mantras repetitively, like a schoolchild writing out lines. This is known as *Likhita Japa* and aids in the development of a wonderful concentration.

Timing and rhythm (allied with studied breath control), sincerity and concentration are major considerations in correct *swadhyaya*, or mantra usage involving chanting or recitation of holy texts. Each syllable intoned carries essential meaning. Some mantric sounds trigger off an emotional response; others evoke images and ideas similar to those experienced in a mystical vision. When mantras are used with consistent and dedicated purpose, there also can occur a profound prophetic awareness.

Power of Mantra

Hindu mythological writings from the medieval period include reference to mantric wars involving *devas* ("shining ones"; gods) and *asuras* (demons) within the confines of the lower astral regions, dimensions parallel but inferior to our world. At least one such conflict is said to have ended in tragedy for a demon who happened to mispronounce a potent chant aimed at an opponent deva. Because of his error in enunciation, it came back at him like an exploding boomerang!

The extraordinary power of mantras—positive and negative—is discussed throughout the *Bardo Thodol*, the Tibetan *Book of the Dead*. In Tibet the *lamas*, or priestly monks, chant mantras (or *mantram*, to use an alternative plural form) while counting beads on a rosary, much in the fashion of a Roman Catholic Christian.

Whatever the place or occasion, the intention remains the same. In India, *sankirtan*, or group chanting, is favored. At such a gathering, mantras and *bhajans* (devotional songs) are sung to the accompaniment of an accordion and/or hand-beaten drums.

The celebrated Swami Muktananda always kept an *ektara*, a one-stringed instrument, at his side with which he accompanied himself during chants. One of his disciples, Swami Nityananda (named after Muktananda's own guru, Bhagavan Nityananda), relates in his book *The Nectar of Chanting* that his master also kept a stick and a few blocks of wood handy during sankirtan—the blocks to throw at older people who dozed off during chanting, and the stick to chastise youngsters who did not pay sufficient attention to correct pronunciation of the mantras.[3]

In summing up, mantras can best be described as words and phrases of power, peace or personal transformation, depending upon individual choice and usage. It is also important to note that their ultimate effectiveness is directly related to the knowledge, intentions and convictions of the user.

The Sound of the Soul

The great sage Sri Ramakrishna was once heard to note that the sacred texts give us information about God and not God Himself. If the old books contain information about God, logic tells us that there must be some form of discipline which leads us to experience God, instead of just gathering information about Him. Mere acceptance of a doctrine that divinity lies within each individual is insufficient. In order to attain some conception of the Ultimate, it becomes necessary to *experience truth*. This is the essence of yogic practice. Constant sounding of a mantra, aloud or silently within the mind, provides protection from the impact of *maya*, or earthly illusion, and allows for intuitive experiencing of spiritual truth.

Such practice will also lead eventually to the perception of *nadas*, the internal "sound of the soul," which forms within and is heard without the aid of the ears.

Some teachers refer to mantras as direct manifestations of the Supreme Being. In his book *Formulas for Transformation*, Eknath Easwaren defines the concept as a "powerful spiritual formula for the highest that we can conceive of."[4]

The correct sounding of the syllables contained in any single mantra serves both *to focus* spiritual energy effectively from within the chanter's own being and *to attract* desirable vibrations from without. These twin energies can be of a protective, healing or motivating nature, depending on the chant used.

It is believed that the greater the accuracy of pronunciation, strict maintenance of rhythm, and frequency of repetition, the most beneficial will be the effect produced through mantra use. However, there are, in effect, many variations of specific mantra intonation, dependent upon regional origin and dialect employed.

According to Hindu tradition, each mantra is imbued with six separate but indivisible aspects:

* The *Devata*, or presiding deity of a particular mantra

* The *Rishi*, or seer who first pronounced it

* The *raga*, or musical melodic aspect

* The *bija*, or primal seed sound

* The *shakti*, or power of the chant

* The *kilaka*, (literally "pillar"), the chanter's own will power

The selection of a particular mantra for a specific occasion is of immense importance and requires the application of both intuition and plain, old-fashioned common sense. No mantra should be used lightly or in a negative fashion. It is a basic cosmic law that all negativity consciously projected will eventually return from whence it came. So, too, will every sincere outward projection of love and goodwill—usually multifold. To a large extent, through our thoughts and our actions we create our own future. And as the power of mantra is generally far more potent than that of any phrase used in everyday speech, we are advised to be ultra-cautious in choice and use of our words of power.

Seed Sounds, Kundalini and the Chakras

In both Tibetan and Indian sacred chanting, certain "seed" sounds form the basis of all mantric syllables. These are known as *bija* (bee-jah) mantras—the first of which is the familiar *Om.* There are numerous other bija sounds, some of which are directly related to the physiological and psychical functioning of the human being.

According to Hindu science, each person possesses seven major *chakras*—cerebrospinal centers or energy points located along the body—through which there is a continuous two-way flow of vital force, or *prana.*

A form of this power, the *Kundalini* (or goddess power), lies dormant at the base of the spine . . . until it is awakened.

When handled with the utmost caution, this awakening will energize the body's chakras and bring about a raising in consciousness, a heightening of faculties, and an intensified feeling of liberation. In this process it is of prime importance that the chakras all open simultaneously and in perfect harmony.

The seven bodily chakras and their bija seed sounds.

There is, however, a grave warning attached to the practice of Kundalini activation: It is better not to attempt it without the guidance of an advanced teacher, knowledgeable in all aspects of its operation.

In any event, most of us during our progress along our chosen paths will eventually begin to discern the effects of Kundalini awakening, step by step, as a natural unprovoked process. The New Testament Revelation of St. John the Divine contains symbolic exposition of yogic science taught by Jesus which gives reference to the seven chakras or "seals" (Revelation 6-8). Through the seven "divine exits," the yogi, by use of scientific meditation, can escape from his bodily prison and reunite with his higher spirit self.

The seven principle chakras (or seals) are located at:

1—The base of the spine (the sacral ganglion)—the *muladhara   chakra*, the   seat of the Kundalini.
2—Above the organs of reproduction (the prostatic)—the *svadhishthana chakra*.
3—The solar plexus (the epigastric)—the *manipura chakra*, seat of emotional control.
4—The heart (cardiac)—the *anahata chakra*, center for transmission of spiritual or universal love (as opposed to emotional love).
5—The throat (pharyngeal)—the *vishuddha chakra*, extrasensory center for clairaudience or spiritual hearing.
6—The center of the forehead (cavernous)—the *ajna chakra*, so-called "third eye" and center for clairvoyance or spiritual sight.
7—The pineal gland or crown of the head, the cerebral cavity (conarium)—the *sahasrara chakra*, link with the "higher" consciousness and the true "spiritual eye."

There is a correspondence between the chakras and the body's endocrine gland system, and it is possible to regulate or stimulate the ductless glands through the practice of various yogic postures, through meditation, and through the use of certain seed sounds, or bijas:

Lam [lahm] is the bija for the **first** or root chakra at the base of the spine. It corresponds to the element of Earth and is linked with the sense of smell.

Vam [vahm] is the bija for the **second** chakra, linked with the sex organs. Its element is Water, and its sense is taste.

Ram [rahm] is the bija for the **third** chakra, the solar plexus. Its element is Fire and its sense is sight.

Yam [yahm] is the bija for the **fourth** chakra, the heart. Its element is Air and its sense is that of touch.

Ham [hahm] is the bija for the **fifth** chakra, located at the base of the throat. Its element is Ether and its sense is the sense of hearing.

Om [aum] is the bija for the **sixth** chakra, the third eye at the forehead. It represents the vastness of infinity.

The bija for the **seventh** chakra, the pineal gland or the crown of the head, is known as *sahasrara* and is **soundless**, being beyond sound, and yet containing all sound. It is the link with the higher consciousness, and it is represented as a thousand-petaled lotus at the crown of the head.

These bija seed sounds can be intoned as part of a process that cleanses and balances the seven chakras prior to mantric or silent meditation. Continuing sets of chakras of a super-physical nature range beyond the seven bodily energy vortices. The **eighth** chakra, located above the head, is usually visualized in the form of a diamond, the symbol of perfection in the mineral kingdom. It provides a gateway to more advanced dimensions and a link with the Overself, or spiritual portion of each person's being. The **ninth** chakra, beyond the eighth, exists as part of a fifth-dimensional reality of formless or Superluminal Light energy.

In order to reach into these "higher" realms of consciousness activity, it is sometimes necessary during meditation and mantra invocation to temporarily "close off" the two lowest bodily chakra—the root or spinal base chakra and the chakra situated in conjunction with the sexual organs. This is done through an act of will via mental visualization. The object is to remove from the physical body as much consciousness focus as possible while reaching into the realms of super-consciousness.

On Tantra Yoga and the Use of Mantras

Those who take part in the ancient art of Tantra or sex yoga and/or Kundalini yoga generally will not attempt to shut out the two lower chakras—for these are usually essential to the Tantric method of achieving higher union through harnessing of sexual and psychic energies. Tantric principles inform us that all that exists in the universe must also exist in the human body, and the object of Tantric practice is to attain *moksha*, or "liberation," while still living in a physical body (which is the ultimate aim of most yogic practices), but without foregoing any of the experiences of living. It is the method used to awaken cosmic energy through controlled sexual activity, and the body, with its biological and psychological processes, becomes an instrument through which cosmic power is revealed. However, the practice of Tantrism should not be considered as a license to indulge in orgies of pleasure. It is reckoned unwise to concentrate more on the physical pleasure than the mystical opening up of perception that can result from participation in Tantric ritual.

Aside from the more apparent physically sexual magical and occult connotations contained in ancient Tantric texts, there is a subtle and sophisticated spirituality involved. Interested readers are guided to make a careful study of the literature available on the subject.

Although the use of certain mantras and the practice of Tantra yoga can be closely linked, the present work concentrates more on the spiritually transforming aspect of mantra usage. As already indicated, this involves raising of the consciousness primarily from the third through the seventh chakras and into the eighth and ninth and beyond while "closing off," via mental visualization, the two lower chakras, which can be linked with sexual activity. As a method of mantra meditation, it is the result of personal preference over many years of study and participation in Mantra yoga, although it should be expressly noted that there is no hint here of any advocacy of a need for celibacy, outside of specific time periods devoted to selective meditation and mantra usage. The contrary is, in fact, the case as the writers have enjoyed a full and rewarding sex life through some 35-odd years of adult life, and have found that all human activity, including sexual, is perceptibly enhanced by the heightening of physiological and intuitive awareness that comes from frequent use of mantras and invocations in various tongues. However, we have found that as one gets older it is a natural process for sexual activity to diminish, especially if one has embarked upon a spiritual path in which an attempt is made to transform physiological energy into spiritual energy.

12. FIRST OF ALL MANTRAS

The cosmic sound AUM, or its condensed form, OM, is the origin of all other sounds.
—Swami Sivananda Radha

Om (Aum) is everything. It is the name or symbol of God, Isvara or Brahman.
—Swami Sivananda

The *rishis*, or wise men of India, discovered many ages ago that there are distinct laws that govern the sound alliance existing between nature and the human being. Because nature is taken as an objectivication of the "primal sound" or creational word *Om*, the sages then realized that a person may obtain a certain measure of control over a particular natural manifestation through use of certain mantras and chants embodying that initial sacred sound. Om thus represents the essence, the totality, of all other sounds. It is generally accepted in the East as "first of all mantras." Most commonly pronounced *Aum*, it is known as *pranava*, or the sacred syllable, as related to *prana*, the all-pervading life principle.

The Three Principles

Om also symbolizes the three basic principles: initiation, preservation and regeneration, which are the accepted attributes of the major Hindu godly "Trinity" of Brahma (creator), Vishnu (preserver) and Shiva

157

(transformer). The primal sound is found as a component part in almost all potent mantric phrases but also remains highly effective if sung as a mantra on its own. Many mantra-users start their daily mantral meditation session by chanting Om, so as to set the spiritual tone for all that is to follow.

The first part of its sounding ("A") represents the genesis process. The middle portion ("U") relates to the maintenance and preservation of what has been created. Its final part ("M") imbues what has been created and preserved with vital transformational energy, or concentrated power devoid of all ego. Its sounding can be broken up further to signify: "A"—the physical plane; "U"—the mental and astral plane; "M"—all that is beyond the reach of the intellect.

Om (Aum): The Primal Sound.

There are numerous ways of pronouncing Om, and we have found the following rendition to be most in tune with our own inner vibrations. Constant use of this most powerfully moving of sounds will eventually bring to the user a realization of how best it should be intoned to suit any particular individual's physiological, psychic and spiritual makeup.

A Sanskrit term, *ardhamatra* (literally "the half-meter"), is used in connection with Om to signify the shifting tone occurring between the syllables in order to delineate the three resultant tones. When sung on its own, Om/Aum can be most effective if drawn out into a three-part but singly sung *AAH-OOO-MMM*, ending with a humming sound through almost closed lips. Ideally, equal time should be given to each of the three component parts.

Chanting the Om

As a purification ritual aimed at the physical/psychical makeup of the individual, the Om can be sounded 21 times to clear out the ten human sense organs (five senses of action: vocal organs, head, physical eyes, genital and excretory organs; five senses of knowledge: ears, skin, spiritual eyes, tongue, nose); the five basic elements comprising existence (Ether, Air, Fire, Water, Earth); the five breaths in the layers of the mind; and then, with the final vocalization, to create a link with the higher mind, or Spiritual Oversoul.

It is recommended the "AH" be sounded softly, with a stronger "OO" component, softening once again into the "MM."

To sustain contact with the Spiritual Oversoul the following procedure can be used: At the commencement of chanting, the "AH" is visualized as beginning in the region of the navel at the solar plexus chakra (also known as the "astral lotuses"). Moving into the "OO" part of the chant, the sound is raised to the heart chakra. Finally, it should reach the throat chakra for intonation of the "MM" sound.

After repetition for a while through the three indicated chakras, the opening sound of the mantra ("AH") can be recommenced at the throat chakra region, taken to the third-eye chakra on the forehead ("OO"), and then carried up and out of the top of the head, the region of the crown chakra ("MM").

Sung with sincerity and devotion, vocalization of the Om can put the chanter in touch with the source of all creation, providing a bridge between the spiritual and physical dimensions and opening the way for inspirational contact with higher realms and beings. As is the case with most mantras and other words of power, constant repetition builds up individual concentration and promotes universally acquired power. When used as an introduction to meditation, the sounding of Om will provide a powerful catalyst for inspiration and illumination.

Those practicing Tantra yoga will probably prefer to begin the intonation at the base of the spine chakra, the seat of the Kundalini, and then move upward through the chakra situated just above the sex organs and into the solar plexus chakra for the final part of the sounding.

One especially effective method of entering deep meditation is to chant Om for a few minutes, starting quietly, building up intensity, peaking, and then fading away until the sound can be heard only within the mind of the chanter. This results in not only a physical experience but a triune act of perception involving the physical, mental and spiritual on a primary level—and the individual, universal and transcendental on a more elevated plane of action.

While the mantra is being intoned, an advanced meditative state may be reached if the chanter is able to visualize the Sanskrit symbol for Om—preferably in color. As meditation progresses, all of the colors of the spectrum can be introduced into this mind picture. A person in deep meditation may even experience inward sighting of certain unfamiliar colors. These are hues which exist beyond our normal spectral range of vision.

Remember one important fact: All the study in the world will not help in understanding the importance of Om as a generator of power from within and inspiration from without. The only way to discover and experience its true meaning and purpose is to sing the first of all mantras frequently. This can be done aloud during meditation or as a silent chant within the heart and the soul of the individual meditator.

The Jewel in the Lotus

Other than the singular and celebrated Om, probably the most prominent mantra of the East is the six-syllabled Buddhist chant *Om-Mani-Padme-Hum*. This is the multipurpose invocation of Avalokitesvara, the *Bodhisattva* of Compassion—a *Bodhisattva* is a personage who, on reaching enlightenment, delays his entry into *Nirvana*, or Heaven, in order to continue to work among the suffering of humankind as an act of pure compassion. (*Nirvana* can be described as a "state of eternal bliss"—*knowing* God, instead of merely knowing about God.)

Avalokitesvara (his Tibetan name is Spyan-Rasgzigs or Chenrazee), as the Bodhisattva gifted with

The Bodhisattva Avalokitesvara, author of the renowned mantra Om-Mani-Padme-Hum.

complete enlightenment, is reputed to reject no plea made to him by distressed individuals. The Chinese have transformed this supremely compassionate Buddha into the well-known female deity Kuan Yin, and in his Japanese Zen Buddhist form, Avalokitesvara is known as an androgynous god called Kwann-on Bosatsu, who is worshipped in eight forms and 33 manifestations.

An important Buddhist goddess named Tara (Tibetan name: Sgrol) is said to have been born from Avalokitesvara's tears of compassion. Tara, who manifests in 21 forms, plays an indispensable role in the Buddhist Tantra or ritualistic cults in which female energy, and more specifically the act of sex between male and female, is given great prominence. The mantra *Om-Mani-Padme-Hum* is an essential element in the practice of Tantra yoga, although it is also used on many other levels unrelated to ritual sex actions. It is found repeatedly inscribed on copper cylinders in Tibetan Buddhist temples, and is written thousands of times over on long rolls of Tibetan paper as well as on "prayer wheels" used by the devout.

Meaning and Use of
Om-Mani-Padme-Hum

The usual literal translation of Avalokitesvara's mantra *Om-Mani-Padme-Hum* runs something like "Hail to Him who is the Jewel in the Lotus." A more comprehensive analysis of this supremely important mantra reveals an even fuller meaning.

Om, as we know, represents the prime cause of creation, the sum of all sounds in the universe.

Mani-Padme (Jewel in the Lotus) relates to the intrinsic values contained within the Buddhist philosophy—a combination of divine wisdom and supreme compassion, much like the *Chokmah* and *Binah* of the Hebrew Tree of Life.

Hum is an equivalent of Om, but is always used at the closing of a mantra.

On a spiritually esoteric level, *Om-Mani-Padme-Hum* represents, therefore, the Infinite bound within the finite, the union of the Supreme and His creation. This important coupling of energies is, on another level, also apparent in the Tantric rituals in which *Om-Mani-Padme-Hum* plays an important role.

When it comes to chanting it, there are two main pronunciations of the *Mani* (as the famous four-word mantra is popularly known), depending on whether it is recited by an Indian or a Tibetan Buddhist, although, as is the case with any other mantra, intonation varies from district to district, and even person to person.

Om-Mani-Padme-Hum—The Jewel in the Lotus—inscribed on a Buddhist prayer wheel together with a decoration representing the Tibetan "Wheel of the Law."

The most familiar Indian version would sound something like:

Aa-oo-mm Mah-nee-Pad-may Hoom

Tibetan Buddhists might be heard reciting the mantra thus, with the *p* sounding almost like *b*:

Aa-oo-mm Mah-nee-Pay-may Hoong

In each case, *"Mani-Padme"* is voiced, more or less, as one word, with the *"Aum"* and *"Hum"* at either end of the chant more elongated.

The Mani chant is used by Buddhists for a number of purposes: as protection against all manner of hazards, on this plane and in other dimensions of reality; as a method of generating compassion towards other beings (one instance being its use during Tantra or sex yoga); and as a prelude to personal communication with higher levels during meditation—a tuning in, so to speak, with the energy of the great Bodhisattva himself.

The effects to be gained from use of this great mantra are manifold. Already mentioned is its generation of compassion for others, as in the Tantric application (any practitioner of Tantra yoga will no doubt be able to add much to this statement, for the all-embracing love of the deity of the mantra, Avalokitesvara, knows no bounds). On a level involving communication with "higher" levels of activity, the singing of *Om-Mani-Padme-Hum* can place the user in direct contact with the great Bodhisattvas of past, present, and future, bringing thus the appropriate inspiration and aid necessary for spiritual growth.

Each one of us who uses this great mantra may end up with a different experience. What is certain for all is that dedicated and persistent chanting of *Om-*

Mani-Padme-Hum, in whatever circumstance it is used, can only lead to an eventual uplifting of body, mind, and spirit.

As is the case with the Om mantra (and with many other chants), it can be advantageous for the chanter to visualize in color the symbols representing *Om-Mani-Padme-Hum*. This color connection forms a bio-coupling with a higher reality, which in turn aids in increasing the intensity and power of any given meditation session. In higher forms of communication, sound alone is insufficient. It becomes necessary to add the elements of color and pictographic vision to form an effective bonding with extra- and ultra-terrestrial dimensions of existence.

Colors commonly associated with the Mani are as follows:

* *Om*: White—representing the world of the *devas* (gods).
* *Ma*: Green—representing the realms of the *asuras* (spirits).
* *Ni*: Yellow—representing the human realms.
* *Pad*: Blue—representing the realms of the animals.
* *Me*: Red—representing the realms of nature.
* *Hum*: Gray—representing the realms of the underworld.

The Gayatri Mantra

The revered living Master and miracle worker Satya Sai Baba of Prasanthi Nilayam in southern India places very special emphasis on the meaning and usage of a particular mantra known as *Shabda Brahman*, literally "the sound of the all-pervasive spirit" or, more commonly, the *Gayatri Mantra*. The Gayatri Mantra is as important to Hindus as the *Lord's Prayer* is to Christians. The word *shabda* means "sound." The term *gayatri* is derived from *gayantam triyate iti*—"that which rescues (and protects) the chanter is This"—and symbolizes the all-pervading protection of the Creative Principle, or the Shabda Brahman. The goddess Gayatri, incidentally, is known as the "Mother of the Vedas" and is the acknowledged presiding deity of the mantra. Another name for the Gayatri Mantra is, therefore, *Veda Mata*, or the "Mother of the Vedas."

In the *Rig Veda* we read that, prompted by a sacrificial anointment of humankind by the *sadhyas* or demigods, the Creator caused the birth of recited verses and chants in meter form, from which evolved the "formulas," or holy mantras.[1]

The Gayatri Mantra is composed in such a metric fashion, known as *tri-padhi*, consisting of 24 syllables arranged in a triplet of eight syllables each, and is similar to some of the early verses in the *Rig Veda*.

In the ancient Zoroastrian tradition, the Gayatri Mantra bears the name *Mazda-i*, relating to the Persian prime deity Ahura Mazda, whose name is connected with a number of Sanskrit terms, including *medha* ("wisdom"), *mada* ("spiritual intoxication") and *mastim* ("illumination").

The following analysis of the mysteries of the Gayatri Mantra is based on an interpretation given by Sai Baba to one of his devotees, Dr. Eruch B. Fanibunda, as published in the book *Vision of the Divine*.[2]

The Gayatri Mantra in Sanskrit.

The celebrated Gayatri Mantra is broken up into three parts:

* The *Pranavashabda*: the all-inclusive *Om*.
* The *Mahavyahritis*: literally "highest ritual of the breath"—directing the chanter's plea to the three worlds: the Earth (*Bhuh*), the Atmosphere or Subtle Ether (*Bhuvah*), and that which is beyond the atmosphere: the Causal, Heaven (*Svah*).
* The *Mantra*: consisting of a *gayatri* triplet and offering a universal prayer, without asking for any particular benefit or pardon, other than full illumination of the mind and intellect.

When using the *Veda Mata*, the chanter contemplates:

* While chanting the *Pranavashabda* and *Mahavyahritis*: The Glory of the Light which encompasses the three worlds—*Om, Bhuh Bhuvah Svah*.
* While intoning the first two lines of the mantra itself: The Splendor and Grace emanating from the Great Light—*Tat Savitur Varenyum; Bhargo Devasya Dhemahe*.
* While intoning the final line of the mantra: Final Liberation/Transformation through invocation of the Intelligence which pervades the universe in the form of Light—*Dhiyo Yo Na Prachodayat*.

A guide to English pronunciation of the Gayatri Mantra follows. Here again, it must be borne in mind that pronunciations vary from place to place and that the chanter must persevere until a "comfortable" delivery that sounds right to the user's ear is achieved.

> *Om, Bhuh Bhuvah Svah*
> [Aum B'huhr B'hu-vah Svah]
> *Tat Savitur Varenyam*
> [Tat Sah-vee-tur Vah-ren-**yum**]
> *Bhargo Devasya Dhemahe*
> [B'har-goh Dey-vas-ya D'he-ma-hee]
> *Dhiyo Yo Na Prachodayat*
> [D'hi-yoh Yo Na Pra-cho-da-**yaht**]
> *Om*.........
> [Aum..........]

Some consider it customary to end the chant with a second Aum. Other traditions place an Aum between *Svah* and *Tat* (the latter being a short word representing the Ultimate Reality—literally "That!").

A traditional full English translation of the Gayatri Mantra would read something like this:

> Aum! Earth, Ether, Heaven!
> Adore the Divine exemplified by the Sun;
> Contemplate the Luster and Radiance
> of Divine Truth;
> Pray for Illumination of the Intellect.

An alternative translation reads:

> Let us meditate on the excellent light
> of the Creator.
> May he guide our minds
> and inspire us with understanding.

The benefits of this mantra are multifaceted. Other than to generate unusual energy during meditation/mantra chanting sessions, the Gayatri Mantra serves to focus individual consciousness firmly within the Divine, working directly in conjunction with the causal body (the *buddhi*) and taking the chanter outside of the limitations of the personal self and into the "limitless light" of the Supreme Reality—thus leaving behind all cares and considerations of the material existence. Another beautiful Gayatri-type mantra, to be used as an occasional alternative, embodies the names of both the deity or *devi* Gayatri and the Zoroastrian Supreme being Mazda and praises the "Mother of Mantras" itself (key to pronunciation in brackets):

> *Namaste Devi Gayatri,*
> [Nah-mas-teh Dey-vee Gay-atri]
> *Savitri Tripadhakshare Mazdai;*
> [Sav-itri Tri-pad-hak-shareh Maz-d'ai]
> *Ajare Amare Sai Mata-Ha*
> [Aja-re Ama-re Sai Mata-Hah]
> *Loka Samastass Sukhino Bhavantu.*
> [Lo-ka Samas-tass Suk-h'eeno B'hav-antu]

> I bow to Thee, O Divine Gayatri,
> O Savitri, O Three-Syllabled Mazdai;
> O Eternal, Immortal Divine Mother of Mothers,
> Let all the World have Peace and Happiness.

On Sanskrit Pronunciation

Except where contrary acknowledgment or indication is given, the chants presented in this and following chapters are based on traditional Indian and Tibetan mantras. As already indicated, there are many variations of intonation dependent upon location and other factors, and the key to pronunciation accompanying each mantra is provided as a guide only. In the end, it is left to the user to determine how best to intone any particular chant. If the method employed strikes an inner harmonious chord within the self, then it is obviously right for the particular individual involved. This will be in line with the ancient Vedic tradition which claims that all mantric or sacred sound originally emanates from deep within the center of any individual—the "seat of truth," or *rtasya sadas*—and manifests first as a "flash of light."

There are recordings available from various sources which can be used as an aid to pronunciation and which will demonstrate how mantras can be sung instead of merely being spoken. Singing a mantra obviously adds to the quality and beauty of presentation, although it must be emphasized that whether sung, spoken, or used silently the power of the words remains unaltered.

What is of critical importance is the *attitude* of the chanter—sincerity and devotion being the key qualities connected with mantra usage.

The Sanskrit language, known also as *Devanagai*, or "Language of the gods," was brought to India around 1500 B.C.E. by the people known as Aryans (the word *aryan* means, literally, "Noble") and is acknowledged as probably the world's most ancient tongue. It is also possibly the most perfect, with an alphabet consisting of 50 letters, each carrying a fixed, basically invariable pronunciation. This inflexibility of basic pronunciation of the individual letters has aided in maintaining some sort of parity of usage (particularly in relation to the chanting of the mantras) down the centuries, despite an inevitable differentiation of inflection from district to district, which is common to all languages.

Obviously, anyone who has made a serious study of Sanskrit will be able to get closer to the original sounding of any particular letter, word, or phrase. However, for everyday mantra-singing usage, a basic idea of pronunciation is sufficient. As already stressed, it is the motivation behind the actual chanting which mostly determines the end result in mantra usage. This axiom holds good for invocative chanting in any of the ancient languages, as well as for any affirmation or chant expressed in any language at all, ancient or modern.

It is no easy task to transliterate all Sanskrit sounds and intonations into exact English terms. However, a phonetic guide most closely approximating the Sanskrit is given for each mantra.

Readers seeking to develop more definitive Sanskrit pronunciation skills are guided to the appendix "How to Pronounce the Mantras" in the book *The Nectar of Chanting* (SYDA Foundation, PO Box 600, South Fallsburg, New York 12779, USA, 1984).

The following simplified rules can be noted:

Where words in the phonetic guide begin with *s*, the correct pronunciation is "Ss"—i.e., Siva = [Ssiva]. *S* or *sh* in the middle of the word is pronounced as we would pronounce these sounds in English.

a	= *a*	as in *sonata*	ai	= *ai*	as in *aisle*
ah	= *a*	as in *far, alms*	i	= *i*	as in *big*
ey	= *ey*	as in *they*	oh	= *o*	as in *no*
ee	= *ee*	as in *reed*	u	= *oo*	as in *foot*

13. DISPERSING NEGATIVITY

Chanting is not only a means to an end;
the bliss of chanting God's name
is an end in itself.

—Swami Nityananda

Many Sanskrit mantras exhibit a clearing, toning, calming and revitalizing effect. A majority include the name or names of some deity or other, most of which possess two syllables (Ra-ma, Shi-va, Krish-na, etc.). The first such syllable relates to *agni*, or fire—which burns away accumulated negativity. The second syllable symbolizes the *amrith*, or nectar principle—refreshing and restorative. The two form essential parts, the *namah* (name) and the *rupah* (form), of the dualistic whole contained in all creation.

By whatever name we may choose to identify the ultimate reality, the use of mantras calls up the deepest within ourselves. To the wise person of the East, the name of any specific deity is not only a word of recognition but a spiritual force in its own right. A name is not only symbolic of a particular attribute of the Supreme—it *is* that attribute. In effect, the repetition of holy names as mantra is considered better than praise.

175

Holy Names

Ordinary material sounds are unable to awaken spiritual consciousness. Only use of the divine sounds of the actual names of God can set in motion a process of personal and universal transformation. According to Hindu Vedic tradition, the advent of Caitanya, 16th-century leader of the *Bhakti yoga* (devotional yoga) movement and an incarnation of Lord Krishna, heralded the stirrings of a new "Golden Age" of 10,000 years in which chanting of the holy names will reverse the degradation of the present age and bring spiritual peace to our planet.

When it comes to the use of mantras embodying holy names, sincerity and devotion are essential elements. According to one of his devoted disciples, the great Indian sage Sri Ramakrishna was once heard to remark that there are people who repeat the name of a deity and perform pious and charitable acts in the hope of some earthly reward. When misfortune approaches, they tend to forget the names of God: "They are like the parrot that repeats by rote the divine name '*Radha Krishna, Radha Krishna*' the livelong day, but cries 'Kaw! Kaw!' when caught by a cat, forgetting the divine name."[1]

The Maha-Mantra

Because of its persistent chanting on street corners in cities around the world for the past few decades, perhaps the most familiar to Western ears of the deity-linked mantras is the simple, but highly effective, *Maha-mantra*, or "Great Mantra," used extensively by the *Hare Krishna* movement, founded in 1965 by A. C. Bhaktivedanta Swami Prabhupada as the International Society for Krishna Consciousness. However, whether or not one maintains the same unyielding devotion to Lord Krishna as do the mostly shaven (except for the odd pigtail) and saffron-robed young folk who happily beat their drums and chant *"Hare Krishna; Hare Rama"* on our busy streets is relatively unimportant. Traditionally, the Maha-mantra has existed for aeons and remains an ages-old formula designed to liberate the soul from the negative influences of material existence. Ancient Hindu lore tells us that when the renowned *rishi* Narada approached Brahma, the Creator, at the commencement of a *Kaliyuga*, an age of destruction, and asked how he would be able to survive such an age, the reply was that he should sing the Maha-mantra unceasingly. Moreover, Narada was informed that even a murderer might be pardoned if he or she were to utter the 16-word mantra 35 million times!

Krishna and Rama

This song to Krishna and Rama is known as the "great chant of deliverance." Hindu lore tells us that the name Krishna is so powerful that anyone chanting it with sincerity and perseverance will soon rid themselves of accumulated negativity of many lifetimes. The name of Rama is as frequently used on the Indian sub-continent as that of his counterpart Krishna—and is every bit as powerful.

Repeated intonation of the combined chant, in the express experience of the authors, induces several results, perhaps the most notable of which is a feeling of intense happiness, even approaching euphoria.

The Hindu deity Lord Krishna, with his familiar blue and beautiful face, has attracted the greatest body

Krishna—The One Who Attracts

of mythology of all the Indian deities—and is probably the most beloved of all the Hindu gods. The name *Krishna* means literally "he who attracts us to him." As the eighth incarnation of the god Vishnu, the musical Krishna was also known as Murlidhar, "he who plays the flute." In Indian sacred art he is generally pictured wearing a crown of brilliant peacock feathers and playing his instrument amidst pastoral beauty. When the shepherdesses who had fallen in love with him became so numerous that they could not all touch him when dancing with him, Krishna multiplied himself into many forms so that each girl would have the illusion that she was holding his hand.

As a symbol of his own divine growth, Krishna left a legacy to humankind in the form of the immortal *Bhaghavad Gita*, which is part of the ancient *Mahabharata*, the main body of Hindu scripture and the longest poem ever written—100,000 verses. The *Gita*, as this revered and inspiring work is generally referred to, consists of a wide-ranging philosophical poem relating how Krishna, acting as a divine charioteer, instructed the great warrior Arjuna prior to battle. Arjuna had initially hesitated to take part in the war, deploring the useless slaughter and the fact that many of his former friends and relations were opposing him on the battlefield. Krishna reminded him that as a member of the *Kshatriya*, the Warrior Caste, Arjuna would not attain Heaven if he displayed any cowardice. Besides, in a world that consists of *maya*, or illusion, the death of anyone was only an appearance. In reality, the soul remains eternal and those who die on the battlefield do not cease to exist. What had to be remembered above all else was that Arjuna (and anyone else) should act without having any concern for the results, or rewards, of his actions.

Rama, the second of the great deities invoked in the Hare Krishna mantra is known as "Rama the Strong" and was the seventh of the more notable incarnations of the prime god Vishnu. Rama was born specifically to contend with Ravana, the much-feared ten-headed demon-king of Lanka (Ceylon), and his eventual overcoming of his terrible foe was as much a tribute to his own moral excellence as to his exemplary warrior skills. His name also carries the meaning "to rejoice" or can be taken to mean "he who fills us with unbounded joy."

The admirable Rama was revered for his three main attributes: heroism, honesty and devotion. His reign as an earthly king coincided with a period of outstanding peace and prosperity, and the vibrations stimulated by his name are at once protective and sustaining and inductive of courage and fortitude.

Valmiki, composer of the *Ramayana*, the great epic poem which describes the deeds of Rama, was, at first, a common bandit who detested the name Rama. He then met a sage who tried to persuade him to alter his viewpoint by repeating the detested name over and over. Valmiki refused.

Knowing, however, that the bandit loved trees above anything else, the canny old rishi eventually got Valmiki to repeat the words *mara, mara, mara*— meaning "trees, trees, trees."

What Valmiki did not realize was that repetition of the word *mara* eventually became "Rama, Rama, Rama"!

He then became so immersed in the chant that he did not move from the spot on which he sat for several months—until an anthill was built over him. Translated, the name *Valmiki* means "he who found enlightenment in an anthill."

A Universal Mantra

A. C. Bhaktivedanta Swami Prabhupada, founder of the Hare Krishna movement, in line with Vedic literary sources (such as the *Brahmanda Purana*, the *Kalisantarana Uphanishad*, and the *Agni Puranas*), taught that the Maha-mantra is a "universal mantra" especially recommended for the current age. The transcendental vibration evoked by repetitive chanting of "*Hare Krishna, Hare Rama*" is a sublime method for reviving individual and collective transcendental consciousness.

According to Swami Prabhupada, the philosophy behind this statement is that as living spiritual souls we were all originally "Krishna conscious entities," but due to our constant association with matter through the aeons, our consciousness has become adulterated by materiality or *maya* (the word *maya* can be translated as "that which is not"). The Hare Krishna chant is used specifically to disperse this negativity which covers our true nature so that we may cleanse ourselves and thus revive our original true god consciousness.[2]

The full chant runs as follows:

Hare Krishna, Hare Krishna
[Hah-ray Krish-nah Hah-ray Krish-nah]
Krishna, Krishna, Hare, Hare.
[Krish-nah Krish-nah Hah-ray Hah-ray]
Hare Rama, Hare Rama;
[Hah-ray Rahm-ah Hah-ray Rahm-ah]
Rama Rama, Hare Hare.
[Rahm-ah Rahm-ah Hah-ray Hah-ray]

Hail to Krishna, Hail to Krishna;
Krishna, Krishna, Hail, Hail.
Hail to Rama, Hail to Rama;
Rama, Rama, Hail, Hail.

During chanting of this mantra, it is not unusual to experience, at first, a sense of inner conflict—the inner, Krishna-conscious self responds to the sounding of the Holy Names, while the outer, maya-encrusted self resists any attempt at cleansing. If the chant is intoned with regularity and determination, this disturbance will eventually disappear to be replaced by a marvelous sense of well-being and peace. The timing involved will vary from individual to individual, being dependent upon numerous accumulated factors relating to that particular person's present life and past incarnations. However, once the process is started, it is seldom reversed.

Om Namah Sivaya

In some instances, a mantra based on the Holy Name of Shiva, the destroyer of negativity, is thought to be even more powerful than the Hare Krishna chant, particularly when employed to disperse misguided and destructive personal illusions.

This ageless invocation is said to have been composed thousands of years ago by the great *Siddha* Yogis, or "Perfected Beings" who were particularly adept in the strictly controlled use of psychic forces for spiritual purposes. The Siddhas are acknowledged as having rediscovered a direct way of reaching a spontaneous awareness of universal consciousness, which had for thousands of years been buried under masses of abstract scholarly learning and monastic practice. *Siddha yoga* is very much a "hands on" discipline which uses mantras and meditation as tools to attain personal awareness.

The mantra *Om Namah Sivaya* was much used in recent times by the revered Siddha masters, Swami

Muktananda and Swami Sivananda, and is still sung constantly by their many disciples. Swami Muktananda's interpretation of *Om Namah Sivaya* placed it as a chant invoking the supreme *guru* (teacher), the "Self of All." According to Hindu lore, the Lord Shiva is acknowledged as dispenser of gifts of the soul and the transforming deity who destroys negative tendencies in preparation for personal renewal and/or transformation. The mantra *Om Namah Sivaya* serves to draw towards the user the power needed to attain effective balance in the three *gunas*, or human-based characteristics of life. These are:

* *Sattva*: knowledge, wisdom, happiness, light and harmony
* *Raja*: passion, desire, the need for action
* *Tama*: ignorance, negativity, inertia

The three gunas are active in our lives at all times and the preponderance of one over the others determines any individual's character and/or path of destiny. Ideally, the gunas should be well balanced, although, paradoxically, it is a preponderance of *sattva* which will ultimately lead to illumination.

The prime lesson to be learned here is that we must be prepared at all times to let go of out-of-date concepts and beliefs, and be ever ready to accept new challenges and capitalize on fresh opportunities for growth and service to our fellows.

As with the Hare Krishna mantra, but usually in a perceptibly more severe fashion, use of *Om Namah Sivaya* can bring with it a certain amount of personal suffering prior to an opening up of the inner consciousness. This suffering is, under most circumstances, of a psychological nature and only occurs during that period when long-suppressed negative emotions and attitudes are still being sorted out and dealt with. Thereafter, once the dross covering the inner spiritual light has been cleared away, the reward for those who are prepared to endure possible initial discomfort is enormous and wonderfully uplifting.

When using this mantra, do not become alarmed if the body's limbs begin to move spontaneously. This is all part of the cleansing process and the condition will soon pass. If it does persist, rest and meditate awhile before continuing with the mantra chanting.

It has been our own experience and that of others for a blue light to appear to the inner eye while chanting *Om Namah Sivaya* with eyes closed. This is a sign of breakthrough—of contact with the Divine Self. Concentration upon this blue light within the head will usually lead to inspirational promptings from the higher self, which is in contact with the realms of the great Siddha Masters.

There are a number of melodic versions of this important supplication to the Lord Shiva. Sai Baba devotees, for instance, prefer to chant it over and over at a quick tempo. However, of the various chants in different languages used by myself and my wife (a yoga teacher) during more than 20 years of mantra practice, *Om Namah Sivaya* has proved to be one of the two or three most effective *when sung slowly*—dragging out each syllable as if it were a mantra on its own.

This is, incidentally, similar to the method used on occasion by the late Swami Muktananda and his many followers around the world. An aid to pronunciation follows:

Om Namah Sivaya
[Aaaaaauuuuuummmmmm Na-**mah**-aaah Ssee**va**-ah-ah-ah-**yah**!]

Om, reverence to the Name of Shiva

The sacred symbol Om and the Hindu trinity: Brahma (center);
Vishnu (left); Shiva (right).

Sarasvati—Goddess of Learning

The Three-in-One Mantra

According to Hindu mythology, the deity Dattatreya was the son of Atri, one of the *Prajapatis*, the ten beings created by Brahma in order to carry out the detailed creation of the world, and his consort Anasuya. More importantly, Dattatreya was reputed to have been a triple-incarnation involving all of Brahma, Vishnu and Shiva.

Chanting of the "Three-in-One mantra" dedicated to this threefold manifestation of the Supreme creates for the user an activation of all of the qualities embodied in the names of the three named principle Hindu deities: righteousness (Brahma), proper activity (Shiva), and universal love (Vishnu).

It also serves to confirm the inseparable relationship existing between each of the numerous aspects of living and service.

The energy released through correct intonation and concentrated use of this chant attracts to the supplicant firm direction in life, clear inspirational thought, and manifold protection in every circumstance.

Its immediate effect on the user is warming, uplifting and vitalizing. This mantra is a great "energizer," especially useful when self-motivation needs to be cultivated.

Om Sri Dattatreyaya Namah
[Aum Ssree Dah-tah-trey-**yai**-ah Nah-mah]

Om, Honor the name of Dattatreya

Honor to the Great Sarasvati

Hindu deities represent visible attributes of the one Universal Force and, of the numerous gods and goddesses of India, the striking Sarasvati, consort to the Hindu first deity Brahma, is known as the patron of learning, eloquence, music and the arts.

Sarasvati supplies the creative knowledge that backs up the self-motivational qualities exemplified by the creator-god Brahma. She is also a role model for the "Universal Mother," Devi.

The mantra noted below, which incorporates the name of Sarasvati, will aid the user, not only in eventually gaining some perception of the universe and how it operates, but in personally experiencing some of its many mysteries.

Stimulation of the intuitive faculty and unfoldment of artistic expression may also become manifest, and this action will serve to alleviate any negativity in the make-up, fitting the chanter for confident activity in the material world. As is the case with the Three-in-One mantra, use of this tribute to Sarasvati fosters self-confidence and self-motivation on all levels.

Om Sri Maha Sarasvatyai Namah
[Aum Ssree Mah-**hah** Sahr-ah-svaht-**yai**
Nah-mah]

Om, Honor to the Great Sarasvati

Kali and the Great Ages

According to Hindu tradition, there are, in human terms, four "Great Ages" or *Yugas* of varying lengths from around 432,000 to 1,728,000 years.

The first Great Age, *Kritayuga*, lasts for 1,728,000 years and is known as the perfect "Golden Age" when Dharma, deity of justice, walks on all of his four legs.

The second is called *Tretayuga*, extends for 1,296,000 years, and is marked as a slightly less happy

Kali—Goddess of Destruction

period when Dharma walks on only three legs.

Third comes *Dwaparayuga* (864,000 years), with Dharma balancing on only two legs and, with virtue half absent, problems for humanity abound.

At present, we live in the fourth Great Age called *Kaliyuga* (432,000 years), the "Age of Destruction." At this time, with Dharma perched precariously on only one leg, our social and spiritual lives are destined to sink to their lowest point.

This unhappy situation is apparently set to continue until the advent of the next incarnation of Vishnu as *Kalki*, an *avatar* or perfected one. The mythological vision of this coming of Vishnu sees him riding a white horse, bearing a drawn sword, and blazing across the sky (a possible analogy for a great comet or other hitherto undiscovered heavenly body).

This current fourth Great Age is named after Kali, goddess of destruction, and one of the several aspects of the female consort allied with Shiva, who himself symbolizes the transformational principle, as exemplified in the mantra *Om Namah Sivaya*.

One of Kali's other manifestations is as Durga, the "Earth Mother," who, like Shiva, assists to eradicate all unwanted and played-out emotions and conditions.

A short mantra using the name of Kali is designed to help disperse all manner of negativity swiftly and effectively, and can be chanted anywhere in time of urgent need.

Om Kali

[Aum **Kah**-Lee]

Om, Honor the Name of Kali

14. MORE MANTRAS OF INDIA AND TIBET

If you recite a mantra with Love,
God will accept it.
—Sathya Sai Baba

The mantric phrases that follow are designed for various applications. Brief explanations of the use and value of each are given as we move along, but as many of the chants are loosely linked with the concepts known as reincarnation and karma, some explanation of these important terms may be necessary.

Reincarnation and Karma

For the most part, spiritual philosophy in the East is indivisible from a firm belief in reincarnation and karma. A story that serves to illustrate these concepts concerns a particular Indian *guru* who was once sorely pestered by a young man, who complained incessantly about financial and other worldly problems. Showing no interest in the man's material affairs, the guru asked him one question only: "How good is your credit in God's bank?"

The shamefaced young petitioner, who held some basic knowledge of Hindu beliefs, knew immediately what his spiritual master was referring to—the omnipresent and irreversible *Law of Karma*.

Life is full of challenges, and we may sometimes wonder at their origin. Most people in the East, and an increasing number in the West, hold some belief in the doctrine of reincarnation—the system whereby our souls transmigrate on death of the body and take up residence again in a newborn child, carrying with them the essence of the wisdom (and the folly) of previous lives.

Out of the reincarnation principle flows the concept of karma, whereby, in the simplest interpretation of a rather complicated process, we are rewarded in our present existence for good works done in past lives and, conversely, chastised for our ill-doing in former times.

Although their actual operation may be rather more complex, when put simply, the karma and reincarnation doctrines explain in an easy-to-understand fashion the reason for those many unexpected disasters (and strokes of good fortune) which appear to be unrelated to anything attempted or experienced in a particular single lifetime.

In Sanskrit, the word *karma* is derived from the word *kri*, which means "to do." The essential meaning of the expression karma is, therefore, "to work." If the Hindu belief in karma is to be accepted, it would appear that, in order to comply with its injunctions, we have to *work* at our defects and in our service to others—and sometimes even suffer a little—so as to attain true wisdom and reach a balanced and orderly life.

A Mantra for Victory and Success

A mantra said to specially aid in the wiping out of past karma—and to promote victory and success in the everlasting battle with dark or negative forces—invokes the name of Skanda (also Subramanya), Commander-in-Chief of the Heavenly Army in the Hindu pantheon. It is intoned as follows:

Om Sri Skandaya Namah
[Aum Ssree Skahn-**dai**-ah Nah-mah]

Om, Honor to Skanda

Use of this chant does not always bring immediate results, and perseverance over a long period may be required. What generally occurs is the user receives during chanting and meditation sudden flashes of insight relating to action that can be taken to redress personal karmic imbalances and disturbances. If this guidance is faithfully adhered to, life can take on a new aspect as old and outworn conditions are dealt with and eliminated.

Sun Mantra

The symbolism of the sun as representative of heavenly bounty is prevalent throughout the mystical traditions of both East and West. Included in the Hindu religious system are several so-called "sun mantras." These are usually intoned at sunrise and are designed to draw health and vitality towards the chanter.

A favorite sun mantra for the promotion of good health is:

Om Suryaya Namah
[Aum **Sur-yai**-ah Nah-mah]

Om, Salutations to the Supreme

It is recommended that this sun mantra be chanted prior to early morning yoga or other exercises, preferably facing the rising sun and with arms outstretched.

194 / Words of Power

The Theosophical Mantra

The Theosophical Society was founded by the colorful and multitalented Madame Helena Petrovna Blavatsky in 1875, and still flourishes in many countries around the world over 100 years later. The word *theosophy* means "divine wisdom" or, as Blavatsky would have it, "the wisdom of the gods." The basic tenets of the organization formed by her revolve around the attainment of true, unfettered knowledge.

The ancient Hindu *Hitopadesa* informs us:

> Amongst all things, knowledge, they say, is truly the best thing; from its not being liable ever to be stolen, from its not being purchased, and from its being imperishable.[1]

From knowledge issues truth, and this concept of truth and knowledge above all else is repeated throughout the Hindu scriptures. It is also echoed in the foundation principles of Theosophy and is clearly exemplified in the Society's official Sanskrit mantra, which translates: "There is no religion higher than Truth."

Satyam Nasti Paro Dharma
[Saht-yam Nahs-tee Pah-roh D'hahr-mah]

There is no religion higher than Truth

Vocalization of this phrase serves to program the subconscious into accepting the principle that truth and knowledge are essential ingredients in all successful effort on this earthly plane. Continued use will manifest in a personal build-up of determination to assess the truth in all situation—and then to act in accordance with that truth.

Two Prosperity Mantras

Most people will contend that it is generally a more simple task to reach a state of spiritual peace when material affairs are already in good order. There are numerous Sanskrit mantras directed at achieving a balance of spiritual and material prosperity, two of which are here recommended to the reader—the first calling upon the grace of Krishna, "the one who attracts," and the second on Devi, consort of Shiva, the Hindu deity of personal transformation.

Krishna, Krishna, Maha-Yogin
[**Krish**-nah **Krish**-nah Mah-hah-Yoh-gihn]
Bhaktanama, Bhayamkara
[B'hakh-tah-**nah**-mah B'hah-yahm-kah-rah]
Govinda Paramananda
[**Goh**-vihn-dah Pah-rah-**mah**-nahn-dah]
Sarva Me Vishamanaya
[Sahr-vah Mey Vih-shah-**mah**-nah-yah]

O Krishna! Krishna!
Thou art the Greatest Teacher;
O Govinda! Thou art Bliss.
I Pray Thee, Favor Me.

This mantra is a particular personal favorite which, in its very construction, lends itself to song instead of mere enunciation. Try singing it out loud, without worrying about any specific preconceived tune. It was our own experience when first using this mantra many years ago that a tune became immediately apparent, as if it were somehow a built-in component of the word structure.

For us, this great supplication to Krishna, who symbolizes the Universal Teacher in the same way as does Jesus, has always produced results, particularly when invoked in times of real and not imagined material and spiritual distress. Its bounties are usually two-fold: a heightening of spiritual consciousness (as if a "gift of the spirit" is bestowed); and a stimulation of insight into methods which may be employed to alleviate and improve individual material conditions.

All of the above is also true when applied to the second of these favored "prosperity mantras" which invokes the name of Devi (or Dehi), who, like her consort Shiva, is a destroyer of negativity and a transformer of the human condition, the goddess of two aspects—fierceness and benevolence:

Ayurdehi Dhanam Dehi Vidyam Dehi
[Ah-yoor-day-hee D'nahm Day-hee
Vihd-**yahm** Day-hee]
Maheshvari Samastamakhilam Dehi
[Mah-**hesh**-vah-ree Sah-mahs-tah-mahk-heel-um
Day-hee]
Dehi Me Parameshvari
[Day-hee Mey Pah-rah-mesh-vah-ree]

Grant me long life, wealth, knowledge,
O Goddess Devi, Consort of Shiva.
O Goddess Devi, give me all that I desire.

Mantra of Peace

Om Santi is known as the Great Mantra of Peace and is another of those chants very familiar to Westerners because of its use by so many individuals, groups and organizations throughout the world. As is the case with two Middle Eastern counterparts, the phrase *Om Santi* is used both as an invocation for peace and as a personal greeting. It is also remarkably similar in sound and in content to the Hebrew *shalom* and the Arabic *salaam.*

The sounding of this beautifully cadenced mantra provokes conditions of both inner and outer peace:

Om, Santi, Santi, Santi
[Aum **Ssan**-tee, **Ssan**-tee, **Ssan**-tee]
Om. Peace! Peace! Peace!

There is an especially important and very beautiful Sanskrit mantra which includes *Om Santi* as a closing affirmation, and which is dedicated to the eternal quest for transition from Darkness into Light, from the physical into the super-physical and immortal:

Aasathoma Satgamaya
[Asa-t'homah Sat-gama-yah]
Thamasoma Jyothirgamaya
[T'hama-sohma J'yoi-t'hir-gam-ah-yah]
Mrthyor Maa Amiritham Gamaya
[M'rit-h'yorr Ma-ah Ahm-ree-t'ham Gam-ah-yah]
Om, Santi, Santi, Santi
[Aum, **Ssan**-tee, **Ssan**-tee, **Ssan**-tee]

From the Unreal, lead me to the Real;
From Darkness, lead me to Light;
From Death, lead me to Immortality;
Om. Peace! Peace! Peace!

Aiding the Departed

As is the case elsewhere in the world, much store is placed in the East, and India specifically, on the use of correct procedures in the dispatch of the departed—rituals that will aid the party concerned in safely negotiating the transition from this sphere of existence into the next. In line with the beliefs of the Jews and others, people of the Hindu and other Indian traditions consider it of express importance that the deceased leave this world with the sound of sacred syllables on their lips and in their ears. Mantras are thus inevitably used at Hindu funerals. Much the same as a devout Jew would wish to pass from this life into the next uttering the *Sh'mah*, the Hindu will meet death with a smile while intoning *Sri Ram, Sri Ram*. Mahatma Ghandi was apparently one great personality who was known to die while voicing the name of Rama. When he was tragically assassinated in January 1948, he fell to the ground murmuring the words *"He Ram; He Ram."*

Another sacred sound much used at funerals is the concise *Om Tat Sat*, which is also intoned as an endpiece to meditation or prayer, something in the manner of the Judeo-Christian *Amen*. The full meaning of *Om Tat Sat* can be translated as "Thou art the Inexpressible Absolute Reality." It is intoned as follows:

Om Tat Sat
[Aum **Taht Saht**]

Another version of the *Om Tat Sat* mantra incorporates one of the many names of the deity Vishnu—in his aspect as Hari, the "Disperser of Sins." This chant can also be used as a purification mantra, clearing the mind and senses in preparation for inflow of illuminating thought.

Hari Om Tat Sat
[Hah-ree Aum **Taht Saht**]

Om, The Divine Absolute Reality

The simple two-word chant, *Hari Om*, is frequently heard at funerals—and on just about every other occasion when people gather together in remembrance or worship.

Hari Om
[Hah-ree Aum]

Om, Salutations to Vishnu as Hari

Liberation Mantra

In his book *Japa Yoga* Swami Sivananda pays special attention to an unusual "liberation" mantra, designed to aid the user in the quest for victory over death, or over the effects of *samsara*, the universal state of flux in which all beings are doomed to wander for as long as their ego-born delusions of independent existence persist.

This liberation mantra is called the *Maha-Mrityunjaya* mantra and can aid in the perception of our own physical world as but an infinitesimal fraction of the whole of creation. On a more mundane level, the liberation mantra is said to help in gaining mastery over the complex results of physical mishaps, such as snakebite, lightning, and diseases and accidents of all descriptions. The liberation mantra is dedicated to Shiva and runs as follows:

Om Tryambakam Yajamahe
[Aum Trah-yahm-bah-kahm Yah-**jah**-mah-hey]
Sugandhim Pushti Vardhanam
[Suh-gahnd-him Push-tee Vahrd-hah-nahm]
Uruvarukamiva Bhandhanan
[Uru-**vah**-ru-kah-mee-vah Bahnd-hah-**nahn**]
Mrityor Muksheeya Mamritat
[M'riht-yohr Muk-**shee**-yah **Mahm**-rih-**taht**]

*Stylized portraits of Guru Nanak hang on the walls
of most Sikh homes.*

We worship the three-eyed One (Lord Shiva), who
is fragrant and nourishes us;
May he liberate me from death and make me immortal,
Just as the cucumber is severed from its
bondage (to the creeper).

Use of the liberation mantra is only recommended
to those already well-versed in the principle of universal cosmic responsibility, or universal karma, and who
have long practiced use of mantras as a form of stimulating growth into elevated realms of mental and spiritual activity.

Sivananda told his devotees to repeat it 50,000
times on their birthdays!

Many Names of the One

Of the numerous religious groups and sects of India, the turbanned and heavily-bearded Sikhs of the
Punjab are among the more colorful in their dress, and
in their religious beliefs and practices. The main Sikh
precepts include elimination of caste distinctions and
the total equality of women. The central place of Sikh
worship is the imposing Golden Temple at Amritsar.
All Sikh men carry the same surname, *Singh*, which
means "lion." Sikh women hold the surname *Kaur*, or
"princess."

The Sikhs trace their origins back to a holy man of
the 15th century C.E. named Guru Nanak. Ten great
Sikh gurus followed him, the last being the Guru
Gobind Singh, who organized the Sikhs into a strong
militant group.

The philosophy and doctrine of Sikhism's founder
Guru Nanak was based on a synthesis of the personal

devotion, or *bhakti*, of Hinduism, the mystical side of
Islam, or *Sufism*, and the ritualistic *Tantra yoga* of Tibetan and other Buddhists.
    Guru Nanak synthesized the basic Sikh creed in
the first hymn he composed, the *Mool Mantra*, which,
although not regularly used by us, is included here because of its display of profound truth, put simply and
beautifully:

Ik Onkaar
Sat Naam
Karta Purkh
Nirbhau
Nirvair
Akaal Moorat
Ajooni Sabh
Gur Parsad

There is only one God
Truth is his name
He is the creator
He is without fear
He is without hate
He is timeless and without form
He is beyond death—the enlightened one
He can be known by the Guru's grace

Sikhs are now found in almost every part of the
world, with temples in many Western as well as Eastern countries. The keynote of Sikh worship is the conviction that God is singular and personal, a transcendent Creator with whom each individual is duty bound
to form an intimate relationship. In line with Judeo-
Christian, Islamic and other beliefs, the Creator is considered formless (*nirankar*), eternal (*akal*), and ineffable (*alakh*).

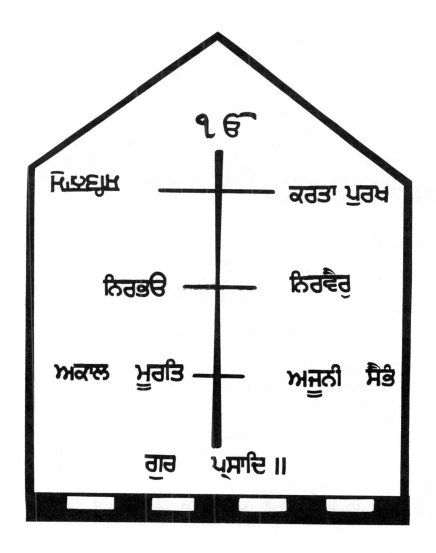

The Mool Mantra

In addition, and again in consort with most of the other major religions, Sikhism teaches that God is capable of many forms of manifestation and is symbolized by many names.

There is another well-known Sikh mantra which illustrates the essential Oneness of the Supreme Being, despite the use of many names to describe Him. Intonation of this mantra reminds the user that although life may appear to consist of many levels of manifestation there is an underlying unity linking all things. It is vocalized as follows:

Eck Ong Kar Sat Nam Siri Wha Guru
[Ehk Ohng Karr Saht Nahm Ss-iree Whah Gu-ru]

The Supreme is One, His Names are Many

Tibetan Mantras

For the most part, Tibetan worship is based on the principles and traditions of Buddhism, whose founder, Siddharta Gautama, lived in a time period spanning the 6th and 5th centuries B.C.E. Son of King Suddhodana and Queen Mahamaya, the young man who was to become known as Buddha lived his early life in the foothills of the Himalayas, protected by his father from the negative influences of the world. Destined at first to become a king like his father, he was reared and schooled as a prince.

In a fairy-tale-type scenario, Prince Siddharta married a beautiful princess, Yasodhara, who bore him a son. But it was soon after this happy occasion that Siddharta first became aware of the suffering that existed beyond his protective home circle. On his initial foray into the outside world, he met up with a succession of cases of misery and illness before he came upon a wandering, shaven-headed beggar in a yellow robe who, despite his poverty-stricken circumstances, radiated peace and goodwill. This was the turning point for the young prince who, in material terms, appeared to have the world at his feet.

It was the time of Siddharta Gautama's *great renunciation*, when he left his wife and infant son to take up the life of an ascetic.

Siddharta then received what has become known as *the great enlightenment* while meditating under a Bodhi-tree by the river Gaya, and began preaching to his companions, the first Buddhist order of monks.

The basic precept expounded by Gautama Buddha pinpointed *desire* as the root cause for humanity's suffering. Buddha taught that this desire could be controlled by following the "Middle Way" between the two extremes of physical sensuousness and spiritual asceticism.

One of the numerous sayings of Buddha tells us that the wise test gold by burning, cutting and rubbing it (on a piece of touchstone). What is implied is that mere acceptance of his words out of simple regard for the Buddha is not enough—they should be examined thoroughly so that their verity may become manifest in practice as well as in theory.

For the Tibetans, the importance of speech, or *chos-adon* ("verbalized religion"), in ritual observance is paramount. Contemplation and meditation alone are not enough. In his daily routine, the Tibetan *lama*, or priest-monk, moves from attitude to action, exercising constantly the power of sound in the form of chanting. Up to the 7th century, Tibetan religious life was dominated by the shaman, the magician-priest. Thereafter, Buddhism began to take hold, and the Tibetans developed their own observances and practices based

Buddha experiences "The Great Enlightenment."

on the original Indian systems, including that known as *Tantra*. The *Tantras* are the scriptures of a Hindu school of mysticism that played a large part in the development of Tibetan Buddhism. Later developments saw a partial domination of the *Tantra* system by a sexual element which emphasized the spiritually creative potential inherent in the psychic tension existing between male and female. The basic *Tantra* way is threefold, embracing the use of *mudras*, ritual gestures, *yantras*, diagrams of symbolic meaning, and verbalized *mantras*.

The universally used "Jewel in the Lotus" mantra, already discussed in Chapter 12, is one of an almost countless selection of specifically Tibetan mantras, tabulation of which would require an extended separate study. A small selection of chants used by the Tibetans to, amongst other things, calm what they call the *namtok*, literally "the chattering mind," follows. Two of these chants are:

Om Ah Hum
[Aum Ah Hum]

Come towards me, Om

Padma Siddhi Hum
[Pahd-mah Sih'd-hee Huhm]

Come to me, O Lotus Power

The next two mantras, placed together with *Om-Mani-Padme-Hum*, complete the trinity of so-called "essence" mantras of the "Three Protectors of Buddhist Lamaism." As already recorded, *Om-Mani-Padme-Hum* is the mantra of the *Bodhisattva* of Compassion, Avalokitesvara (Chenrazee). The second of the great Lamaist triune is the mantra of the Bodhisattva Manjughosha (or Jampalyang), the "God of Mystic Wisdom." It runs as follows:

Om Wagi Shori Mum
[Aum Wah-gee Sho-ree M'm]

Hail to the Lord of Speech!

The third principle Buddhist mantra is that of the Bodhisattva Vajra-Pani (or Chakdor), "The Wielder of the Thunderbolt." The "'thunderbolt" (*vajra* or *dorje* [dorr-jay]) referred to is similar to that wielded by the Hindu Vedic deity Indra, shaped like an *omega* eight on its side, and also holds certain phallic connotations.

Om Vajra Pani Hum
[Aum Vaj-rah Pa-a-nee Hum]

Hail to the Holder of the Dorje!

Another well-known Tibetan chant is dedicated to the Buddha known as the "Precious Guru" and represents the supreme embodiment of *Tantra* or ritualistic power:

Om Ah Hum Vajra Guru Padma Siddhi Hum
[Aum Ah Hum Vaj-rah Gu-ru Pahd-mah
Sih'd-hee Huhm]

The Union and Oneness
of Initiation, Inspiration and Expression,
teaches us the Power of Fearless Compassion

15. IN THE NAME OF JESUS

If ye shall ask any thing in my name,
I will do it.
John 14:14

And they were astonished at his doctrine:
for his word was with power.
Luke 4:32

Other than the Holy Name of God Himself—in
times of sorrow and distress, and in times of joyful
thanksgiving—no name has been more called upon
down the centuries than that of the Jewish teacher who
would have been known to his contemporaries as
Yehoshua (Joshua) or Yeshua, but is now known universally as Jesus Christ.

Yehoshua translates as "God (Yahweh) saved."
Yeshua means literally "he shall save" or "salvation."
Other versions of these names given in the Bible include: Hosea, Hoshea, Osea and Oshea, all meaning
"Deliverer." Jesus, or IESU, is, of course, a Greek
transliteration for Yehoshua / Yeshua. Christ or *Chris-
tos* is also Greek and means "the anointed"—or more
specifically "anointed by God," referring to the Messianic aspect of Jesus. The word *Christ* also alludes to
the apparent kingship of Jesus. In ancient times, the
King of Israel was always regarded as the "anointed
one," or *meshiach*, and the concept of an "End Times"
messiah of supernatural form only came afterwards.

Yeshua (Jesus), the Jewish miracle worker who used words of power to cure the sick and raise the dead.

Jesus the Jew

Historically, Jesus was a devout Jew involved in the contemporary issues of his time. His attitude towards the religious practices and rites of Judaism was firmly grounded in the Temple and the Law, despite his tendency to sometimes circumvent the traditional in favor of the spontaneous, and he was, at heart, a Jew deeply rooted in the religious tradition of his ancestors and wholly absorbed by it.

During the time of Jesus, the Holy Land was filled with different religions and cults, mainly as a result of the Roman occupation which had brought people of many nationalities into Palestine. The Jews themselves, however, were divided up into three main groups (four, if the schismatic Samaritans, unaccepted by other Jews, were to be included), and orthodox Judaism embraced the priestly Sadducees, the more flexible Pharisees, and the ascetic Essenes. Of several smaller splinter-groups, the most important were the Zadokites or *Tzaddikim*, a remnant group from the days of the Hebrew high priesthood who claimed descent from Aaron, and the Zealots, who were to become famous for their defense of the fortress of Masada around 79 C.E.

There is evidence that Jesus may have been primarily a Pharisee, and it is likely that early on he came under the influence of another famous Pharisee teacher, Hillel—whose main lessons were based on the principle "Do unto thy neighbor as thou would unto thyself." There is also some probability that at some stage Jesus came into contact with the strict desert-living order known as the Essenes. Essene scribes compiled the famous Dead Sea Scrolls, found during our own century in a cave at Qumran in the Negev Desert opposite the ruins of one of their settlements. The scrolls reveal, among other startling facts, that some of the teachings of Jesus echo those of a personage referred to by the Essene scribes as the "Teacher of Righteousness." An example is the famous Sermon on the Mount, attributed to Jesus, but containing ideas and teachings, and even whole sentences, written a century before by the Qumran scribes.

The Tzaddikim

Jesus almost certainly also came into contact with the Zadokites or *Tzaddikim*, and it is highly likely that he even was one of them. A *tzaddik* was considered by the Jewish sages to be the supremely righteous person who bows to the will of the Father, lives by the *Torah*, and performs charitable works—that is, someone who fully observes both the letter and the spirit of the Law. The true tzaddik is said to be able to control the laws of nature and to influence others merely by his presence.

At any given time there are said to be 36 especially righteous tzaddik instructors on Earth, who may be of any faith, and who are spread around the world in various countries, their true identities usually hidden. By their very existence they sustain the world through their daily link with the Divine Presence or *Shekinah*. Collectively, this group of ultra-righteous tzaddikim embodies the Tree of Knowledge that is necessary for humankind's continuing evolvement into a more superior state of being. Moreover, one of the 36 is considered a Priest of Righteousness, or *Kohen Tzaddik*, which is something in line with a living Messiah—a role that can easily be applied to Yeshua/Jesus. Jesus, in any event—and as was the case with characters like Abraham, Isaac, Jacob and Moses before him—can be considered a *tzaddik gamur*, a great one who fulfilled the whole *Torah* from *aleph* to *tau*. Until well after his death, when Paul appeared on the scene to start the Christian Church, there appears to be no hint that Jesus was anything more than a man, albeit an extraordinarily righteous and charismatic personality, for there can be no challenging the fact that he was a uniquely remarkable person who, at times, displayed definitively super-human or magical characteristics. Although none of the Gospels refer to Jesus as God in totally unambiguous terms—not even the writings of Paul, generally accepted founder of the Christian Church as we know it today—the title "Very God" was conferred upon him at the Council of Nicea, presided over by Emperor Constantine in 325 C.E. At the time Constantine was a High Priest of the *Sol Invictus* sun-worship religion, and it is certain that, with probably political motive, he brought pressure to bear on the delegates to the council to mix elements of Christianity with the *Sol Invictus* cult. The result was an image of Jesus that became visibly removed from that of the original essentially Jewish teacher, albeit a rather unorthodox one.

The Power of His Name

The use of the name of Jesus down the centuries has carried with it an enormous power far and beyond what may be reasonably expected of the name of any mere mortal. The most quoted witness to the great authority inherent in the name of Jesus is that given by Paul in his Epistle to the Philippians (2:9 and 10). In this text Paul reminds his readers that Jesus himself remained obedient to God, even unto death. He goes on to state:

> Wherefore God also hath highly exalted him, and
> given him a name which is above every other
> name: That at the name of Jesus every knee would
> bow, of (things) in heaven, and (things) in earth,
> and (things) under the earth.

Paul's emphasis seems to be that the vibrations contained within the name of Jesus exhibit a unique command or control over the whole of creation, with even spiritual beings of a higher order than humankind remaining subject to him. The name of Jesus has been used by priests and laypeople in healings, exorcisms and intercessions for nearly 2,000 years. There is also ample evidence in old magical texts that in his own lifetime his name was more frequently employed than any other by Middle Eastern magicians in their spells—and even by certain Jewish mages after his death, as is told in Acts 19:13:

> Then certain of the vagabond Jews, exorcists, took
> upon them to call over them which had evil spirits
> the name of the Lord Jesus, saying, We adjure you
> by Jesus whom Paul preacheth.

In the New Testament, there are many references to the authority of the name of Jesus. His personal instruction to his disciples to use it *as a name of power* is clearly recorded in John 14:13-14:

> And whatsoever ye shall ask in my name, that will
> I do, that the Father may be glorified in the Son. If
> ye shall ask anything in my name, I will do it.

One of Jesus' most oft-quoted statements relates to drawing down of his energy and presence into any place where people meet in his name; Matthew 18:20 refers:

> For where two or three are gathered together in
> my name, there am I in the midst of them.

However, according to all of the four main Gospels, Jesus always makes it overwhelmingly clear that he had come to perform his ministry strictly *in the name of the Father*. In Matthew 7:21-23, he places definitive emphasis on the necessity of being absolutely true at all times to the *will of God*, which goes far beyond mere use of Jesus' own name, as a prerequisite to spiritual progress.

In the Name of the Father

Before and after its official ban in Temple worship, the four-lettered Holy Name of God enjoyed widespread secret use in ancient times. This is confirmed in the *Sefer ha-Razim* ("The Book of Secrets"), a Jewish magical work of the late Roman era, and in Origen's *Contra Celsum*, which describes the magical power of certain Jewish formulae as well as the power of the name of Jesus when used in the realm of the spirits. As has been the case with the name of Jesus for the past 1900-plus years, the Tetragrammaton has been an essential ingredient in countless spells and exorcisms used by pagan, Jew and Christian alike—from long before the birth of Jesus, through the Middle Ages, and right up to the modern era.

In his intriguing book *Jesus the Magician*, Morton Smith, professor of history at Columbia University, postulates that Jesus "did his miracles and even raised himself from the dead by magical use of the divine Name, the greatest of all spells."[1]

It is quite clearly stated in the New Testament (and in many of the so-called apocryphal books, or texts of doubtful authenticity) that, as was most probably the case with Moses and other great Hebrew sages of the past, Jesus frequently used the Ineffable Name of

God in his invocations—and instructed his disciples to follow his example. John 17:25-26, provides a classic instance:

> O righteous Father, the world has not known thee: but I have known thee.... And I have declared unto them your name, and I will declare (it); that the love wherewith thou hast loved me may be in them, and I in them.

Jesus the Miracle Worker

By all accounts, Jesus the Nazarene was a miracle worker of remarkable achievement, perhaps unsurpassed by any other in that his reputed miracles involved bringing back from the dead, not only other persons, but Jesus himself.

Traditional scriptures relate that in addition to demonstrating this profound life-restoring power Jesus healed the sick and lame by the score, cast out devils and exorcized unclean spirits aplenty, walked on water, stilled a terrible storm at sea, once fed 5,000 people with five loaves of bread and a few fishes, and even turned water into wine. Apocryphal Gnostic texts list many more of Jesus' miracles, with a number of the healings and exorcisms described including the use of special words to accomplish specific effects. According to Morton Smith, the method used by Jesus to exorcise unclean spirits might have involved spells actually screamed out by him, plus a certain amount of gesticulation which matched the mad in their fury—this being normal practice for magicians of the time. There is an allusion to this possibility in Mark 3:21 in which Jesus is described as being "beside himself." He is then immediately accused by some scribes from Jerusalem (Gali-

In the Name of Jesus / 217

lean Pharisees in one account) as being himself pos-
sessed by the demon Beelzebub, the "prince of devils."
Jesus immediately corrected them by asking pointedly:
"How can Satan cast out Satan?"

As it was (and still is) the custom among exorcists
to call an evil spirit by its name, if that name is known,
it is quite possible that Jesus, in this instance, might
have used the name Beelzebub in his cleansing invocation.

When Jesus performed his well-tabulated exorcism in the country of the Gerasnes near Galilee (Mark
5:1-20; Matthew 8:28-34; Luke 8:26-39) involving the
driving of demons from a man (one account says two
men) into a herd of swine, he first asked of the supposed possessing spirit: "What is thy name?" The reply
came: "My name is Legion—for we are many." The fact
that Jesus was able to get the spirit / spirits to reveal a
name was in itself remarkable, for, as we have learned
in our study of Egyptian names of power, possession of
any entity's secret name gave the holder absolute command over that entity.

Jesus also appears as a miracle worker in the Islamic holy book, the *Qur'an*. A notable instance occurs
in *sura* (or chapter) 5 in which the founder of Christianity, when still a child, is described as breathing life into
the clay figurine of a bird. Tradition says that he made
several figures of sparrows and other birds for his play-
mates, which flew about or stood on his hands as he ordered them and also ate and drank at his command.
The *Qur'an*, incidentally, confirms the virgin birth of
Jesus and claims that he began to speak while still in
Mary's womb and as a baby in the cradle. However, according to the Muslims' holy book, Jesus was not cruci-
fied "but was represented by one in his likeness" on the
cross (sura 4).

Words of Power Used by Jesus

Once, when Jesus was visiting Capernaum, a Roman centurion came to him and implored that the Jewish healer cure his servant, who was at home, sick of the palsy. When Jesus agreed to come with him to heal the man, the centurion stopped him, claiming that his home was not a worthy place for such as Jesus. Matthew 8:8 continues the story, with the Roman going on to say:

> ... but *speak the word only*, and my servant shall be healed." (our emphasis)

Marveling at the centurion's great faith, Jesus complied, and the Roman went home to find his servant cured. The New Testament scribe Matthew does not reveal the actual word spoken by Jesus on this occasion, but one of the most singular healing miracles by Jesus involving a known word of power occurred when he once traveled inland towards Lake K'nesseret or the Sea of Galilee from the coastal direction of Tyre and Sidon.

At Decapolis on the Sea of Galilee, Jesus' followers brought to him a pathetic deaf and dumb man with the request that the master lay his hand upon the man. Jesus proceeded to place his fingers in the deaf mute's ears, and then spat and touched the man's tongue (at the time spittle was considered efficacious in cases of diabolical possession—sometimes considered a reason for disease). The tale is continued in Mark 7:34:

> And looking up to heaven, he sighed, and saith unto him, "Ephphata," that is, Be opened. And straightway his ears were opened, and the string of his tongue was loosed, and he spake plain.

Pronounced *ef-fat'h-ah*, the word used by Jesus on this occasion is of Aramaic origin and has its roots in the words *pat'hah* ("to open" or "to loosen") and *pet'hah* ("an opening" or "a gate").

Another Gospel according to St. Mark reference (5:41) records the words used by Jesus to revive the departed daughter of Jairus, one of the rulers of the synagogue at Decapolis. While Jesus and Jairus were on their way to see the stricken girl, news reached them that she was already dead. Jairus was distraught in his grief but was told by Jesus not to be afraid, but to believe. On arrival at Jairus' house, amidst much weeping and wailing, Jesus upbraided the people gathered there for mourning the dead girl. He was laughed to scorn but, ignoring the throng outside the girl's room, made her father and mother enter with him. Once inside, Jesus took the apparently dead girl by the hand and pronounced the words *Talitha Koumi*. To the amazement of all, the 12-year-old girl stirred, rose up immediately, and began walking, fully healed.

The word *talit'ha* means "fresh" or "young girl." *Koumi* translates as "Arise!" Used together they would be pronounced something like ta-lee-t'ha koo-mee.

Talit'ha stems from the Aramaic / Chaldean *taleh*, or "lamb." The derivation of the word *koumi* is the root word *quwm*, "to rise."

In another case involving a raising-from-the-dead miracle, Jesus gave a simple command to the dead son of the widow of Nain: "Young man, I say unto thee, Arise!"

What the aforementioned incidents seem to indicate is that Jesus sometimes used common-day words and phrases in his healing, but invested them with extraordinary authority and power. Of course, it also remains possible that he combined the words given in the

Gospels with the four-lettered Holy Name of God, but this fact has not been recorded—or was simply omitted somewhere along the line from our versions of the scriptures.

Resurrection—and Ascension

The Gnostic *Pistis Sophia*, a Coptic codex of the 5th and 6th centuries taken from a Greek original, is a work which details the supposed secret metaphysical teachings of Jesus given to a company that included some of his former Apostles, his mother Mary, Mary Magdalene, and Martha, sister to Lazarus (the man Jesus raised from the dead), when he returned to be among them after his resurrection. According to the text, Jesus was with them for eleven years following his ordeal on the cross.

The pages of the *Pistis Sophia* abound in descriptions of powerful mystical ceremonies using incantations. Included are the words alleged to have been used by Jesus in his own resurrection process and in the famous case of the raising of Lazarus, brother of Mary and Martha, from the dead (John 11:1-46 refers). This intriguing Aramaic phrase is given in the *Pistis Sophia* as *Zama Zama Ozza Rachama Ozai*, without any strictly literal translation offered.

The non-traditional Gnostic Gospels provide a variety of invocation and prayers allegedly used by Jesus when instructing his disciples and when guiding them through various stages of spiritual development. Another of the apocryphal books, *The Book of the Resurrection of Christ* by Bartholomew the Apostle, describes the scene when Jesus took his apostles up onto the Mount of Olives. Bartholomew relates: Jesus "spoke to us in an unknown tongue, which he revealed to us, saying: *Anetharath* (or *Atharath Thaurath*)," and then records that, following delivery of this mystical phrase of ascension, Jesus and the apostles proceeded to go up into the "Seventh Heaven."[2]

Using the Name of Jesus

On several occasions down the years we have been called upon to perform exorcisms of one kind and another. An exorcism involves the expulsion by adjuration or other means of evil influences from a place or a person, and is, in effect, a form of ceremonial magic. The following simple formula which invokes the name of Jesus has proved to be one of the most effective ways to quickly combat and expel any form of negativity, from place or person:

In the Name of Jesus, Jesus, Jesus:
Let that which cannot abide depart!
(Repeat three times)

Such an invocation of the all-powerful name of Jesus might be compared in terms of power and potency with the Hebrew *Qadosh, Qadosh, Qadosh, Adonai Tzeba'oth* (see Chapter 6) and the Sanskrit *Om Namah Sivaya* (Chapter 13).

The Secret Name

There are schools of thought that consider either of the original Hebrew *Yeshua* or *Yehoshua* as the only possible correct forms of the name of the historical character generally known as Jesus. One of the strongest proponents of the name Yeshua for Jesus is the controversial orthodox Jewish Rabbi Simcha Pearlmutter, formerly of Boston and Miami, but resident at Kibbutz Ir-Ovot in the Negev Desert, south of the Dead Sea, Israel, for some 20 years. Significantly, Ir-Ovot is at the site of the newly discovered ruins of the city of Tamar, described in Ezekiel (47:19 and 48:28) as the marker for the southeastern border of *Eretz Israel*, the original land of Israel accorded by God to the Jews. It is also an important venue in relation to prophecy about the coming (or return) of the Messiah.

Rabbi Pearlmutter has caused quite a stir among both Jews and Christians by claiming that the patently orthodox Rabbi Yeshua of Nazareth was indeed a Messiah, was recognized as such by many orthodox Jews of his time, died on the cross, and was then resurrected. In his opinion, the Christianized Jesus is a distorted version of the original, exclusively Jewish personality. His own stated mission in life is to bring the Messiah of 2,000 years ago back into Judaism, and to reconcile Jew and Gentile by getting them to accept the original Yeshua.

The charismatic rabbi of Ir-Ovot points out that in ultra-orthodox editions of the Jewish prayer book, or *Siddur*, there are many key references to Yeshua / Jesus, including the very explicit *Yeshua Kohen Gadol*— "Yeshua, the Great High Priest"—in the important *Shofar* Service of *Rosh Hashanah*, or New Year. Other references include an expression made up of the letters *yod* (comma) *hey* found in numerous places in the *Siddur* and a secret name, *Yenon*, in which the two letters *nun* replace the *shin* and *ayin* of the name Yeshua. These attempts to keep reference to Yeshua hidden were apparently prompted by the desire that the name of the true Jewish Messiah be not desecrated or profaned by the enemies of the Jews.

According to Rabbi Pearlmutter, the traditional

Jewish *Pesach*, or Passover Festival celebration of the Hebrews' release from Egyptian bondage, is also an allegory for the death and resurrection drama of the Messiah Yeshua. That he has gained some acceptance for his ideas from other orthodox rabbis, from mainstream Jews, and even some Christians, is certainly food for thought. It is also, in a fashion, fulfillment of New Testament prophecy which relates to the acceptance of Jesus (Yeshua) by the Jews prior to the End of Times. Equally important would perhaps be a return to the correct Hebrew enunciation of the Messiah's true name, Yeshua, as a word of power.

Adding a Letter to the Name of God

In Jewish lore, the three-pillared Hebrew letter *shin* (**ש**) is the symbol of Divine Power, and also of Earthly Corruption. In addition, it represents a third element—the crossing-over point between the Human and Super-human, the bridge between earthly existence and existence in the Many Mansions of the Father's Heavenly Kingdom. *Shin* is also clearly exemplified in the symbol associated with Yeshua or Jesus— the cross. Basically, *shin* stands for physical mastery and spiritual peace. In kabalistic terms its three pillars can be said to represent, on the right, the *Chokmah* or Wisdom of the Father Principle, on the left, the *Binah* or Understanding of the Mother Principle, with the central pillar embodying the qualities of both *Chokmah* and *Binah* to create the culminating point of the kabalistic *Ets Cha-yim* or Tree of Life, namely the *Kether* or Crown (of thorns?).

Another interpretation views the three separate units as alluding to the three worlds in which we reside: This World, the Messianic World, and the World

to Come. This transliteration refers to: The "body"—
the vehicle used on Earth; the "soul"—the vehicle of
Spiritual Transformation; and the "spirit"—the Spiritual Body of Light we need to create for ourselves in order to enter into and transverse the Higher Universes.

Moreover, when the letter *shin* is set as a central
additional letter among the four letters that make up
the Tetragrammaton, the Holy Name of God, a new
name is formed, which can be vocalized as *Yehoshua*.
This single-letter name alteration suggests that, apart
from its accepted historical content and numerous religious and spiritual connotations, the life story of
Yeshua/Yehoshua/Jesus provides an allegorical mystery which portrays the method to be used by any individual for personal transformation from human into
super-human, from earthly into heavenly, from body
into spirit or Body of Light, via "crucifixion of the soul"
on the "cross of space and time."

16. THE LORD'S PRAYER

When thou prayest, enter into thy closet,
and when thou hast shut thy door,
pray to thy Father...
Matthew 6:6

One of the most powerful invocations of all time, and in any language, remains the Lord's Prayer, used daily by millions of people around the globe. According to the New Testament (Matthew 6:9-13; Luke 11:1-4), Jesus gave his disciples this important statement on being asked how they should pray. A recording of the events that led up to this occasion is of some relevance if one is to understand the importance placed by his followers on correct praying.

During the reign of Emperor Hadrian at the start of the 2nd century C.E. (when Palestine was still under the yoke of Rome), Roman decree forbad use by the Jews of their beloved *Sh'mah* in public worship. The early pre-Nicene followers of Jesus were known as the Nazarenes and were, in effect, practicing Jews and members of what was then regarded as a somewhat heretical, but definitely Jewish, cult which based its religious observances on those used in the orthodox synagogue. There is, incidentally, some evidence that the town of Nazareth did not yet exist in the time of Jesus, appearing in the 3rd century—thus the popular

225

title "Jesus of Nazareth" is possibly incorrect. Some sources assert that the term *Nazarene* (which is the correct translation of the original Greek version of the New Testament reference) alludes to a specific Jewish religious and/or political party in Palestine during Jesus' day.

Following the mentioned Hadrianic decree, the Nazarenes substituted the *Sh'mah* with the Lord's Prayer, and the various elements contained in it can be aligned with Old Testament Jewish worship and with the Ten Commandments originally given to Moses.

Correspondences

Taking the most comprehensive version of the Lord's Prayer, as given in Matthew 6, some of the correspondences with Jewish ritual liturgy are as follows:

Our Father who art in Heaven.
(One of three general forms of address
in Jewish liturgy)
Hallowed be Thy Name. Thy Kingdom come.
(Parallels the Jewish *Kaddish, Kedusha* and
Amidah—based on Ezekiel 38:23)
Thy will be done in Earth, as it is in Heaven.
(The Jewish *Tosephta Berakoth* 3:7)
Give us this day our daily bread.
(Parallels Proverbs 30:8: "... feed me with food con-
venient for me.")
And forgive us our debts, as we forgive our debtors.
(The Jewish *Amidah* and *Megillah*)
And lead us not into Temptation,
But deliver us from Evil.
(Parallels the standard Jewish *Morning Prayer*)
For Thine is the Kingdom, and the Power,

and the Glory, For Ever. Amen.
(The Jewish *Evening Prayer* and I Chronicles 29:11:
"Thine, O LORD *is* the greatness,
and the power, and the glory, etc.")

According to Solomon Ben Yehuda Ibn Gebirol
and other early kabalists of note, correspondences between elements of the Lord's Prayer and the Ten Commandments (Exodus 20) run approximately as follows
(with the order of the 7th and 8th Commandments pur-
posely transposed):

Our Father
(First Commandment:
Thou shalt have no other gods before me.)
Who art in Heaven.
(Second Commandment:
Thou shalt not make unto thee any graven image,
etc.)
Hallowed be Thy Name.
(Third Commandment:
Thou shalt not take the name of the Lord thy God in
vain.)
Thy Kingdom come.
(Fourth Commandment:
Remember the Sabbath day, to keep it holy.)
Thy will be done in Earth,
(Fifth Commandment: Honor they father and thy
mother, etc.)
As it is in Heaven.
(Sixth Commandment:
Thou shalt not kill.)
Give us this day our daily bread.
(Eighth Commandment:
Thou shalt not steal.)
And forgive us our debts, as we forgive our debtors.

(Seventh Commandment:
Thou shalt not commit adultery.)
And lead us not into Temptation,
(Ninth Commandment:
Thou shalt not bear false witness, etc.)
But deliver us from Evil.
(Tenth Commandment:
Thou shalt not covet, etc.)

Earliest Text

The earliest known New Testament text, the *Codex Sinaiticus*, was first discovered in the mid-19th century in the monastery of St. Catherine at the foot of Mount Sinai and later brought to the attention of the world by a German scholar, Constantin Tischendorf. It includes a version of Mark's Gospel which varies from the standard in a number of notable respects, including omission of any reference to the appearance of Jesus to his disciples after his Resurrection. The *Codex Sinaiticus*, which now rests in the British Museum, London, after first having been presented to Russian Tsar Nicholas II by the monks of Mount Sinai, also contains a truncated form of the Lord's Prayer—which specifically excludes the normal closing phrase based on I Chronicles ("For thine is the kingdom, etc.").[1]

It may be worthy of mention that the omitted portion is an important element in the Western hermetic tradition as it forms the key phrase of the so-called kabalistic cross used in occult and other ritual.

Father, Hallowed be thy name,
Thy kingdom come.
Thy will be done, as in heaven, so upon earth.
Give us day by day our daily bread.

And forgive us our sins, as we ourselves also forgive every one that is indebted to us. And bring us not into temptation.

Hebrew Version

Listening to any Hebrew rendition of the great invocation known as the Lord's Prayer is, musically, a marvelous experience that takes the listener and singer into a new dimension of participation in the use of the sacred Language of Light. Using a shortened form of the text, similar to that given in the *Codex Sinaiticus* version, a translation would run something like this:

Avenu Sh'ba-Sh'maiyim
[A-**vay**-noo She-**bah**-Sh'mai-**yeem**]
Yitkadash Shemeycha
[Yit-ka-**dash** Shem-maiy-**chah**]
Tavo Malkutecha
[Ta-**voh** Mal-khoo-taiy-**chah**]
Y'asseh Retzoncha
[Y'ah-**seh** Re-tzon-**cha**]
K'mo Ba-Sh'maiyim Kain B'Aretz
[K'**moh** Bah-Sh'**mai-yeem** Kay-**in** B'Ah-**retz**]
Et Lechem Hukeynu Ten-Lonu Ha-Yom
[Et Le-**chem** Hoo-**kay**-inoo Ten-**Loh**-noo Hah-**Yom**]
U'Slach Lonu Et Hovetheynu
[Oo'**slach** **Loh**-noo Et Hoh-veht-**t'hay**-inu]
K'Asher Solachnu Gam Anachnu L'Ha Yaveynu
[K'ah-**sherr** Soh-**lach**-noo Gum
Ah-**nach**-noo L'Hah Yah-**vaiy**-noo]
Vi-al Tivi-Aynu Li-Y'Dey Nisa-Yon

[Vih-ahl Tee-vee-**Aiy**-noo Li-Y'**Daiy** Nih-sah-**Yohn**]
Ki Im Hal-Tzeynu Min Hara
[Kee Eem Hahl-**Tzaiy**-noo Min Hah'**rah**]

Our Father who art in the heavens.
Hallowed be thy name.
Thy kingdom come.
Thy will be done,
On earth, as it is in the heavens,
Give us this day our daily bread.
Forgive us our debts,
As we forgive our debtors.
And lead us not into temptation,
But deliver us from the evil ones.

The usual English version of the Lord's Prayer, in full, is:

Our Father who art in Heaven,
Hallowed be Thy Name.
They Kingdom come.
They Will Be done,
On earth as it is in Heaven.
Give us this day our daily bread,
And forgive us our sins,
As we forgive those who sin against us;
And lead us not into temptation,
But deliver us from evil.
For Thine is the Kingdom,
and the Power and the Glory,
for Ever and Ever, Amen.

The Lord's Prayer is only one of the many marvelous legacies left us by the personality known today as
Jesus the Christ. The prophet Daniel once wrote: "They
that be wise shall shine as the brightness of the firma-

ment." (Daniel 12:3) Recorded history has yet to provide us with any one individual who has shone brighter than the Jewish Rabbi Yeshua bar Yosef, Jesus son of Joseph, whose unique message, on whatever level it is comprehended, has inspired so many millions since he walked and talked and taught in Palestine, nearly 2,000 years ago.

Greek and Latin Liturgy

The language of the New Testament is rich in expressions of great power, and Greek Orthodox and Roman Catholic liturgy is redolent with songs and prayers of praise, healing and redemption of great efficacy and beauty. There are many fine Greek affirmations relating to the coming together of *Sophia* (literally "Wisdom of Ultimate Things") and *Phronesis* (practical application of wisdom) to achieve *Sunesis*, or personal "Unification." Phrases incorporating such terms as *Agape Christou* ("Love of Christ") and *Agios Pneuma* ("Holy Spirit") can be utilized in a similar fashion to the chants and mantras of the Middle East and India.

But although the early members of the Christian Church were familiar with Greek expressions (and many of the apocryphal scriptures are written in that language), as a unifying force promoting a central focus for the Christian faith around the globe, Latin soon superseded Greek. Latin was last used as a *lingua franca* during the Middle Ages, in Byzantine times when Greek took over, but due to its continued use in the Roman Catholic Church, it has remained a living language.

The cornerstone of the Roman Catholic Church is its *Credo*, a statement of profound authority which, in its declaration of the basic foundation of Roman Catholic faith, ranks some comparison with the Hebrew *Sh'mah* and the Muslim *Kalimah*:

Credo in unum Deum,
Patrem omnipotentum,
Factorem coeli et terrae,
Visibilium omnium, et invisibilium
Et in unum Dominum Jesum Christum,
Filium Dei unigenitum
Et ex Patre natum
ante omnia saecula,
Deum de Deo, lumen de lumine,
Deum verum de Deo vero ...

I believe in one God
the Father Almighty,
Maker of heaven and earth,
And of all things visible and invisible:
And in one Lord Jesus Christ,
the only begotten Son of God,
Begotten of his Father
before all worlds,
God of God, Light of Light,
Very God of very God ...

Very familiar to Roman Catholics will, of course, be the confession—the *mea culpa*. Taken from the *Daily Missal*, it reads:

Confiteor Deo omnipotenti,
et omnibus Sanctis,
quia peccavi nimis cogitatione,
verbo et opere,
mea culpa,
mea culpa,
mea maxima culpa.

I confess to Almighty God,
and to all the saints,
that I have sinned exceedingly in thought,
word and deed,
through my fault,
through my fault,
through my most grievous fault.

Another famous Catholic chant, the *Sanctus*, is the Latin version of the Isaiah (6:3) and Revelation (4:8) texts, which describes the activity surrounding the throne of the Almighty (see Chapter 6 for the Hebrew version, *Qadosh, Qadosh, Qadosh...*).

Sanctus, Sanctus, Sanctus,
Dominus Deus Sabaoth.
Pleni sunt coeli, et terra gloria tua.
Hosanna in excelsis.

Holy, holy, holy.
Lord God of Sabaoth.
Heaven and earth are full of thy glory!
Hosanna in the highest.

It is also worth recording the Lord's Prayer as it reads in Latin:

Pater Noster,
qui es in coelis,
sanctificetur nomen tuum:
Adveniat regnum tuum.
Fiat voluntas tua,
sicut in coelo, et in terra.
Panem nostrum quotidianum da nobis hodie.
Et dimitte nobis debita nostra,

sicut et nos dimittimus debitoribus nostris;
Et ne nos inducas in tentationem,
sed libera a nos a malo.

Our Father,
which art in heaven,
Hallowed be thy Name.
Thy kingdom come,
Thy will be done,
in earth as it is in heaven.
Give us this day our daily bread.
And forgive us our trespasses,
As we forgive them that trespass against us.
And lead us not into temptation;
But deliver us from evil.

Mother of Christ

For the millions of adherents to the Catholic faith, the name of Mary, mother of Jesus, has become almost as important as that of Jesus himself. For over 2,000 years the Virgin Mary has been venerated as the focal point of what has almost amounted to a separate cult. She has replaced the pagan mother goddess and provided a sympathetic and merciful face of Christianity as the mother who is always ready to intercede with God on behalf of her children in order to obtain forgiveness for their misdeeds. This has offered a sharp contrast to the harsh, hell-fire image of judgment and damnation created by the Church down the centuries in order to keep its flock in line.

Indeed, the *Salve Regina*, sung in Latin, *O clemens, o pia, O dulcio Maria* ("O merciful, kind, sweet Mary"), has become, for Catholics, one of the most familiar and well-loved hymns of petition, and an invocation of some considerable power. So too has the *Ave Maria,* perhaps the most beautiful of all Roman Catholic chants:

> *Ave Maria,*
> *gratia plena,*
> *Dominus tecum;*
> *benedicta tu in mulieribus,*
> *et benedictus fructus ventris tui, Jesus.*
> *Sancta Maria,*
> *Mater Dei,*
> *ora pro nobis peccatoribus,*
> *nunc et in hora mortis nostrae. Amen*

> Hail Mary, full of grace!
> the Lord is with thee;
> blessed art thou amongst women,
> and blessed is the fruit of thy womb, Jesus.
> Holy Mary, Mother of God,
> pray for us sinners,
> now and at the hour of our death.

In closing this chapter, it might be appropriate to record the standard Latin *Gloria* used at the beginning and ending of most Catholic ritual:

> *Gloria Patri*
> *et Filio,*
> *et Spiritui Sancto.*
> *Sicut erat in principio*
> *et nunc et semper*
> *et in saecula saeculorum.*

> Glory be to the Father,
> and to the Son

and to the Holy Ghost;
As it was in the beginning,
is now, and ever shall be,
world without end. Amen!

17. THE ISLAMIC CALL TO PRAYER

La ilaha illa-llah:
Muhammedan rasul Allah!
(There is no god but God:
and Muhammed is the apostle of God!)

As we have touched on the traditions of the Jews and the Christians and their sacred chants, it would be appropriate to spend some time with the third great religious grouping that claims as an original founding father a singular, desert-dwelling man—Abraham, former resident of the city of Ur, the "City of Light," whom the Muslims consider as neither Jew nor Christian but "an upright man who had surrendered himself to Allah" (*Qur'an, sura* 3:64).

Throughout the world, in the Arab countries, in India, and in every other land where Muslims dwell, the *Kalimah*, or principal Islamic profession of faith citing one God only called Allah and Muhammed as His messenger is repeated five times daily by the faithful—after they have removed their shoes, made their ablutions, and bowed low to the East towards Mecca. This potent phrase, which is used every day at pre-appointed times, has constituted both the rock and the banner of Islam for over 1400 years. It also fired a period of phenomenal Muslim conquest and conversion across Asia, Africa and Europe during the first thousand or so years of the existence of Islam as a religious system. Although continued territorial gains have since dwindled, Islam remains probably the fastest-growing faith in the world today.

La ilaha illa-llah: Muhammedan rasul Allah—
"There is no god but God: and Muhammed is the apostle of God."

In the Name of Allah

The great Muslim sage Ibn Sina, also known as Avicenna and as physician and vizier at an Arab court, was a philosopher-scientist who was an acknowledged master of the religious sciences by age ten. His profound studies embraced philosophy, ontology and metaphysics. Ibn Sina described the *Shahadah*, the first fundamental formula of Islam, *La ilaha illa-llah*—"There is no god but God"—as translating even more fully to reveal that there is no power, agent or reality, if it is not *The Power, The Agency, The Reality.*

Jalal ud-Din Rumi, founder of the Muslim Sufi order known as the Dancing Dervishes, was a 13th-century Persian sage (he was actually born in Afghanistan in 1207) who has been described as possibly the greatest mystical poet of any age. Rumi took 43 years to compile his great work, the *Masnavi*. Among his numerous recommendations for a successful life for anyone who chooses a spiritual path was the observation:

When the day dawns, the night takes flight.
When the pure name (of Allah) enters the mouth,
Neither does impurity nor the
impure mouth remain.[1]

Rumi once told the story of a man in grave distress who was persuaded by Satan to cease calling on the name of Allah. When confronted by the saint Khizt, who asked why he no longer called upon the Mighty Name, the man replied that it was because he had never received the clear answer: "Here am I." Khizt immediately chided the man because the mere fact that he had called upon "The Name" meant that Allah was already with him.

To further illustrate this concept, Rumi goes on to tell of a proud and wicked Pharaoh who was given by Allah excellent health, riches in abundance, and absolute dominion in the world. The Pharaoh, however, neglected to even once call upon the Holy Name, not even in thankfulness. Paradoxically, Allah withheld from the Pharaoh all pain and sorrow, leaving him with nothing at all to complain about, "Because pain and sorrow and loads of cares are the lot of God's friends in the world." The reasoning is that those who suffer are constantly reminded to seek union with their Creator. Rumi concludes:

The cries of those free from pain are dull and cold,
The cries of the sorrowful come from
the burning hearts.[2]

Islam

Other than to bring the human being into closer accord with the Supreme, one of the principal functions of most religions of the world has been to bestow some

*Jalal ud-Din Rumi, author of the famous Sufi mystical book,
the Masnavi.*

semblance of order on human life. This is especially true of Islam, one of the world's three great monotheistic faiths—alongside Judaism and Christianity. Both of these religions claim the same starting point as Islam. The Arabic word *islam* comes from a root denoting "surrender" or "commitment." Total commitment and surrender to the will of God as Allah (literally "The God") is at the heart of the Islamic system. The phrase *insha Allah*, "if God wills," is used incessantly in daily discourse. To the devout Muslim, God or Allah is at once the First (*al-awwal*) and the Last (*al-akhia*). Religion is the means whereby the faithful may return to their spiritual origin through participation in a threefold revelation: *Shari'ah* (the Sacred Law or Divine Will); *Tariqah* (the Path); and *Haqiqah* (the Truth).

Although all Muslims are expected to obey the Sacred Law to the letter, there are two discernible holy paths in Islam, the outward and the inward. In order to die in grace and enter into Paradise, it is enough for a person to live according to the *Shari'ah* and in surrender (*islam*) to the Divine Will. This is the outward path of Islam. However, those who wish to experience God on Earth follow the inward path, so as to enter into the more esoteric dimension of the *Tariqah*, which leads to *Haqiqah*, the Ultimate Truth.

Muhammed, the Qur'an and the Ka'aba

Muhammed, founder of Islam, was born around 570 C.E. in Mecca, Arabia. His father died before he was born, his mother soon after. He was raised by his grandfather and later by an uncle. As a boy, Muhammed traveled with the trading camel caravans across the desert from Mecca to Syria. At 25 he married a rich widow, Khadija, who was 15 years his senior, but who remained devoted to him and to his later cause. Although a pagan like most of the Arabs of his day (worshipping a variety of deities, local and universal), Muhammed early on came under the influence of Jewish and Christian teachings. He always enjoyed a reputation as a wise and honest man. He first received his call as a Prophet of God at the age of 40 when he was confronted one day by the Archangel Gabriel, who revealed to him what all Muslims believe to be the infallible "Word of Allah"—the *Qur'an* (or *Koran*), the holy book of the Islamic world.

Just as the twin external pillars of the Jewish faith are represented by a book, the *Torah*, and a building, the Temple, so, too, do the Muslims hold two similar objects sacred above all else—the *Qur'an* and the *Ka'aba*.

In Arabic the word *qur'an* means "the Recital" or "the Reading." In the Muslims' holy book, other than its opening verses in which Muhammed or the Angel Gabriel speaks in the first person, the narrator throughout is Allah himself. The *Qur'an* is arranged into chapters known as *suras* and contains not only religious, mystical and historical data but also practical instruction for the day-to-day running of any Muslim community. In essence, it preaches the Oneness of God and emphasizes divine compassion and forgiveness.

Mecca, where Muhammed was born, is to this day the site of the holy *Ka'aba* (literally "cube"), a massive granite-built structure, ten meters wide and fifteen meters high, in which is set a black stone said to have fallen from the heavens. This monument is regarded as the central shrine of Islam and is visited by many thousands of pilgrims each year. The *Ka'aba* is believed to have been built by Adam, the first of all men, then rebuilt by the common Islamic / Hebrew patriarch Abraham, and finally restored by Muhammed, who destroyed more than 300 pagan idols housed within when he returned triumphantly to Mecca in the year 630. For Muslims, the *Ka'aba* is the center of being. In Sufi mystical terms, anyone who turns towards Mecca and the *Ka'aba* symbolically makes an inward return in a reintegration of the finite individual self with the infinitude of the Divine Self.

Muhammed died in the year 632, two years after the conquest by his followers of his city of birth and the consolidation of Islam as a vibrant new religion. He had turned to Mecca two years previously only after having first chosen Jerusalem as the center for his new faith. He was, however, rejected by the Jews there, whom he had initially hoped to convert.

Comparisons with Judaism

There are, indeed, many close comparisons between Islam and Judaism. Of the 25 prophets listed in the *Qur'an*, 19 are from Jewish scripture, including Abraham, common first forefather of both Arab and Jew (and perforce of Christians, because of their own Jewish heritage). In Hebrew, the name Abraham (*Ibrahim* in Arabic) means "father of the nations." Abraham's appearance on the scene around 2000 B.C.E. was to alter the whole course of history—for out of the Judaism which eventually became the religion of his descendants was born both Christianity and Islam. Many Muslim dietary and social laws also parallel closely the equivalent customs and beliefs of the Jews.

Jesus, founder of Christianity, also features prominently in the pages of the *Qur'an*, although mainly as a revered prophet of high standing and not directly as the Son of God. However, in sura 3 of the

Qur'an the advent of Jesus is described in the following interesting terms: "Verily the likeness of Jesus in the sight of God (Allah) is as the likeness of Adam: he created him out of dust, and then said unto him 'Be'; and he was."

The Call to Daily Prayer

Fundamental to the daily practice of Islam is *salat*, or daily prayers. Salat is one of the five acknowledged major pillars of Muslim observance. The others are: *arkan* (profession of the Muslim creed); *sawm* (fasting); *hadj* (pilgrimage to Mecca); and *zakat* (tithing to aid the underprivileged). Some traditions add a sixth pillar—*jihad*—and interpret the word to denote "holy war." A more accurate translation of *jihad* places it as an expression specifically illustrating the eternal inner spiritual battle (the "striving"), rather than the outward war of conquest and conversion (the "lesser *jihad*").

Although all of the other fundamental pillars of Islam may be attended to at some time or another, the one practice common to all faithful Muslims every single day is the call to prayers. To establish the fact that prayer is the express duty of the believer, the name of Allah and his Prophet Muhammed are spoken into the ear of each Muslim baby soon after birth. When a Muslim child reaches the age of four years and four days, a ceremony called *Bismillah* takes place, at which ritual the child is taught the principal introductory phrase prefacing each of the suras of the *Qur'an*, bar one: Sura 9—"Repentance." According to traditional commentators, sura 9 does not begin with the Bismillah because it is in fact an extension of sura 8, "Spoils."

The Bismillah runs as follows:

Bismillah al-rahman, al-rahim

In the name of Allah, the Compassionate,
the Merciful.

For the record, it can be noted that in Arabic pronunciation the letter "*l*" (*lam*), when used as a final letter of the definitive article in front of certain consonants, is elided into a sound approximating "*r.*" Thus the appellations *al-rahman* and *al-rahim* would sound more like "ar-rahman" and "ar-rahim." Most other rules are similar to those for Hebrew.

The Bismillah can be equated with the Hebrew sacred phrase *Adonai Adonai El-rahum ve-hammun*—"Lord, Lord, merciful and compassionate." The two divine appellations, *al-rahman* and *al-rahim*, are derived from the same root *rahama*. *Al-rahman* symbolizes the transcendent mercy of Allah; *al-rahim* is its earthly manifestation.

An Arabic prayer known as the *Tawhid* (the term means "Unity at once with the Divine and with all *things*," indicating a true relationship with God) is a favorite of many who attend the five-times-a-day Muslim prayer sessions. This prayer alludes to the oneness of Allah with all creation, His eternal presence, and His almighty omnipotence. It runs as follows:

Qol hua Allahu achaol
Allahu as-samad
Lam yalid wa-lam yulad
Wa-lam yaqul lahu kufwan achad

Translation:

Say: He is Allah the One!
Allah the eternally besought of all!

He begetteth not nor was begotten.
And there is none comparable to him.

The five-times-a-day Muslim call to prayer is known as *adhan* and is traditionally given by a *muezzin* from the *minaret*, or tower, of the mosque, or *masjid*. *Masjid* means literally "a place for prostration," but the mosque is much more than just a meeting house for prayer. It is a place for worship, school, council chamber, law court and community center, and an indispensable part of the life of any Muslim community.

The Mystical Path

Sufism is the name given to the metaphysical expression of Islam, and the *Sufis* have played a vital role in Muslim history and theology, especially in Muslim literature. One probably erroneous legend tells us that the term *Sufi* is taken from the word *suf*—a plain woolen garment said to have been worn by Islam's early mystics. Another possible derivation is the expression *Sa fa*, "he was pure." But according to Idries Shah, author of *The Way of the Sufi* and other notable books on the subject, the actual sound or mantra *SSSUUUFFF*, derived from a combination of the Arabic letters *soad, wao* and *fa*, is the root for the expression *Sufi* simply because of its direct effect upon the organized mental activity of any individual. Moreover, Muslims who follow this mystical path will not refer to themselves as Sufis, this, according to Idries, being a term coined in Germany in 1821. Idries refers to the expression *Mutassawif* as being nearer the correct one, which is confirmed by another well-known contemporary writer on Sufism, Seyyed Hossein Nasr, who uses the term *Tasawuwuf*—both versions meaning roughly "he who strives to be a Sufi."[3]

Idries Shah, incidentally, was born into a family that traces itself through the Prophet Muhammed and beyond, back to the year 122 B.C.E., which is possibly the oldest recorded lineage on Earth.

Stages of Spiritual Progress

According to Sufi precepts, there are three stages of spiritual progress:

* *Sair ita-Ilah:* progress towards God—a stage which leads towards *fana* ("annihilation"), the Sufi equivalent of the Hindu *Nirvana.*
* *Sair fi-Ilah:* progress in God—the various stages of *fana.*
* *Sair'ani-Ilah:* progress beyond God—the attainment of *fana* or permanent "non-being."

The final state of "non-being" can be reached only through direct experience. It cannot be attained indirectly or intellectually. The four basic Sufi practices on the mystical path are *Dhikr*: remembrance, or repetitive chanting of the name of Allah; *Riyadat*: constant and rigorous fasting; *Inkisar*: detachment from the worlds of illusion and conditioning; and *Subha*: consciousness of the Absolute reached only through "annihilation."

Of the four basic mystical practices required to reach "progress beyond God," the first, known as *Dhikr*, involves repetition of the Supreme Divine name of Allah as a kind of rhythmic breathing—with no restriction placed on when or how often this practice of "remembrance" should be made. Although the Sufis may use other invocations to promote mystical union with Allah (for instance, *Hu el-haiy el quaiyum*—"He, the living, the Self-Subsistent"), it is said that all other invocations and litanies become redundant when placed alongside the Name of Divine Majesty.

For the Sufi, mere repetition of the Name of Allah is not sufficient unless the act is backed up by fulfillment of all other obligations of the Muslim Holy Tradition. The invocation of the Name itself, although the most powerful of all rites, is only acceptable to God when all of the other traditional prerequisites have been met.

Before moving on to a discussion of the many Names of Allah as related to the practice of *Dhikr*, it may be of some passing interest to note here that it has been claimed that certain Western Masonic rituals, words and terms can often be "decoded" by using Sufi mystical systems. Celebrated Jewish sages who lived in Spain under Muslim domination during the 12th century and beyond most certainly came under the influence of Sufi schools, and nearer to our present time that enigmatic mystic and teacher G. I. Gurdjieff made no secret of the links his teachings had with Sufism, particularly with the branch dominated by the so-called whirling dervishes. Moreover, Father Cyprian Rice, a Catholic priest, has even proposed in his book *The Persian Sufis* that there are Catholic mystics and academicians who ascribe to the possibility that a future purpose of Sufism will be to "make possible a welding of religious thought between East and West."[4]

18. MANY NAMES OF ALLAH

The real nature of intelligence is ultimately
to come to realize that
there is only one Absolute Reality.

—Seyyed Hossein Nasr

Islamic legend tells of the day the famous Sheikh Bayezid Bastami was asked: "Which is the greatest name of Allah?" The Sheikh retorted: "Communicate thou to me His least name, that I may give it thee in return as His greatest."

The venerable Sheikh's inference was, of course, that *all* the many names of Allah are of equal importance.

There have been claims that there are in total 3,000 names of Allah. One thousand of them are known only to the Angels; a further one thousand are known only to the Prophets; three hundred are found in the pages of the Hebrew *Torah* and three hundred in the Psalms of David; while another three hundred occur in the New Testament.

There are, however, according to most references, just 99 known names of Allah mentioned in the *Qur'an*. These are called *Asma al-Husna*, the "Excellent Names," with one hidden name known to Muslims as *Ism Allah al-a'zam*, "The Greatest name of Allah"—the name which is *khafa*, concealed, mysterious. It is said

"Allah!"

that anyone who reads the *Qur'an* right through will unwittingly sound the hidden Holy Name.

The 99 Names

There are several lists available noting the alleged 99 names of Allah, but they are not all consistent, there being some argument over what actually represents a Name of Allah. The following list is taken from *The Gospel of Islam* by Duncan Greenlees:[1]

1. Allah (The Self-Subsisting); 2. Ar-Rahman (The Gracious); 3. Ar-Rahim (The Merciful); 4. Al-Malik (The Master); 5. Al-Quddus (The Holy); 6. As-Salam (The Peace); 7. Al-Mu'min (The Faithful); 8. Al-Muhaimin (The Guardian); 9. Al-Azim (The Infinite); 10. Al-Jabbar (The Strong); 11. Al-Mutakabbir (The Superb); 12. Al-Khaliq (The Creator); 13. Al-Bari (The Shaper); 14. Al-Musawwir (The Fashioner); 15. Al-Ghaffar (The Forgiver); 16. Al-Qahhar (The Almighty); 17. Al-Wahhab (The Bestower); 18. Ar-Razzaq (The Provider); 19. Al-Fattah (The Victorious); 20. Al-Alim (The All-Knowing); 21. As-Sari (The Swift); 22. Al-Basit (The Wide-Spreading); 23. Al-Khafiz (The Abaser); 24. Ar-Rafi (The Exalter); 25. Al-Mu'izz (The Blissful); 26. Al-Muzill (The Giver of Shade); 27. As-Sami (The Hearer); 28. Al-Basir (The Seer); 29. Al-Hakim (The Wise); 30. Al-Fasil (The Decider); 31. Al-Latif (The Subtle); 32. Al-Khabir (The Aware); 33. Al-Halim (The Considerate); 34. Al-Aziz (The Mighty); 35. Al Ghafir (The Pardoner); 36. Ash-Shakur (The Grateful); 37. Al-Ali (The Sublime); 38. Al-Kabir (The Great); 39. Al-Hafiz (The Protector); 40. Al-Hasib (The Reckoner); 41. Al-Jamil (The Beautiful); 42. Al-Karim (The Noble); 43. Ar-Raqib (The Watcher); 44. Al-Mujib (The

Answerer); 45. Al-Wasi (The All-Embracing); 46. Al-Hakim al Mutlaq (The Absolute Judge); 47. Al-Wadud (The Loving); 48. Al-Majid (The Glorious); 49. Ash-Shadid (The Stern); 50. Ash-Shahid (The Witness); 51. Al Haq (The Truth); 52. Al-Wakil (The Defender); 53. Al-Qawiy (The Powerful); 54. Al-Matin (The Firm); 55. Al-Wali (The Friend); 56. Al-Hamid (The Praiseworthy); 57. Al-Qabil (The Acceptor); 58. Al-Badi (The Originator); 59. Al-Muhit (The Surrounder); 60. Al-Muhyi (The Giver of Life); 61. Al-Mumit (The Giver of Death); 62. Al-Haiy (The Living); 63. Al-Qayyim (The Eternal); 64. Al-Yu'id (The Affectionate); 65. Al-Wahid (The One); 66. As-Samad (The Resource of All); 67. Al-Qadir (The Capable); 68. Al-Muquit (The Support); 69. Al-Qarib (The Near); 70. Al-Muakhkhar (The Latter End); 71. Al-Awwal (The First); 72. Al-Akhir (The Last); 73. Az-Zahir (The Manifest); 74. Al-Batin (The Unmanifest); 75. Al-Wuli (The Assister); 76. Al-Muta'al (The Exalted); 77. Al-Barr (The Just); 78. At-Tauwab (The Relenting); 79. Al-Ghafur (The Forgiving); 80. Al'Affuw (The Mild); 81. Ar-Rauf (The Pitiful); 82. Malikul-Mulki (The Master of the Kingdom); 83. Dhuj-Jalal wa Akram (The Mighty and Glorious); 84. Al-Ghalib (The Triumphant); 85. Al-Ghaniy (The Absolute); 86. Al-Mughniy (The Enriched); 87. Al-Maula (The Befriender); 88. An-Nafi (The Profitable); 89. An-Nasur (The Helper); 90. An-Nur (The Light); 91. Al-Hadi (The Leader); 92. Ar-Raziq (The Sustainer); 93. Al-Baqiy (The Everlasting); 94. Al-Azaliy (The Purifier); 95. Ar-Rashid (The Pioneer); 96. Al-Malik (The King); 97. Al-Ghafaw (The Benign); 98. Dhul-Fadli (The Generous); 99. Rabbul-Alamin (The Providence or Lord of all Creatures).

In line with the controversy over definition, the above list differs somewhat from that given in a more recent English-language book on the Names of Allah: *Ninety-Nine Names of Allah* by Shems Friedlander (with al-Haij Shaikh Muzaifereddin).[2]

Sounding the Names

Repetition of specific names of Allah is believed to produce varying effects and benefits for the devout chanter. For example:

* Sounding of the phrase *Ya-Rahman* (God The Beneficent) 100 times is said to result in the acquisition of a good memory and freedom from care and worry.

* Calling out *Ya-Salaam* (The Source of Peace) 160 times to anyone who is ill will bring him or her to health.

* Repetition of *Ya-Mutakabbir* (God The Majestic) by a man before having intercourse with his wife will see him blessed by Allah with a righteous child.

* Devout use of *Ya-Ghaffar* (God the Forgiver) will result in forgiveness of all sins.

* Calling out the name *Ya-Fattah* (God The Opener) will result in the heart of the petitioner being opened for victory to be bestowed by Allah. (Significantly, *Al-Fattah* was the name chosen by Yasir Arafat for the military arm of his Palestine Liberation Organization [PLO].)

* For personal protection, calling out the name *Ya-Hafiz* (God the Preserver) 16 times is recommended.

* Anyone in trouble who cares to repeat the name *Ya-Sabur* (God The Patient) 3,000 times will be rescued from his or her difficulty.

Some Muslims recite successive Divine Names of Allah while running a string of beads through their fingers, much in the manner of a Christian Roman Catholic. The many *asma*, or names of Allah, highlight the multifaceted *sifat*, or attributes of the One God. They may also be said to parallel to some extent the qualities of the pantheon of deities found in, for instance, the Hindu and Egyptian religious systems and the many aspects of God found in the Christian gallery of saints and martyrs.

Some Strange Events

Sufis and other Muslim mystics place great store in the power generated during *majalis adh-dikhr*, sessions at which litanies invoking the Divine Names are chanted. In many orders sacred dance is also performed as is the case with the *Mawlawi tariquah*, the "whirling dervishes" of Turkey and elsewhere.

One of the authors has been a witness at several such gatherings—but with a difference and usually by invitation only—by so-called *khalifa* groups from among the large community of Muslims of Malay origin living in Cape Town, South Africa. Their forebears were brought there as slaves by the Dutch East India Company during the late 1600s, and later as political exiles when the British ruled the Cape. They have mixed little with other races and have, for the most part, remained devout Muslims noted for their law-abiding character and high set of morals. The religious ceremony concerned is known by Cape Malays as *Ratiep* and was originally designed to prove the strength of Allah over the material flesh. The leader of the group, usually a Sheikh who has been to Mecca, is known as the *Khalifa* (caliph or vice-regent). At these sessions involving incessant chanting and beating of *ghomma* drums and tambourines, participants slash themselves with razor-sharp swords and pierce their faces, tongues and other parts of their bodies with red-hot skewers—without any blood being drawn or any scar or mark being left once the swords or skewers are withdrawn! The performance can last an hour or a night, depending on the mood of the performers, and cannot be interrupted. At the end, the chanting and beating of drums and tambourines ceases on a single note and a sudden, almost tangible silence fills the air.

For the reader's interest, Cape Town is rich in its Islamic heritage, and the city is almost encircled by a string of *karamats*, Muslim holy burial places, some placed high on mountain paths on the massive Table Mountain and its accompanying Signal Hill overlooking the city. These tombs of especially holy persons have been buried beneath colossal stone slabs, and miniature mosques, some quite grand, have been built over the resting places. Muslims of our acquaintance have affirmed that the positioning of these buildings will forever ensure the safety of the city from any great catastrophe. This claim is based on the prophetic words of a famous seer, Sheikh Khardi Abdusalem, sent from Turkey over 250 years ago to lead the then straying Cape Malay community back onto the path of Islam:

> Be of good heart my children, and serve your masters; for one day your liberty will be restored to you, and your descendents will live within a circle of karamats safe from fire, famine, plague, earthquake and tidal wave.

In vindication of Sheikh Abdusalem's prophecy, the Malays of the Cape were long ago freed from direct slavery and, as we enter the 1990s, it seems as if they will sometime soon at last become truly free people in a democratic society.

The magical influences surrounding the karamats of the Cape Peninsula are well known and they are favorite places for prayer and meditation. More than 20 years ago, during a particular early evening session of simple chanting of the Holy Names inside one of these mosque-like buildings (it may even have been the tomb of Khardi Abdusalem), just as the setting sun became lost behind Table Mountain, some who were present (including the teller of this tale) were stunned when, during a high point in the chanting, an unlit candle set in the *mihrab*, a wall niche common to all mosques, suddenly burst into flame as if lit by an unseen hand. No one was sitting within three or four feet of the candle, and there was simply no way in which the event could have been rigged. Regular participants in these rituals took it all as a matter of course. Although the sun was setting fast when they had arrived and there was no electricity for lighting, none of them had even bothered to bring along a box of matches!

The Name of Essence

Returning to discussion of the singular name Allah, the Sufi sage Najm al-Din al-Kubra once noted that the letter *ha* in the Divine Name is the sound we make with every breath. This sound is contained in Allah's "Name of the Essence," *Huwa* (He), and turns the very act of living and breathing into a perpetual invocation. A comparison can be made here with the Hebrew letter *hey*, which appears twice in the Tetragrammaton, and with the "h" sound in the Hindu so-called "Mantra of the Breath"—*Soham-Hamsa* (see Chapter 22).

It also can be recorded that in certain Sufi coordinated breathing techniques sounding of the *Shahadah* (Name of Allah) is taken through the seven *lataif*, which approximate the seven chakras. The other letters in the Arabic spelling of Allah— *alif* and *lam*—are said to represent intensified definite articles emphasizing the uniqueness of God. The central core of the name of Allah is, therefore, the *ha*, which automatically places the power of God over our every breath and makes the whole of life dependent upon constant utterance of the Holy Name.

All of the major Muslim invocations of importance embrace use of the name of Allah in one form or another. Phrases like *Allahu Akbar* ("Allah is Great") and *Al-hamdu lillahi rabbi l'alamin* ("All praise belongs to Allah, Lord of All the Worlds") carry for Muslims tremendous evocative power. The *muezzin's* five-times-daily call to prayer highlights this total dedication to Allah and His name by the followers of Islam:

> *Allah akhbar*
> *Ashhadu anna*
> *La ilaha illa-llah*
> *Muhammedan rasul Allah*
> *hayya ila s-salat*
> *hayya il l-fehah*
> *Ses-salat kher min en-num*
> *Allah akhbar*
> *la ilaha illa-llah!*

> God is greatest:
> I testify that
> there is no god but God!

and Muhammed is the apostle of God!
Up to prayer;
Up to salvation.
Prayer is better than sleep.
God is greatest:
There is no God but God!

As a final comment, would it not be marvelous if one day the still unreconciled Sons of Abraham would settle their differences and bury the sword in the desert sand to create a new combined nation of the "People of the Book"—as both the Muslims and the Jews are known—and bring peace at last to the Middle East. Under prevailing conditions, this proposition might be thought of as calling for a miracle of great proportions—but then, the wall that stood for 45 years between East and West Germany was breached in a single day in November 1989...

19. ON MEDITATION

When are liberated all the desires
that lodge in one's heart,
then a mortal becomes immortal.
—Katha Upanishad

The Hebrew, Hindu, Tibetan and Islamic traditions teach us that when we are in harmony with ourselves we are in harmony with all of creation. According to many sages, any attempt to achieve such harmony is based on the perception that the whole purpose of human existence is to further the evolution of consciousness. Such progress can usually only be initiated via deliberate self-transformational activity involving a journey on the inner path of meditation.

Constructive thought is a tool of creation, and creative thought benefits the self and all the self contacts. During meditation we use constructive thought to become centered in the Absolute, at one with the Cosmos. Meditation is, in effect, a mental practice directed towards a spiritual goal that helps us to conserve vital energy instead of dissipating it.

There is really no great secret attached to the practice of meditation. It can be done by anyone anywhere and at any time. For the genuine mystic, meditation is both the staff of life and a daily blessing, and there are people who regard their entire life and all of their activities as a form of meditation. Meditation is, in effect, the key to true wisdom. Regular meditation takes a person way beyond the mere act of relaxation and is not designed merely to calm the nervous system. From its dedicated use there can, in fact, result an invigoration of mental powers, an awakening of the superconsciousness, and a bonding with the Absolute.

Universal Essentials

There are probably as many meditation techniques as there are teachers (or practitioners) of the art. The universal essentials are a quiet place, rhythmic breathing, and, for those who wish to invoke what is perhaps the most dynamic form of meditation, the power of the word, or use of mantras—chanted out loud or intoned silently within the heart and mind—that fan the inner flame of illumination. Some meditation techniques include subtle movements—others involve perfect stillness.

The use of incense and/or a single lighted candle in an otherwise darkened room are also aids to meditation. At times, it can be of great benefit to meditate out-of-doors, particularly on a mountain- or hilltop, in a forest, at the foot of a certain great tree, or overlooking a river, a lake or the sea.

Meditation can be done alone or in a group. Group meditation is a wonderfully useful tool in centering and magnifying divine energy for transmission outwards into the world as a calming, healing and rejuvenating force.

Out of regular meditation there frequently grows the desire to be of service to the community and to humanity as a whole. There can also occur an unfoldment of consciousness and a raising of the individual's level of perception of things, on the physical and other planes—a functional heightening, so to speak. This experience need not be confined solely to specific meditation periods. According to the great yoga Master Patanjali, we should constantly strive to "practice the presence"—that is, to bring the meditative state into the whole of our waking existence.

Times for Meditation

Although there are no absolutely rigid guidelines relating to the most propitious times for meditation— the choice depends entirely upon the individual— many teachers do recommend that there be regular pre-appointed hours for its practice. It is generally believed that meditation just prior to going to bed serves to heighten the capacity for deep cosmic sleep—enabling closer contact with the higher self during the sleep state. Early morning meditation, especially at sunrise, helps set the tone for the day ahead. Some teachers claim that the best time to meditate is around 3 a.m. after a period of deep sleep and when the world outside is normally in its most peaceful state.

It can also be of benefit to perform certain loosening up exercises before meditation, especially yogic stretching routines.

Breathing Techniques

Pranayama, or the practice of Yoga of Breath, can also aid in creating favorable conditions for meditation. One recommended method is alternate nostril breathing, using thumb and forefinger, to balance mind and body. While holding the right nostril closed with the thumb, breathe in easily but deeply through the left, then switch fingers, closing the left nostril with the forefinger. Breathe out and then in again through the right nostril. Close the right and breathe out and in through the left nostril, and so on . . .

Other premeditation breathing techniques can be found in most good books on yoga. These will include, in particular, a method involving "observed" natural breathing, allowing the lungs to breathe with their own rhythm, and an "ignored" breathing technique in which the autonomic nervous system is allowed to take over, sometimes leading to rather long periods when no breath is taken at all. It is recommended, however, that the two mentioned methods only be attempted under the guidance of a suitable teacher.

A Personal Experience

Above all else, meditation is an extremely personal experience. Its results are mostly subjective and largely incommunicable to others, except perhaps to those who themselves practice the discipline. But although the road to true enlightenment and illumination may at first appear a singularly lonely one, anyone who meditates regularly soon realizes that there are interdimensional helpers all along the way. Some like to refer to these inner plane inhabitants as "guardian angels" or "guides." The Sanskrit expression for such a personal guide is *jiva*, a term also meaning "the principle of life." Whatever the appellation used, the fact is that we are not alone, and that our physical world is not the only world existing within our own space and time frames.

According to the teachings of the East, mantras have a direct connection with infinite energy sources that cannot be perceived by the ordinary mortal mind. Words, however, cannot describe the transcendental state to be achieved during mantra meditation. Only through the regular and devoted use of a specific chant or set of chants can a person begin to experience and understand what has been tried, tested and proved by countless sages down the centuries. Of prime importance is to comprehend the full meaning of each invocation used—and the overall effect to be expected.

Introductory Meditation

Those readers who are already meditators will have their own techniques, and the simple meditation given here is basically for those who are new to the concept. Once familiar with the process, the basics can be adapted for use with any of the mantras, chants and invocations given in this book.

The great Indian *guru* Paramahansa Yogananda writes in his *Autobiography of a Yogi*:

> The lotus flower is an ancient divine symbol of India; its unfolding petals suggest the expansion of the soul; the growth of its beauty from the mud of its origins holds a benign spiritual promise.[1]

A simple introductory meditation to be used by anyone incorporates this image of the lotus bloom:
Visualize a lotus bud floating in a pond.... Choose the color you like best.... See the bud flower into a beautiful lotus bloom.... Place yourself in the center of the lotus.... As you become smaller and smaller, so does the lotus flower become bigger and bigger, radiant and iridescent.... Visualize the symbol of the *Om*. ... Introduce into it all the colors of the rainbow.... Now begin to chant the mantra *Om*, slowly, drawing out each of the three components of the word: *Aaaa-uuuu-mmmm*, ending in a humming sound, allowing your consciousness to drift away, until you feel at One with the Cosmos:

Om, Om, Om, Om, Om, Om,
Om, Santi, Santi, Santi;
Peace! Peace! Peace!

Advanced Stage

When an advanced stage has been reached in meditation and breathing technique, special use may be made of the sacred sound *Om* as a resonating agent that stimulates and activates a pyramid-shaped cavity said to enclose the third or spiritual eye. This is possibly the most important point on the entire physical body, providing the bridge where the mind can take control over lower desire and autonomic bodily functions. The approaches to meditation and other spiritual practices are numerous, but all paths must eventually merge at the third-eye entry point.

One mantric method for focusing attention away from the physical and into the spiritual third-eye region is to gather mentally all of the body's energies and random thoughts into the center of the forehead while chanting *Aaa-uuu-mmm*. However, when using this great key that opens a door between two worlds, the final *mmm* part of the chant should be vocalized with lips tightly sealed—sending the sound upward and inward into the third-eye pyramidal cavity. Closing the ears with the thumbs while resting the other fingers lightly on the forehead can aid in this process. Once the ingathering is complete, the *mmm* sound is gently forced further upward, until it resonates within the head prior to touching and activating the Crown chakra, which is the entry and exit point to other dimensions.

20. SOME PERSONAL FAVORITES—MANTRAS FOR EVERYDAY USE

Rock of ages, let our song
Praise Thy saving power.

—Maoz Tzur
(adaptation by Gustav Gottheil)

Anyone who begins to understand and use ancient sacred words and phrases will inevitably come across some that are more personally appealing than others. Before moving on to our final discussion about certain universal principles relating to sound, it may be of some benefit to our readers if we represent for easy reference a few of the mantras and chants which have become our own personal favorites, for a variety of reasons. These are listed under easily recognizable headings and can be used at any time of the day or night (with some qualifications) whenever they are needed. Fairly comprehensive explanations have been given for most of them in previous chapters, but, for easy understanding, additional appropriate notes are added below.

It should be stressed that this is a personal selection and that there is no suggestion that any mantras, chants or invocations included elsewhere but not given below have any lesser value than those we now recommend. Readers who have already made some serious study of the variety of expressions already dealt with will no doubt find more than a few items that can be added.

A note of warning: In certain instances, it may be necessary to invoke a needed phrase while busily engaged in some activity, and this can be done quite safely. It is, however, strongly recommended that following any unusually repetitive use of any of these mantras, such as in a formal meditation session, a period of time be allowed to elapse (say 10-15 minutes) before any participant resumes normal daily activities, such as driving a car or operating any kind of equipment or machinery.

Chanting the Aum

Opening and Closing Meditation

The ideal opening chant for starting and finishing any meditation, be it alone or in a group, remains the Sanskrit expression which, according to the traditions of most Eastern countries, embodies the first of all sounds: *Om* or *Aum*. The merits of this great three-syllabled invocation have already been discussed. In brief, when used as a meditation opener, sounding of the Om puts the user in touch with the Source of all creation, and provides a sound-bridge between spiritual and physical dimensions. When selected to close a meditation session, it acts as an enfolding and protective force. Full notes on vocalization can be found in Chapter 12. The introductory statements immediately preceding each mantra are taken from the book *Love is Life* by Esther Crowley (Bennu Books, Cape Town, 1975).

> *Lord of the Universe*
> *enrich our lives with Thy love.*
> *Guard the treasure*
> *of our innermost souls.*
> *Aum*
> [Ah ... oo ... mm]

The Hebrew chant *Qadosh, Qadosh, Qadosh* equates with the "music of the spheres." From our own experience we have found that as a premeditation protection mantra it has few equals, particularly when a visualization is performed which places a golden helmet of protection around the user's head. This visualization process is described in full in Chapter 6. Intonation of this important Hebrew mantra serves to induce harmony of purpose into any group meditation as its sounding replicates the beating of the human heart and brings the vibrations of the individual meditators in tune with each other. It can also be used as a protective mantra by any individual at any time.

> *Hearken to the inner voice:*
> *tune in to the heartbeat of thy neighbor.*
> *If all would listen thus,*
> *we would live in a glorious world.*
> *Qadosh, Qadosh, Qadosh,*
> [Qa-**dosh**, Qa-**dosh**, Qa-**dosh**]
> *Adonai Tzeba'oth;*
> [Ad-o-**noy** Tze-ba-**ot'h**]
> *M'lo Kol Ha'aretz K'vodo*
> [M'lo Khol Ha'**ah**-retz K'vo-**do**]

(Repeat entire chant 12 or 24 times for best effect)

Holy, Holy, Holy!

Calming Body and Mind

The first mantra in this section can be listed as a particular favorite that has proved of inestimable value for many years, both as a personal cleanser of mind, body and soul, and as a vehicle for the initiation of personal transformation. Whenever agitation or fear has taken over, a quick resort to the chanting of *Om Namah Sivaya* has, for us, always brought swift results—calming, healing, soothing. It is the great "clearing out of negativity" mantra. Repetitive intonation leads to upliftment of the consciousness that motivates mind, body and soul to be at one with the higher self, or the spirit. See Chapter 13 for a full description of the many qualities and effects that come from use of this beautiful chant. Vocalization of *Om Namah Sivaya* is suitable for individual or group chanting, and, like so many of the wonderful sacred phrases available to us, it can be invoked wherever and whenever it is needed. After use of this remarkable mantra, it is advisable to rest awhile before resuming daily activities.

> *Justice is our karma.*
> *We reap what we sow in life.*
> *The law is immutable,*
> *and is the key to all things.*
> *The door closes;*
> *,we turn the key—*
> *it opens . . .*
> *Om Namah Sivaya*
> [Aaaaauuuuummmmm Na-**mah**-aaah
> Ssee**va**-ah-ah-ah-**yah**]
> *Om, reverence to the Name of Shiva*

Details regarding the esoteric significance of the so-called "Mantra of the Breath," *Soham-Hamsa*, can be found in Chapter 22. On a practical level we have discovered that the greatest benefit emanating from its use as an everyday chant is the swift stimulation of easy and correct breathing. Its sounding promotes a calming and soothing effect on both the respiratory and nervous systems, and its vocalization is of special value for those who find themselves short of breath through tension. On a higher level, it serves to release the soul, free the mind, and fill the body with life-giving *prana* force.

> *We breathe in the essence*
> *which forms our souls;*
> *We breathe out*
> *to radiate His love.*
> *Soham, Hamsa*
> [So-hahm, Hahm-sa]
> *He Am I; I Am He.*

For anyone who may be feeling drained of energy and who is finding it difficult to maintain their attention at a sharp level, repetition of the Arabic phrase *Ya-Rahman*, "God The Beneficent," which is one of the 99 known names of Allah, can bring immediate clarity to a tired mind and a more active clear-sightedness. It is also a memory stimulant of some value.

> *Our vision becomes clear,*
> *nature will become alive for us;*
> *We will become vital,*
> *and the Spirit will shine*
> *in our hearts.*
> *Ya-Rahman*
> [Yah Rach-maan]
> *God the Beneficent*

Another attention stimulator is the Egyptian statement *Asar-djedu,* which invokes the spine-strengthening qualities of the "Pillar of Osiris." Repeated use can generate a rise in energy levels on both the physical and paraphysical level. A résumé of the other qualities of this revivifying invocation are tabulated in Chapter 10.

United, we are as one!
Unity is the strength of God,
for He is all thought.
Ȧsar-djedu
[Os'r dje-doo]
Pillar of Osiris

Healing Mantras

Most mantras and other sacred invocations stimulate healing processes in one form or another. Those listed below, however, have been specifically designed for the purpose of bringing relief to persons who are ill in body, mind, soul or spirit. It is recommended that after chanting is completed the names of the person or persons to whom healing is directed should be vocalized.

An especially powerful Hebrew healing mantra invokes the name of *Geburah* (see Chapter 6), who is notable as an Angel of Healing. *Geburah* is invoked to "break the seven seals,"—that is, to restabilize and revitalize the sevenfold chakra system of any person who is in distress. For maximum effect, intone the words *Shel Shem Geburah* aloud six times, then add the name or names of those who need healing. Then repeat the chant six more times. This healing invocation is especially effective in group healing sessions.

Center of the macrocosm,
direct Thy rays of power
to those who are part of Thee.
Shel Shem Geburah
[Shel Shem Ge-bu-**rah**]
In the Name of Geburah

The sun has always been a symbol of good health, and many cultures have placed great store on sun-chants as a source of bodily healing. *Om Suryaya Namah* is a Sanskrit sun mantra best intoned at sunrise to promote general health and vitality for the user (see also Chapter 14).

O nature, fill us with thy essence;
fill us with divine life,
so that we may radiate the life force.
Om Suryaya Namah
[Aum **Sur-yai**-ah Nah-mah]
Om, Salutations to the Supreme

Invoking the sun mantra

An Egyptian sun mantra that invokes the name of the sun-god Ra can also be employed to good healing effect, if intoned at sunrise (see Chapter 9 for more details).

O Sun, the giver of life,
our sustenance
is in the elements of nature—
the food of life.
Ra-Neṭer-Àtef-Nefer
[Reh N'tjir O'tef N'fer]
The Divine god Ra is gracious

An Arabic mantra that incorporates another of the 99 known names of Allah, *Ya-Salaam*, "The Source of Peace," can be utilized as a promoter of physical, mental and spiritual health. It also stimulates a feeling of great peacefulness in the chanter, especially if repeated, according to Muslim tradition, 160 times after morning prayers.

When we find ourselves involved in the
quest for spiritual realization, we will
ultimately return to the source . . .
Ya-Salaam
[Yah Sah-laam]
The Source of Peace

Mantras for Protection

The Sanskrit threefold invocation *Om Sri Dattatreyaya Namah*, which invokes the energies of the Hindu trinity, Brahma, Shiva and Vishnu, is a mantra for personal or group protection at any time. Its energy brings firm direction into life and the promotion of clear inspirational thought. It is also a highly useful self-motivation tool. The full esoteric meaning of this chant is given in Chapter 13.

> *When we join the circle*
> *of His spirit,*
> *we become whole.*
> *Remaining on the fringe*
> *will leave us incomplete.*
> Om Sri Dattatreyaya Namah
> [Aum Ssree Dah-tah-trey-**yai**-ah Nah-mah]
> *Om, Honor the name of Dattatreya*

The Egyptians placed great store on the Eye of Horus symbol as a protective device, and invocation of the phrase *Heru-Udjat* whenever needed is designed to bring immediate personal protection, particularly against psychic attack of any kind. Its sounding also promotes strength and vigor.

> *May our lives be firmly linked*
> *with God, the center,*
> *by glittering strands of light.*
> Ḥeru-Udjat
> [Che-roo Oo-dgot]
> *Eye of Horus*

The Archangel Michael has long been accepted as a protective force by Jew, Christian and Muslim alike. The oldest known form of the name of the Prince of Angels can be called upon confidently at any time whenever a threat of any kind is encountered. Our own experience has been that help often comes in the most unexpected way.

> *Glory be to the Angels above...*
> *Mik-kah-eylu*

(Repeat 12 or 24 times for best effect)

It has already been stressed in Chapter 15 that the name of Jesus carries with it marvelous protection and other powers. Mention has been made of its value as an exorcism tool, but it can also be invoked whenever danger threatens. Personally, in more recent years, we have come to prefer the use of one or other of the original Hebrew/Aramaic forms of Jesus' name. However, repeated invocation of the Greek form by so many millions down the ages has made certain that this great name of power has maintained its potency, no matter the preferred sounding.

We ask for protection
from all evil and negative
thoughts and acts,
in the name of:
Jesus ... Jesus ... Jesus
(alternatively)
Yeshua ... Yeshua ... Yeshua
(alternatively)
Yehoshua ... Yehoshua ... Yehoshua

For Upliftment

For Jews in particular, the *Sh'mah* prayer represents possibly the most powerful of all invocations for the general upliftment of any individual. A shortened version incorporating only the first two lines of the full prayer is recommended for utterance just prior to falling asleep and again on awakening, as a protective and elevating influence while in the dream state, and as a rejuvenating power on awakening. For a full exposition on this important invocation, see Chapter 5.

El Eliyon

We can choose God,
and by our choice,
He lives in each and every
one of us.
We are but sparks of His life force.
Sh'mah Yisrael!
[Sh'**mah Yis**-ro-ail]
Adonai Elohainu Adonai Echad
[Ad-o-**noy** El-o-hayi-noo Ad-o-**noy** E-**chad**]
Hear O Israel!
The Lord our God, the Lord is One!

When it comes to a raising of the general vibratory level of any group meditation, and the creating of a firm connection with ultra-terrestrial levels, we have discovered that the most efficient tool for the job is an ancient Hebrew temple blessing, *El Eliyon*. This is one of the several titles of God (see Chapter 6). While chanting this wonderfully uplifting phrase from atop one of the pyramids at Tikal in Guatemala, one of our colleagues has even had the experience of being joined in his song by an ultra-terrestrial voice of unbelievable purity.

We raise our consciousness,
we expand our auras,
our thoughts of love.
El Eliyon
[El Eli-**yon**]
The Most High

The Hebrew word *Shalom*, as described in Chapter 5, is both a greeting and a plea for peace, and makes a fitting final item but one in our personal short list of favorite words and phrases of power. Its overall function is basically the same as *Om Santi*, and both mantras, Sanskrit and Hebrew, incorporate the universal *Om* in their sounding.

Hold this world perfect in thy thought—
hold the thought of a world of love—
and, on the ethereal plane,
our thoughts of peace will manifest a thousandfold.
Shalom
[Sha-lom]
Peace

There is a deep inner peace known in the Hebrew context as "the peace which passeth all understanding"—*Shulamit Shalom*. Uttering of this phrase certainly helps towards attainment of inner peace, and it is highly recommended for intonation just prior to silent meditation, individually or in a group sitting.

In a world of contradictions
there is but one truth...
Shulamit Shalom
[Shoo-lah-meet Sha-lom]
Peace which passeth all understanding

Finding Peace

The Sanskrit phrase *Om Santi* is one of the best known of Eastern mantras and is especially effective as a key for opening the door to that inner peace we all need to experience from time to time if we are to progress favorably on our selected spiritual paths. It has already been included as part of a special meditation presented in Chapter 19, but is repeated here as an essential invocation for all who aspire to get the best out of the words and phrases of power and beauty handed down to us by antiquity. Other than its value on a personal level, *Om Santi* is a focal sound for distribution of peaceful vibrations towards any place or person of choice.

Brethren, we join together
to pray for peace on Earth;
peace and goodwill unto all.
Om, Santi, Santi, Santi
[Aum **Ssan**-tee, **Ssan**-tee, **Ssan**-tee]
Om. Peace! Peace! Peace!

21. UNIVERSAL SOUND

*And the whole earth was of one
language, and of one speech.*
Genesis 11:1

*The student has but to practice himself in sensitivity
for all the several sounds—there are no more than
thirty-two or thirty-three altogether—and the
corresponding feelings will come, if he will only
make up his mind to become conscious of them.*
—Rudolf Steiner
(*Speech and Drama Course*,
September 1924)

In our ongoing study of sacred words of power we
frequently come across words and phrases that are
similar in sound and meaning but from different language sources. This has naturally led to a raising of the
question as to whether there is some single original
source for all communicative expression. Most readers
will be familiar with the Genesis story about the Tower
of Babel. At a time when everyone on Earth apparently
spoke a single language, an attempt was made by the
"children of men" to build a tower to reach Heaven itself. God was so displeased at this display of effrontery
that He came down to Earth to deal with His subjects
personally. Genesis relates that He confounded their
language "that they may not understand one another's
speech" and scattered the races of men all over the face
of the planet.

The word *babel* is a derivative from the Hebrew word *balal*, meaning "to mix, to confuse, to confound," which was also used in the context of "overflow" as in the mixing of oil. It has been said that God's reason for confounding the one common language of the time and dividing it into different dialects was because He considered humanity unready to ascend into the heavens, and the confusing of tongues served to disunite a previously united race.

Whatever the origin and merits of this story may be, there has been evidence to suggest that all of our world's languages do have a common source—if not, perhaps, in direct transfer down the ages from one race to another of actual words and phrases, quite possibly in relation to the meanings and values placed on certain key sounds that are common to the tongues of all peoples.

Visible Speech

The well-known teacher of occult sciences, Dr. Rudolf Steiner, was one researcher who uncovered several conclusive universal language connections based on sound values, his major work on the subject being *Speech and Drama*.[1]

Born in Austria in 1861, Steiner enjoyed a brilliant academic career before entering the late 19th-century world of the occultists and theosophists. In 1912, he broke away from Theosophy and formed his own Anthroposophical Society, which still flourishes in many countries around the globe. Steiner's prime premise was that the human mind has incalculable potential which can be developed for humanity's lasting benefit. His teachings ranged over a wide spectrum, from meditation and mind exercise to revolutionary education techniques and organic farming methods. In the present context, some of his most absorbing work was connected with sound and movement. To describe the interrelationship between the two, he used the term *eurythmy*, which means literally "a system of harmonious body movement to the rhythm of music and spoken words" or "speech and music made visible."

For Steiner, as, indeed, for Hebrew kabalists and others, speech was not considered merely as a means of communication; it was and is part and parcel of creation itself. He proposed that each word we produce takes on a definable form in the air, and that if all the letters of the alphabet from *A* to *Z* were to be uttered in a certain way, a human etheric body would be created. This is, of course, completely in line with several ancient teachings, including, as one instance only, the Hebrew tradition, which considers the sounds and forms inherent in the 22 letters of the Hebrew language as the actual protoplasm of creation. We have also learned of kabalists of our own day who refer to language as a sort of computer program that works directly on our "walking bio-computers," or physical/psychic bodies. It follows, therefore, that every word we utter can take on importance as a generator of either a positive or negative (and in some cases, neutral) impulse that will have some effect on our existence.

In a collection of some of his lectures on sound and movement, given mostly in 1924, the year before his death, and published under the title *Eurythmy as Visible Speech*, Steiner theorizes that consonants represent "an imitation of external happenings," and vowels, "an inner experience." He also informs that the letter *H* is midway between consonants and vowels and is related to breath itself. Here again, there are correlations with ancient teachings. In the Vedic tradition, *apana*, or "inspirational breath," is regarded as a catalyst for mind transformation, and the Sanskrit "Mantra of Breathing," *Soham-Hamsa*, conclusively embodies in its vocalization the mentioned *h* sound. In the Hebraic system, the letter *hey* is actually equated with the breath of the Lord Himself, as is the Arabic expression *huwa*, which again embodies the *h* sound.[2]

Steiner equates the use of words with body movement and color, as well as with a human being's actual relationship with the world of form. He suggests that there are 12 basic gestures linked with speech that signify the whole being of any person and that these are in turn related to the 12 signs of the zodiac. Of most interest to us here is what he said about some of the sounds themselves.

Steiner states that the first sound in the alphabet, represented by the letter *A* (as pronounced in German, or "ah" as in "far"), "proceeds from our inmost being when we are in a state of *wonder* and *amazement*." It is connected with birth and creation and stimulates the growth of philosophy, which begins with wonder. Significantly, the first of all mantras—*Aum*—has *A* as the initial syllable of its tripartite sounding. Moreover, a full translation of the Sanskrit term *vach*, which holds the *A* as its central sound, places it not only as a word meaning "speech," but as the mystical personification of speech. In a deeper sense, *Vach* is the subjective Creative Force which emanates from the Creative Deity to become concrete expression in our vision of reality. The Greek equivalent is the well-known expression *Logos*. And, for the record, the Hebrew letter *aleph* or *A* is at once taken as the symbol of God as the Creator and considered to be the prime element used in any combinations of letters employed to form the very elements of creation.[3]

We have already been told that, according to Steiner, every vowel sound is, in effect, bound up with an experience of the soul—which may even bring us back to the posited seven-vowel version of the Name of God discussed in Chapter 4—or to the fact that the five vowels *AEIOU* vocalized in succession sounds remarkably like the word Yahweh, the Name of God derived from the Hebrew Tetragrammaton. Consonants, on the other hand, are different in that they are not sounds that arise from inner promptings but are "images of that which is outside our own being."[4]

It is, however, of more than passing interest to note that the letter *B*, and all other consonants for that matter, cannot be uttered without the addition of a soul-produced vowel sound. This points to the proposition that nothing in our physical world can take on existence without stimulation from the power of the spirit. For the record, Steiner equates the sound of *B* (the first letter in the English "build") as creating a form that is something in the nature of a shelter or a house—which, of course, is precisely what the Hebrew letter *bet* means, in its most direct sense. *Bet* is also, incidentally, a symbol for the Holy Temple in Jerusalem.

In the Beginning

Placing important emphasis on the value of Hebrew as a language of creation, Steiner described the ancient tongue of the descendants of Abraham as "a language which works upon the soul quite differently from any modern language." Moreover, he affirmed that the sounding of Hebrew calls up in the soul of a person a picture, even a whole world, such as when utterance is made of the words that mark the start of Genesis: *B'reshiyth bara elohim et ha'shmayim v'et h'aretz*—"In the beginning God created the heavens and the earth."[5]

Much in line with what we have already written about Hebrew, Sanskrit and other ancient tongues, Steiner posited that the creative power inherent in Hebrew sound sequences could be utilized to allow for elevation of consciousness from the sensible to the supersensible, an action which might be compared in some ways with the clairvoyant experience of a modern-day seer or channeler. He also put forward the suggestion that use of ancient sound forms could create a bridge to penetrate the primeval records of our existence in a way that is entirely different from the methods used by modern research. To Steiner, true reality is spiritual reality, and our physical life form is only a secondary existence brought into being by the actions of discarnate and ultra-terrestrial forces. In one of his lectures, "The Mystery of the Archetypal World," presented in Munich in 1910, he described the first three letters of the Bible as indicative of this process, and of what lived inside any Jewish sage when the sounds penetrated his soul:

> *Bet*, the first letter, called forth the weaving of the habitation of substance; *Reysh*, the second sound, summoned up the countenances of the spiritual Beings, who wove within this dwelling, and *Shin*, the third sound, the prickly, stinging force which worked its way out from within to manifestation.[6]

The underlying principle back of all this is, of course, the supposition that ancient sound correctly intoned stimulates a creativeness unknown to modern-day abstract speech.

A Universal Foundation

Steiner's work regarding sound and movement has been carried several steps further in recent times by the Israeli-born speech and drama teacher and counselor Yehuda Tagar, now resident in Adelaide, Australia, who has given workshops in Australia, Switzerland and England, and as part of a joint Jewish-Arab educational program, in Israel and Palestine. Tagar came under the influence of Steiner's Anthroposophical teachings early on in his career when studying in his home country and later in England. His research and experimentation has been directed mainly at Steiner's approach to drama, but he has also adapted certain elements of Steiner's propositions for use not only as a teaching aid for classes on acting but in psychological counseling and self-therapy by direct confrontation with the forces that lie hidden in the sounds of language. His method, known as *Philophonetica*, has been recently included in several tertiary and other educational courses in Australia.

The term *Philophonetica* can be translated as "love of sounds" or "soul relationships with sounds." It is a method of exploring and experiencing the phenomenon of the single sounds of language and of their effects and impressions on the body and on the soul.

In the present context, Tagar's most interesting conclusions relate to his views and findings on a universal foundation for all languages. In his studies he has uncovered those elements which emphasize the differences between various languages, but has also discovered other elements which can be used to create a bridge between two or more tongues.

This attempt by Tagar at bridging the gap between cultures calls to mind the experiences while in

North America of our good friend Credo Vusamazulu Mutwa, current High Sanusi and Keeper of the Tales of the Zulu nation, whom one of the authors first met over 20 years ago in the famous black city of Soweto, near Johannesburg, South Africa. When it comes to the tongues of the black tribes of Africa, Mutwa is an accomplished multilinguist. In 1975, he was invited to the United States to lecture and to assist with research on a film project. On his return he told us that while in the USA he had spent some time with the elders and medicine men of the Zuni Indian tribe, and that to the amazement of both his hosts and himself, he was able to converse with them in a language that approximated their own. This was accomplished by use of a combination of words and phrases taken from several Southern African dialects and root-languages, which were almost identical in pronunciation and meaning to the Zuni Indians' own spoken form.

The question still remains as to whether these similarities have come about as a result of an initial universal language that spread all around the globe, which then became confused into numerous subsidiary forms—or, as Steiner and Tagar would have it, because certain seed sounds universally represent the same or similar objects and/or experiences. Steiner, incidentally, did posit a universal language in Atlantis, the famed continent of antiquity that sunk into the sea. Perhaps both propositions are true and there was a universal language once *because* certain sounds represent and express the same experience.

Sounds are Experiences

There are numerous examples in the *Philophonetica* system, based on the original Steiner find-

ings and developed by Tagar, through whi
sonal discovery can be made of powerful ar
ate connections between particular sounds a
lated inner experiences. Some of these unusu
cepts contained in Tagar's working proposition
noted for the reader's comprehension:

The letter *B*, when spoken with the active partici
pation of the whole body, results in an experience of
embracing, holding; *K*—of breaking through a barrier;
G—of guarding and fending off; *S*—of penetrating (like
a sword); *V*—of invading, and of strong movement; *M*—
mothering; *D*—consolidating; *F*—firing, dispersing,
and mastering confidence; *R*—of scattering and
spreading; *P*—of exploding; *Sh*—of calming down; *L*—
of the water element, of flowing and molding; *T*—of
pointing, and of incarnating; *H*—of expanding in all directions; *O*—of sympathy; *I* [ee]—of self-knowing and
asserting the self; *U* [oo]—of fear and deepening; *E*
[eh]—of offending and countering; *A* [ah]—as already
mentioned, of wonder and openness. (It should be recorded that the above examples represent but a sample
of typical inner and outer expressions and responses
that occur during exposition of *Philophonetica* exercises.)

All these sounds also have their cosmic as well as
natural elemental dimensions, for every consonant is
an utterance of a particular constellation:

Aries	= V	Leo	= T	Sagittarius	= G
Taurus	= R	Virgo	= B	Capricorn	= L
Gemini	= H	Libra	= Ts	Aquarius	= M
Cancer	= F	Scorpio	= Z	Pisces	= N

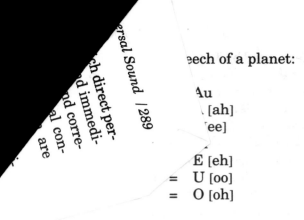

The sounds evoked by the letters of the alphabet are also manifestations of the four elements of nature. They are the forces behind these elements: *B, P, T, K, G, D, M, N* are **Earth** sounds; *S, F, H, V, Sh, Z, Ch* are **Fire** sounds; *L* and *W* are **Water** sounds; three versions of *R* are **Air** sounds.

From the few examples shown above, it would not be too difficult to accept comprehension of sound as a possible all-embracing "language of life" that extends over the whole gamut of human physical, psychic and spiritual experiences. Practice of *Philophonetica* exercises can result in these connections becoming conscious for direct use of appropriate sound as tools for inner healing and change through the medium of the body's ability to express all these experiences in gesture and movement.

Babel or Babble?

In propounding his thoughts on the matter, Yehuda Tagar places initial emphasis on those elements which lie in the foundation of all languages—and points out immediately that, in all the different races and cultures around the globe, babies all babble in exactly the same way:

While on the way to learning how to speak the specific language of the tribe or culture they have been born into, babies naturally go through a stage of what may be called universal language... babbling consists of what is universal to all languages, namely, consonants and vowels. As adults, we are normally only aware of consonants and vowels in their capacity to form words in endless possibilities. But for babies these curious groups of single sounds seem to hold a value of their own. They taste them, they experiment with them, and express much of their inner experience through these sounds alone.[7]

And, still according to Tagar, the babbling of babies takes us right back to what is left of the primal language that existed before the Biblical Tower of Babel episode:

If it be true that the growing embryo, baby and child repeats in his development all of the previous stages mankind has gone through in its evolution, then babbling may be understood as a retracing of a previous stage of human language. Only later in their development do babies relate names to objects, in their particular mother tongue.

When a child begins at last to articulate clearly in the tongue of his or her people, only then does some division from the original universal language begin.

The next stages in the development of personal expression led to both the loss of a universal understanding between cultures and a partial loss of communication between individuals in the same culture. Tagar uses a comparison of the poetry of ancient cultures with the poetry of the 20th century to illustrate part of this evolution away from divinely inspired imagery and vocalization:

In reading the *Iliad* of Homer, pictures come flowing into one's imagination, nearly ready-made.

> There is no need to understand Homer's situation personally in order to understand his poetry, for he does not speak about himself at all. According to his own invocation in the opening words of the *Iliad*, it is the Muse, a heavenly being, who speaks through him, when he is inspired. In comparison, there is nothing "ready-made" in T. S. Eliot's poetic work "The Waste-Land." The Muse speaks not through him, but he himself...

What this all leads to is that we have through the course of time somehow gained individual language at the expense of universal—and have, along the way, even lost much of our social ability to communicate. Asked if this process might be reversible, Tagar has expressed the opinion that it is not, for it is inevitable that human evolution must move forward so that "the fruits of one epoch turn in time into the seeds of another." The development of individual language can be considered as a great human achievement, which need not be reversed. What needs to be done is to take another step or two forward and try to uncover the way in which our "inner content finds its expression, through words." This can lead to a new understanding of one's own language and also of the universal character of the single sounds of any language.

From this new comprehension of expression and communication through speech, the lost universal language may become re-awakened in a more contemporary and individualized sense. A natural process that started with a universal inspirationally based language and worked its way through culturally based languages to develop into the present-day more individual form of communication can, in theory, become part of a conscious process. But any such conscious effort to improve language forms would have to be based on a fresh approach to, and resultant deeper understanding of, the entire foundation of all language. The words used to describe specific objects or incidents usually echo in their sounding some aspect of those forms and/or occurrences, no matter the language used. What must eventually become understood and accepted is that two or more words designating the same object are not necessarily mere substitutes for each other, but rather, "different aspects of the same, shedding their light on each other, enriching the experience of that object."

Moreover, once people of variant cultures begin to realize that their basic communication methods rest firmly on the same foundations, they may also, perhaps, begin to acknowledge common links regarding their cultural and other differences.

Ultimately, one day, we may well have reached full cycle in the evolution from "babble," via cultural language and individualized language, to whatever lies beyond. This will, we hope, consist of a universal form of communication even more complete than the original common tongue in use at the time of the Tower of Babel—a form of communication that can be understood and used by all, regardless of race or culture.

According to Steiner, commencing the last third of the 19th century, the spiritual guidance of humankind was placed in the hands of the Archangel Michael whose characteristics include universal aspects. Developments in recent times that cut across boundaries of race, color, creed and language demonstrate this. It is only natural that this characteristic of our time may ultimately reflect itself in a moving away from the separation of languages towards a unification or synthesis of communicative sound.

Ehyeh Asher Ehyeh—"I Am That I Am."

22. A REMINDER OF OUR SUPERNATURAL ORIGIN

And God said unto Moses,
I AM THAT I AM!
Exodus 3:14

We may have strayed a little from our main theme—the meaning and use of selected words of power—but must emphasize that what is written above is of more than just passing interest when related to our own continual search for correlations of mantric and other expressions that point towards a basic unity in all human experience. An old Indian legend helps to illustrate the meaning of one of the most significant sacred phrases we have come across that is, indeed, common to several ancient cultures.

That and This is One

One day, a village temple dedicated to the deity Krishna was due to be consecrated. As an act of homage to their favored god, the villagers arranged for a large rock that had originally stood outside the door of their brand-new temple to be carved into an image of Krishna. The statue was duly installed, just in time for the consecration, but the chips off the original block of stone were left lying outside the temple door. When

295

worshipers arrived for the ceremony, these devotees of Krishna kicked the rock chips aside before entering.

The chips, like all things in heaven and Earth, enjoyed a life of their own, and appeared to be unconcerned by this harsh treatment. Anyone present who happened to be psychically attuned might have heard them say simply to each other: *Tat Twam Asi*—"That (Krishna) and this (the chips) is one."

What has still to be noted is that the phrase *Tat Twam Asi* can be comfortably equated with the well-known biblical statement of Hebrew origin, "I Am That I Am," and that it has equivalents in other languages as well.

We have already related the tale of how Moses asked God by what name He should be called—and received the reply: "I Am That I Am" (Exodus 3:14). This profound metaphysical statement, which reads in Hebrew *Ehyeh Asher Ehyeh*, symbolizes the trans-substantiation of spirit (I Am) into flesh (That), and back into spirit (I Am). The great "I Am That I Am" mantra, in whatever language it is presented, serves to remind us very forcibly of our supernatural origin, and of our destined ultra-terrestrial future. It is surely a fallacy to insist that as the human species we originate solely from dust and return only to dust. That the most important part of our being is of spirit, and returns to spirit, is clearly stated in Ecclesiastes 12:7: "Then shall the dust return to the earth as it was: *and the spirit shall return unto God who gave it.*" Indeed, all mystical and religious teachings of any worth inform us that we would do well to become aware that we are not in essence material beings and, moreover, that once we have liberated the spirit that resides within each of us we will no longer be fully subject to the material laws of our physical universe.

In our present lifetime we are continually given the opportunity to recognize that we are all sparks of the Divine, the Infinite. We should, naturally, also learn to acknowledge the Divine in those around us. For those who subscribe to a belief in reincarnation, it is of value to note here that there is really no need for us to continually reappear in different bodies on this physical planet. Through correct metaphysical practice (including the use of the sacred sounds handed down to us), and in a single lifetime, we are perfectly capable of subverting the negative reincarnation program and building for ourselves a "body of light" that can transverse physical dimensions and take us into the more elevated realities of the Creator's domain. After all, what is the ultimate message of the story of Yeshua / Jesus but to remind us of this possibility?

Other Versions

The Latin version of I Am That I Am is *Ego Sum Qui Sum*, which will be especially familiar to Catholics, but of special note here is the fact that there are at least two ancient Egyptian versions of this potent statement. Throughout the Egyptian *Book of the Dead* can be found the expression *Nuk Pu Nuk*, which means literally "I Am He, I Am," while a less used but more than exceptionally interesting alternative (also in the *Book of the Dead*) is *Au-u Ur-Se-Ur Au-u*. This utterance is remarkable for its similarity to the Hebrew and Sanskrit counterparts *Ehyeh Asher Ehyeh* and *Tat Twam Asi*. Its full interpretation is rather ponderous: "I Am The Great One, Son of the Great One, I Am," but the meaning is basically the same as "I Am That I Am."

For the reader's interest, the well-known Sanskrit and Tibetan mantric phrase *Om-Mani-Padme-Hum* (see Chapter 12) can also be comfortably equated with the "I Am That I Am" concept. One interpretation of the Jewel in the Lotus mantra places the *Om* part of the chant in an "ascending" role, moving upward towards the Absolute, the words *Mani-Padme* conveying a sense of "merging" with the Absolute, with *Hum* as the return or "descent" back into the physical—carrying with it some of the attributes of the Absolute.

Mantra of the Breath

According to Eastern teachers, there is another significant universal mantra with a similar meaning to *Tat Twam Asi, Ehyeh Asher Ehyeh*, and so on, which is used unconsciously by all living creatures at all times. This is the so-called "Mantra of Breathing," *Soham-Hamsa*. Its roots are contained in the Sanskrit expressions *sah-he-aham*, meaning "He, the Immortal, Am I," and *hamsa*, "I Am He."

The sounds generated by this mantra are directly related to the inhaling of life-sustaining breath, but perhaps its greatest significance is in its function—to release the cords that bind an individual's soul, free the mind, and fill the body with life-giving *prana* force.

Like the water of a river reaching the sea, intonation of *Soham-Hamsa* leads the devotee onwards to reach intimate union with the Supreme, and to forget the physical self. Constant meditation on the phrase while breathing in and out with regular motion aids the individual in identifying totally with the universal soul of Brahman:

Soham, Hamsa
[So-ham, Hahm-sa]

He Am I; I Am He.

The Nadas

While on the subject of identification with the Ultimate, mention must be made of the so-called *nadas*, or logoic sounds of the Universe. Traditionally, there are seven variations to the Sounds of the Logos (the Sufis claim ten). These are the mantras of the cosmos that are not initiated by any human chanter or meditator but are "tuned in to" by the inner ear while a person is in the correct state of receptivity. These wonderful inner tones can vary from an almost excruciatingly tender high-pitched hum through sweetly pure tinkling bells, superbly pitched flutes, and Indian *tabla* drumming, to the deep roar of a raging river or the sound of the sea or wind.

It is said that for the *sravaka*, one who has the ear to hear, the first six nadas eventually merge into a seventh tone which is beyond all sound—the "soundless sound," or Voice of Silence.

Constant meditation and use of mantra can eventually lead us towards the required state for manifestation of the sounds of the silence. What should be borne in mind during this preparatory period is that when we chant sacred invocations it is never sufficient to merely transmit a string of words into space. In order to be of any value, mantra meditations should have a preselected form and objective—for the true aim of invocation or prayer is not to transverse distance, but to *transcend* it. The Ultimate exists all around us *and* within us, permeating our very beings all the time. Separation only occurs within any individual's own consciousness, and contact with the Supreme is limited only by the level of any given individual's personal awareness.

Chanting I Am That I Am

In whatever language is chosen, the "I Am That I Am" mantra, when used with conscious sincerity as an invocatory phrase of great antiquity, can serve as a potential principal introduction to the Voice of the Silence. Just as importantly, it serves as a reminder that the expression "I Am" (indicating the self only) is of no use without the addition of the words "That I Am" (an acknowledgment of our spiritual heritage and connection). In other words, the more any person merely goes into the self without transcending self and acknowledging the overriding presence of the Divine, the more likelihood there is of developing nothing more than an oversized ego.

Indeed, the phrase "I Am That I Am" in its various expressions has been given to us to assist in raising our physical vibrations so that we may experience something of the super-physical while still resident in a material body. It can be vocalized in several forms and languages as follows:

Egyptian

Although there must always be some doubt as to the actual intonation of ancient Egyptian expressions, the following are possible vocalizations of the two given examples:

Nuk-Pu-Nuk
[N'uhk P'oo N'uhk]

I Am He I Am

Au-u Ur-Se-Ur Au-u
[Oh-oo-o Oor-Seh-Oor Oh-oo-o]

I Am The Great One, Son of the Great One, I Am

Sanskrit

When we use this important Sanskrit phrase in mantra meditation, it serves to remind us very succinctly of our spiritual roots and origin, and of our ultimate return to spirit:

Tat Twam Asi
[Taht Th-wam Ah-see]
That and This is One

Hebrew

Recital of the Hebrew phrase *Ehyeh Asher Ehyeh* serves as an activator of the cosmic spark of the Godhead which resides within us all. Its effect when chanted out loud is of an all-embracing nature that will attune the singer's vibrations with those of the *B'nai Or*, the Brotherhood (or Peoplehood) of Light, the non-denominational fraternity of all worlds who co-exist with us in the multidimensional realities which make up the Many Mansions of the Kingdom of the Creator, as recorded in St. John's Gospel 14:2: "In my Father's house are many mansions: if it *were* not *so*, I would have told you."

Ehyeh Asher Ehyeh
[Ay-**yeh** Ah-**shehr** Ay-**yeh**]
I Am That I Am

Notes and References

Chapter 1:

[1] (London: Rider & Co., 1974), p. 63.

[2] (Pasadena, CA: Theosophical University Press, 1977), facsimile edition I, p. 94.

[3] Joan Halifax, *Shamanic Voices*. (London: Penguin, 1980), p. 13.

Chapter 2:

[1] (Secaucus, NJ: The Citadel Press, 1978), p. 6.

[2] Dr. Sant Ramah Mandal, *Aum and Other Words of Power*. (San Francisco, CA: The Universal Brotherhood Temple, undated).

[3] *The Kabbalah Connection*. (Jerusalem: Research Center of Kabbalah, 1983), pp. 81-82.

[4] *Zohar* (Ashlag edition). (Jerusalem: Research Center of Kabbalah, 1970), vol. 4, Parshat B'shalakh, pp. 50-51.

Chapter 3:

[1] J. J. Hurtak, *The Book of Knowledge: The Keys of Enoch*. (Los Gatos, CA: The Academy for Future Science, 1976), pp. 272-273.

[2] Ibid., p. 189f.

[3] *Torus: The Journal of the Meru Foundation*, Vol. 1, (Summer/Fall 1983), and following issues.

[4] Mary Krosney and Ellen Shmuelhoff, "Who wrote the Bible?" in *The Vineyard* (Melbourne, Australia: David Press, August 1986).

Chapter 4:

[1] Reb Zalman Schachter, *Fragments Of A Future Scroll.* (Germantown, PA: Leaves of Grass Press, 1975), p. 10.

[2] Robert Graves, *The White Goddess.* (London: Faber and Faber, 1962), pp. 285-287.

[3] E.A. Wallis Budge, *Egyptian Magic.* (London: Routledge & Kegan Paul, 1979), p. 177.

Chapter 6:

[1] Hurtak, p. 388.

Chapter 7:

[1] This Balancing of the Chakras/Centers meditation in Hebrew is adapted from a meditation originally devised by J. J. Hurtak. Ref: "Visualization: for Breaking the Seven Seals of Revelation," in a privately published booklet "The Academy for Future Science/An Introduction" (Lynne East, South Africa: The Academy for Future Science, undated).

Chapter 8:

[1] *The Book of the Dead* referred to throughout is the translated version by E. A. Wallis Budge: *The Book of the Dead: The Hieroglyphic Transcript of the Papyrus of Ani* (Secaucus, NJ: University Books, 1960).

[2] Numerous works are available dealing with the Egyptian language. A small selection is given here:

E. A. Wallis Budge, *Egyptian Language: Easy Lessons in Egyptian Hieroglyphics with Sign List* (London: Kegan Paul, Trench, Trubner and Co., 1910), (reprinted New York: Dover, 1983); Norma Jean Katan, *Hieroglyphics: The Writings of Ancient Egypt* (London: British Museum Publications, 1980); Joseph and Lenore Scott, *Hieroglyphs for Fun* (New York: Van Nostrand Reinhold Company, 1974).

Chapter 9:

[1] Rex Houston, *Songs of Fire, Tongues of Light*. Words and linear notes by J. J. Hurtak. Burning Bush, 1983. (Available from The Academy for Future Science, P.O. Box FE, Los Gatos, CA, 95031.)

Chapter 10:

[1] Budge, p. 123.

[2] *Songs of Fire, Tongues of Light*.

Chapter 11:

[1] Swami Sivananda, *Japa Yoga*. (Tehri-Garhwal [Rishikesh], U.P., India: The Divine Life Society, 1972), pp. 7-8.

[2] Ibid., p. xxviii.

[3] Swami Nityananda, *The Nectar of Chanting*. (New York: SYDA Foundation, 1983), p. vii.

[4] Eknath Easwaren, *Formulas for Transformation*. (Berkeley: Nilgiri Press, 1977), p. 3.

Chapter 12:

[1] *Hymn 10.90:7-9*. See Wendy Doniger O'Flaherty, translator, *The Rig Veda* (Harmondsworth: Penguin, 1981), p. 30.

[2] Dr. Eruch B. Fanibunda, *Vision of the Divine*. (Prasanthi Nilayam: Shri Satya Sai Books, 1976), pp. 79-88.

Chapter 13:

[1] Swami Abhedananda. *The Sayings of Ramakrishna*. Retold in *The Bible of the World*, Robert O. Ballou, ed. (London: Kegan Paul, Trench, Trubner and Co., 1940), p. 167.

[2] For more information on the specific teachings of A. C. Bhaktivedanta Swami Prabhupada relating to the *Hare Krishna* mantra, the reader is referred to the booklet *Chant and be Happy* (Los Angeles: The Bhaktivedanta Book Trust, 1982).

Chapter 14:

[1] Robert O. Ballou, ed., *The Bible of the World.* (London: Kegan Paul, Trench, Trubner and Co., 1940), p. 155.

Chapter 15:

[1] Morton Smith, *Jesus the Magician.* (London: Victor Gollancz, 1978), p. 49.
[2] Montague Rhodes James, *The Apocrypha New Testament.* (London: Oxford University Press, 1924), p. 184.

Chapter 16:

[1] James Bentley, *Secrets of Mount Sinai.* (London: Orbis Publishing, 1985), p. 130.

Chapter 17:

[1] *Masnavi Book 3:1.* See E. H. Whinfield, translator, *Teachings of Rumi* (London: The Octagon Press, 1979), p. 114.
[2] Ibid., pp. 114-115.
[3] Seyyed Hossein Nasr, *Ideals and Realities of Islam.* (London: George Allen and Unwin, 1966), p. 121.
[4] Fr. Cyprian Rice, *The Persian Sufis.* (London: George Allen and Unwin, 1964), p. 10.

Chapter 18:

[1] Duncan Greenlees, *The Gospel of Islam.* (Adyar, Madras, India: The Theosophical Publishing House, 1948), pp. 201-203.
[2] Shems Friedlander, *Ninety-Nine Names of Allah.* (New York: Harper & Row, 1978).

Chapter 19:

[1] Paramahansa Yogananda, *Autobiography of a Yogi.* (New Jersey: Wehman, 1946).

Chapter 21:

¹ Rudolf Steiner, *Speech and Drama*. (London: Anthroposophical Publishing Co, 1959). Republished by Rudolf Steiner Press.

² Rudolf Steiner, *Eurythmy as Visible Speech*. (London: Rudolf Steiner Press, 1984 [first published 1931]), p. 13.

³ Michael L. Munk, *The Wisdom in the Hebrew Alphabet*. (New York: Mesorah Publications, 1983), p. 43.

⁴ Ibid., p. 33.

⁵ Rudolf Steiner, *Genesis Secrets of the Bible Story of Creation*. Ten lectures given in Munich August 17-26, 1910. (London: Rudolf Steiner Press, 1959), reprinted 1982, pp. 9-11.

⁶ Ibid., p. 14.

⁷ Yehuda Tagar, "On the universal foundation of all human languages, and on the way in which the method called Philophonetica can contribute towards the experience of it." Y. Tagar, c/o The Anthroposophical Society in Australia (S.A. Branch), 84 Halifax Street, Adelaide 5000, Australia, 1989.

Selected Bibliography

Abhedananda, Swami. *The Sayings of Sri Ramakrishna.* New York: The Vedanta Society, 1903.

Authorised Daily Prayer Book of the United Hebrew Congregations of the British Commonwealth of Nations. London: Eyre and Spottiswoode, 1962.

Ballou, Robert O., Spiegelberg, Friedrich, and Friess, Horace L. *The Bible of the World.* London: Kegan Paul, Trench, Trubner and Co., 1940.

Barborka, Geoffrey A. *Glossary of Sanskrit Terms.* San Diego, CA: Point Loma Publications, 1972.

Barclay, William. *New Testament Words.* London: SCM Press, 1964.

Bentley, James. *Secrets of Mount Sinai.* London: Orbis, 1985.

Berg, Dr. Philip S. *The Kabbalah Connection.* Jerusalem: Press of the Research Center of Kabbalah, 1983.
_____."Extra-Terrestrial Life in Outer Space/The Forces Behind the Future." Paper presented at "Forecast 84" Congress, Jerusalem, December 1983.

Bezzant, Reginald, and Pridham, Reginald Poole. *The Promise of Ezekiel's City.* Norwich: Jarrold and Sons, 1952.

Blavatsky, H. P. *The Secret Doctrine.* 2 vols. London: The Theosophical Publishing Co., 1888.
_____. *The Voice of the Silence.* London: The Theosophical Publishing Co., 1889.

Blofeld, John. *Mantras Sacred Words of Power.* London: Mandala, 1977.

The Book of Common Prayer. London: Oxford University Press, [no date].

The Book of Mormon. Salt Lake City, UT: The Church of Jesus Christ of Latter-day Saints, 1980.

Brasch, R. *The Supernatural and You.* Sydney: Cassell Australia, 1976.

Budge, E. A. Wallis. *The Book of the Dead: The Hieroglyphic Transcript of the Papyrus of Ani.* Secaucus, NJ: University Books, 1960.

_____. *Egyptian Language: Easy Lessons in Egyptian Hieroglyphics with Sign List.* London: Kegan Paul, Trench, Trubner and Co., 1910.

_____. *Egyptian Magic.* London: Kegan Paul, Trench, Trubner and Co., 1901.

_____. *The Mummy: A History of the Extraordinary Practices of Ancient Egypt.* New York: Bell Publishing Company, 1989 (reprint, with new foreword).

Chant and Be Happy: The Power of Mantra Meditation. Los Angeles, CA: The Bhaktivedanta Book Trust, 1982.

Charles, R. H. (ed., et al). *The Apocrypha and Pseudepigraphia of the Old Testament.* 2 vols. London: Oxford University Press, 1913.

Chatterji, Mohini M. *The Bhagavad Gita or The Lord's Lay.* New York: Causeway Books, 1960.

Cragg, Kenneth. *The House of Islam.* Encino, CA: Dickenson Publishing Company Inc., 1975.

Crow, W. B. *A History of Magic, Witchcraft & Occultism.* London: The Aquarian Press, 1968.

Crowley, Brian and Esther. *Understanding the Oriental Martial Arts.* Sydney: Recorded Book Corp., 1987.

Crowley, Esther. *Joga in die buitelug.* Cape Town: Bennu Books, 1974.

_____. *The Living Waters of Yoga and Meditation.* Sydney: Recorded Book Corp., 1987.

_____. *Love is Life.* Cape Town: Bennu Books, 1975.

Danby, H. and Segal, M. H. *A Concise English-Hebrew Dictionary.* Tel Aviv: The Dvir Publishing Co., [no date].

Day, Harvey. *The Hidden Power of Vibrations.* London: Pelham Books, 1979.

De Lubicz, Isha Schwaller. *Her Bak: Egyptian Initiate.* New York: Inner Traditions International, 1978.

Driver, G. R. *Semitic Writing from Pictograph to Alphabet.* London: Oxford University Press, 1976.

Easwaren, Eknath. *Formulas for Transformation.* Berkeley: Nilgiri Press, 1977.

Ekvall, Robert B. *Religious Observances in Tibet.* Chicago: University of Chicago Press, 1964.

Evans-Wentz, W. Y., ed. *The Tibetan Book of the Dead.* London: Oxford University Press, 1927.

Fanibunda, Eruch B. *Vision of the Divine.* Prasanthi Nilayam, India: Sri Satya Sai Books and Publication Trust, 1976.

Fortune, Dion. *The Mystical Qabalah.* London: Ernest Benn Limited, 1935.

Friedlander, Shems (with al-Haij Shaikh Muzaffereddin). *Ninety-Nine Names of Allah.* New York: Harper and Row, 1978.

Gaddis, A. and Seif, G. *The Book of the Dead and Elysian Fields.* Luxor, Egypt [no publisher, [no date].

Caster, Theodor H. *Festivals of the Jewish Year.* New York: William Sloane Associates Publishers, 1952.

Graves, Robert. *The White Goddess.* London: Faber and Faber, 1962.

Graves, Robert and Podro, Joshua. *The Nazarene Gospel Restored.* London: Cassell and Company, 1958.

Greenlees, Duncan. *The Gospel of Islam.* Adyar, Madras, India: The Theosophical Publishing House, 1948.

Halevi, Z'ev ben Shimon. *Kabbalah and Exodus.* London: Rider, 1980.

_____. *Kabbalah Tradition of Hidden Knowledge.* London: Thames and Hudson, 1979.

Halifax, Joan. *Shamanic Voices.* London: Penguin, 1980.

Harrison, R. K. *Biblical Hebrew.* London: Teach Yourself Books, 1955.

Hewitt, James. *The Complete Yoga Book.* London: Rider, 1983.

The Hitopadesa. Trans. Francis Johnson. London: Chapman and Hall, 1928.

Hodson, Geoffrey. *The Kingdom of the Gods.* Adyar, Madras, India: The Theosophical Publishing House, 1953.

The Holy Bible. King James Version.

The Holy Qur'aan. 2nd ed. Trans. Muhammad 'Abdul-Haleem Eliasi. Transliteration in Roman script: The Burney Academy, Qur'aan Manzil, Hyderabad, India, 1981.

The Holy Qur'an. Trans. A. Yusuf Ali. Brentwood, MD: Armana Corp, 1983.

Hornung, Erik. *Conceptions of God in Ancient Egypt.* London: Routledge and Kegan Paul, 1983.

Hotema, Hilton. *The Lost Word.* Mokelumne Hill, CA: Health Research, 1967.

Humphries, Christmas. *Buddhism.* Harmondsworth: Penguin, 1981.

Hurtak, J. J. *The Book of Knowledge: The Keys of Enoch.* Los Gatos, CA: The Academy for Future Science, 1977.

_____. "The Guiding Hand." A lecture presented to The Deutsche UFO Studentgesellschaft (Duist) E.V., Weisbaden, West Germany, 1981.

_____."The Reality of the Masters of Light." A lecture presented to Frau Dr. Dina Rees and associates, Solden, West Germany, 1981.

Hymns Ancient and Modern. London: Oxford University Press, [no date].

The Interlinear Bible. 2nd ed. Peabody, MA: Hendrickson Publishers, 1986.

Iyengar, B. K. S. *Light on Yoga.* London: George Allen & Unwin, 1966.

Jacq, C. *Egyptian Magic.* Chicago: Aris and Phillips, Bolchazy-Carducci, 1985.

James, Montague Rhodes. *The Apocrypha New Testament.* London: Oxford University Press, 1924.

Katan, Norma Jean. *Hieroglyphics: The Writings of Ancient Egypt.* London: British Museum Publications, 1980.

The Koran. Trans. N. J. Dawood. London: Penguin Books, 1956.

The Koran. Trans. George Sale. London: Frederick Warne, [no date].

Lalita. *Choose Your Own Mantra.* New York: Bantam, 1978.

Leadbeater, C. W. *Ancient Mystic Rites.* Wheaton, IL: The Theosophical Publishing House, 1986.

Le Mee, Jean. *Hymns from the Rig Veda.* London: Jonathan Cape, 1975.

Lemesurier, Peter. *The Great Pyramid Decoded.* Wiltshire: Element Books, 1977.

Lings, Martin. *What is Sufism.* London: George Allen & Unwin, 1975.

314 / Words of Power

Luck, Georg. *Arcana Mundi: Magic and Occult in the Greek and Roman Worlds.* Baltimore: The John Hopkins University Press, 1985.

MacGregor Mathers, S. L. *The Kabbalah Unveiled.* London: Routledge and Kegan Paul, 1970.

Maharshi, Sri Ramana. *Upadesa Saram.* Tiruvannamalai, India: Sri Ramanaasram, 1970.

Malinowski, Bronislaw. *Magic, Science and Religion.* London: Condor Books, 1982.

Meiseles, Meir. *Judaism: Thought and Legend.* Jerusalem: Feldheim Publishers, [no date].

Miller, Jeanine. *The Vedas Harmony: Meditation and Fulfilment.* London: Rider, 1974.

Miller, Ron and Kenney, Jim. *Fireball and the Lotus.* Sante Fe, NM: Bear & Company, 1987.

Mookerjee, Ajit. *Kundalini: The Arousal of the Inner Energy.* London: Thames and Hudson, 1982.

Morenz, Siegfried. *Egyptian Religion.* London: Methuen, 1973.

Munk, Rabbi Michael L. *The Wisdom in the Hebrew Alphabet.* New York: Mesorah Publications, 1983.

Nasr, Seyyed Hossein. *Ideals and Realities of Islam.* London: George Allen & Unwin, 1966.

_____. *Islamic Life and Thought.* London: George Allen and Unwin, 1981.

The Nectar of Chanting. South Fallsburg, NY: SYDA Foundation, 1984.

New Larousse Encyclopedia of Mythology. London: Hamlyn, 1968.

Pope, Maurice. *The Story of Decipherment from Egyptian Hieroglyphic to Linear B.* London: Thames & Hudson, 1975.

Potter, Charles Francis. *The Lost Years of Jesus.* New York: University Books, 1963.

Pryse, James Morgan. T*he Apocalypse Unsealed.* New York: John M. Pryse, 1910.

———. *The Restored New Testament.* Los Angeles: John M. Pryse, 1925.

Puharich, Dr. Andrija. "Forecast for, 1984 and Beyond." Paper presented at "Forecast 84" Congress, Jerusalem, December 1983.

Qabbalah: The Philosophical Writings of Solomon Ben Yehudah Ibn Gebriol or Avicebron. Trans. Isaac Myer. London: Robinson & Watkins, 1972.

Radha, Swami Sivananda. *Mantras: Words of Power.* Porthill, ID: Timeless Books, 1980.

Radice, Betty, ed. *The Rig Veda.* Harmondsworth: Penguin, 1984.

Ramacharaka, Yogi. *The Hindu-Yogi Science of Breath.* London: L. N. Fowler, 1960.

Ranganathananda, Swami. *Swami Vivekananda's Synthesis of Science and Religion.* Calcutta: The Ramakrishna Mission Institute of Culture [no date].

Regardie, Israel. *The Golden Dawn: An Account of the Teachings, Rites and Ceremonies of the Order of the Golden Dawn.* St. Paul, MN: Llewellyn Publications, 1982 (fifth printing).

The Religion of the Sufis from The Dabistan of Mohsin Fani. Trans. David Shea and Anthony Troyer. London: The Octagon Press, 1979.

Rice, Fr. Cyprian. *The Persian Sufis.* London: George Allen and Unwin, 1964.

The Rig Veda: An Anthology. Trans. Wendy Doniger O'Flaherty. Harmondsworth: Penguin, 1981.

Robinson, James M., ed. *The Nag Hammadi Library*. San Francisco: Harper and Row, 1977.

Schachter, Reb Zalman. *Fragments of a Future Scroll: Hassidism for the Aquarian Age*. Germantown, PA: Leaves of Grass Press, 1975.

Scholem, Gershom G. *Zohar: The Book of Splendor*. New York: Schocken Books, 1963.

Scott, Joseph and Lenore. *Hieroglyphs for Fun*. New York: Van Nostrand Reinhold, 1974.

Seiss, Joseph A. *The Great Pyramid: A Miracle in Stone*. New York: Rudolf Steiner Publications, 1973 (orig. pub. Philadelphia, 1877).

Sen, K. M. *Hinduism*. Harmondsworth: Penguin, 1981.

Shah, Idries. *The Way of the Sufi*. London: Jonathan Cape, 1968.

Shrimad Bhagavad Gita. Bombay: Parmanand Publications, 1954.

Shusud, Hasan. *Masters of Wisdom of Central Asia*. UK: Coombe Springs Press, 1983.

Sivananda, Swami. *Japa Yoga*. 9th ed. Shivanandanagar, India: The Divine Life Society, 1986.

Smith, Morton. *Jesus the Magician*. London: Victor Gollancz, 1978.

Steiger, Brad. *Kahuna Magic*. Rockport, MA: Para Research, 1981.

Steiner, Rudolf. *Eurythmy as Visible Speech*. London: Rudolf Steiner Press, 1984 (first published, 1931).
_____. *Genesis Secrets of the Bible Story of Creation*. London: Rudolf Steiner Press, 1982 (first published, 1910).

Strong, James. *The Exhaustive Concordance of The Bible*. Iowa Falls: Riverside Book and Bible House, [no date].

Suzuki, Daisetz Teitaro. *Introduction to Zen Buddhism*. Including "A manual of Zen Buddhism." New York: Causeway Books, 1974.

Tagar, Yehuda. "On the universal foundation of all human languages." Y. Tagar, c/o The Anthroposophical Society in Australia (S. A. Branch), 84 Halifax Street, Adelaide 5000, Australia, 1988.

————. "The voice of Persephone—a modern approach to drama." Y. Tagar, c/o The Anthroposophical Society in Australia (S. A. Branch), 84 Halifax Street, Adelaide 5000, Australia, 1980-1987.

————. "Philophonetica—Love of Sounds." Y. Tagar, c/o The Anthroposophical Society in Australia (S. A. Branch), 84 Halifax Street, Adelaide 5000, Australia, 1986.

Teachings of Rumi (The Masnavi). Trans. E. H. Whinfield. London: The Octagon Press, 1979.

Tritton, A. S. *Arabic*. New York: David McKay, 1978.

The Upanishads. Trans. Swami Prabhavananda and Frederick Manchester. New York: New American Library, 1957.

Van Over, Raymond, ed. *Sun Songs: Creation Myths from Around the World*. New York: New American Library, 1980.

Vermes, Geza. *Jesus the Jew*. Philadelphia: Fortress Press, 1981.

Waterson, Barbara. *The Gods of Ancient Egypt*. London: B. T. Batsford, 1984.

Watkins, Peter and Hughes, Erica. *A Book of Prayer*. London: Julia MacRae, 1982.

Wilson, Ian. *Jesus: The Evidence*. London: Weidenfeld and Nicolson, 1984.

Woldering, Irmgard. *Egypt: The Art of the Pharaohs*. London: Methuen, 1963.

The Works of Flavius Josephus. Trans. William Whiston. London: T. Nelson & Sons, 1895.

Yogananda, Paramahansa. *Autobiography of a Yogi.* New Jersey: Wehmen, 1946.

STAY IN TOUCH

On the following pages you will find listed, with their current prices, some of the books and tapes now available on related subjects. Your book dealer stocks most of these, and will stock new titles in the Llewellyn series as they become available. We urge your patronage.

However, to obtain our full catalog, to keep informed of new titles as they are released and to benefit from informative articles and helpful news, you are invited to write for our bi-monthly news magazine/catalog. A sample copy is free, and it will continue coming to you at no cost as long as you are an active mail customer. Or you may keep it coming for a full year with a donation of just $2.00 in U.S.A. ($7.00 for Canada & Mexico, $20.00 overseas, first class mail). Many bookstores also have *The Llewellyn New Times* available to their customers. Ask for it.

The Llewellyn New Times
P.O. Box 64383-Dept. 135, St. Paul, MN 55164-0383, U.S.A.

• • •

TO ORDER BOOKS AND TAPES

If your book dealer does not have the books and tapes described on the following pages readily available, you may order them direct from the publisher by sending full price in U.S. funds, plus $2.00 for postage and handling for the first book, and 50¢ for each additional book. There are no postage and handling charges for orders over $50. UPS Delivery: We ship UPS whenever possible. Delivery guaranteed. Provide your street address as UPS does not deliver to P.O. Boxes. UPS to Canada requires a $50 minimum order. Allow 4-6 weeks for delivery. Orders outside the U.S.A. and Canada: Airmail—add retail price of book; add $5 for each non-book item (tapes, etc.); add $1 per item for surface mail.

FOR GROUP STUDY AND PURCHASE

Because there is a great deal of interest in group discussion and study of the subject matter of this book, we feel that we should encourage the adoption and use of this particular book by such groups by offering a special "quantity" price to group leaders or "agents."

Our Special Quantity Price for a minimum order of five copies of *Words of Power* is $32.85 cash-with-order. This price includes postage and handling within the United States. Minnesota residents must add 6% sales tax. For additional quantities, please order in multiples of five. For Canadian and foreign orders, add postage and handling charges as above. Credit card (VISA, MC, Amex) orders are accepted. Charge card orders only may be phoned free ($15.00 minimum order) within the U.S.A. or Canada by dialing 1-800-THE MOON. Customer service calls dial 1-612-291-1970. Mail Orders to:

LLEWELLYN PUBLICATIONS
P.O. Box 64383-Dept. 135 / St. Paul, MN 55164-0383, U.S.A.

GODWIN'S CABALISTIC ENCYCLOPEDIA
by David Godwin
This is the most complete correlation of Hebrew and English ideas ever offered. It is a dictionary of Cabalism arranged, with definitions, alphabetically, alphabetically in Hebrew, and numerically. With this book the practicing Cabalist or student no longer needs access to a large number of books on mysticism, magic and the occult in order to trace down the basic meanings, Hebrew spellings, and enumerations of hundreds of terms, words, and names.

This book includes: all of the two-letter root words found in Biblical Hebrew, the many names of God, the Planets, the Astrological Signs, Numerous Angels, the Shem Hamphorash, the Spirits of the Goetia, the Correspondences of the 32 Paths, a comparison of the Tarot and the Cabala, a guide to Hebrew Pronunciation, and a complete edition of Aleister Crowley's valuable book *Sepher Sephiroth.*

Here is a book that is a must for the shelf of all Magicians, Cabalists, Astrologers, Tarot students, Thelemites, and those with any interest at all in the spiritual aspects of our universe.
0-87542-292-6, 500 pgs., 6 × 9, softcover $15.00

WHEELS OF LIFE: A User's Guide to the Chakra System
by Anodea Judith
An instruction manual for owning and operating the inner gears that run the machinery of our lives. Written in a practical, down-to-earth style, this fully illustrated book will take the reader on a journey through aspects of consciousness, from the bodily instincts of survival to the processing of deep thoughts.

Discover this ancient metaphysical system under the new light of popular Western metaphors—quantum physics, elemental magick, Kabalah, physical exercises, poetic meditations, and visionary art. Learn how to open these centers in yourself, and see how the chakras shed light on the present world crises we face today. And learn what you can do about it!

This book will be a vital resource for: Magicians, Witches, Pagans, Mystics, Yoga Practitioners, Martial Arts people, Psychologists, Medical people, and all those who are concerned with holistic growth techniques.

The modern picture of the Chakras was introduced to the West largely in the context of Hatha and Kundalini Yoga and through the Theosophical writings of Leadbeater and Besant. But the Chakra system is *equally* innate to Western Magick: all psychic development, spiritual growth, and practical attainment is fully dependent upon the opening of the Chakras!
0-87542-320-5, 6 x 9, 544 pgs., illus., softcover $14.95

THE MIDDLE PILLAR
by Israel Regardie

Between the two outer pillars of the Qabalistic Tree of Life, the extremes of Mercy and Severity, stands THE MIDDLE PILLAR, signifying one who has achieved equilibrium in his or her own self. Integration of the human personality is vital to the continuance of creative life. Without it, man lives as an outsider to his own true self. By combining Magic and Psychology in the Middle Pillar Ritual/Exercise (a magical meditation technique), we bring into balance the opposing elements of the psyche while yet holding within their essence and allowing full expression of man's entire being.

In this book, and with this practice, you will learn to: understand the psyche through its correspondences on the Tree of Life; expand self-awareness, thereby intensifying the inner growth process; activate creative and intuitive potentials; understand the individual thought patterns which control every facet of personal behavior; regain the sense of balance and peace of mind—the equilibrium that everyone needs for physical and psychic health.

0-87542-658-1, 168 pgs., softcover   **$6.95**

THE GOLDEN DAWN
by Israel Regardie

The Original Account of the Teachings, Rites and Ceremonies of the Hermetic Order of the Golden Dawn as revealed by Israel Regardie, with further revision, expansion, and additional notes by Regardie, Cris Monnastre, and others. Expanded with an index of more than 100 pages!

Originally published in four bulky volumes of some 1200 pages, this 6th Revised and Enlarged Edition has been reset in modern, less space-consuming type, in half the pages (while retaining the original pagination in marginal notation for reference) for greater ease and use.

Includes further revision and additional text and notes by noted scholars and by actual practitioners of the Golden Dawn system of Magick, with an Introduction by the only student ever accepted for personal training by Regardie.

Also included are Initiation Ceremonies, important rituals for consecration and invocation, methods of meditation and magical working based on the Enochian Tablets, studies in the Tarot, and the system of Qabalistic Correspondences that unite the World's religions and magical traditions into a comprehensive and practical whole.

This volume is designed as a study and practice curriculum suited to both group and private practice. Meditation upon, and following with the Active Imagination, the Initiation Ceremonies is fully experiential without need of participation in group or lodge. A very complete reference encyclopedia of Western Magick.

0-87542-663-8, 803 pages, 6 x 9, illus.   **$19.95**